Families of the Heart

TRANSITS

LITERATURE, THOUGHT & CULTURE, 1650–1850

Series editors:
Miriam Wallace, New College of Florida
Mona Narain, Texas Christian University

A landmark series in long-eighteenth-century studies, *Transits* publishes monographs and edited volumes that are timely, transformative in their approach, and global in their engagement with arts, literature, culture, and history. Books in the series have engaged with visual arts, environment, politics, material culture, travel, theater and performance, embodiment, connections between the natural sciences and medical humanities, writing and book history, sexuality, gender, disability, race, and colonialism from Britain and Europe to the Americas, the Far East, the Middle/Near East, Africa, and Oceania. Works that make provocative connections across time, space, geography, or intellectual history, or that develop new modes of critical imagining are particularly welcome.

Recent titles in the series:

Families of the Heart: Surrogate Relations in the Eighteenth-Century British Novel
Ann Campbell

Eighteenth-Century Environmental Humanities
Jeremy Chow, ed.

Political Affairs of the Heart: Female Travel Writers, the Sentimental Travelogue, and Revolution, 1775–1800
Linda Van Netten Blimke

The Limits of Familiarity: Authorship and Romantic Readers
Lindsey Eckert

"Robinson Crusoe" after 300 Years
Andreas K. E. Mueller and Glynis Ridley, eds.

Transatlantic Women Travelers, 1688–1843
Misty Krueger, ed.

Laurence Sterne's "A Sentimental Journey": A Legacy to the World
W. B. Gerard and M-C. Newbould, eds.

For more information about the series, please visit www.bucknelluniversitypress.org.

Families of the Heart

SURROGATE RELATIONS IN THE EIGHTEENTH-CENTURY BRITISH NOVEL

ANN CAMPBELL

BUCKNELL
UNIVERSITY PRESS

LEWISBURG, PENNSYLVANIA

Library of Congress Cataloging-in-Publication Data

Names: Campbell, Ann, 1933– author.
Title: Families of the heart : surrogate relations in the
    eighteenth-century British novel / Ann Campbell.
Description: Lewisburg : Bucknell University Press, [2023] |
    Series: Transits: literature, thought & culture 1650–1850 |
    Includes bibliographical references and index.
Identifiers: LCCN 2022008843 | ISBN 9781684484232
    (paperback) | ISBN 9781684484249 (hardback) |
    ISBN 9781684484256 (epub) | ISBN 9781684484270 (pdf)
Subjects: LCSH: English fiction—18th century—History and
    criticism. | Women in literature. | Social groups in literature. |
    Group identity in literature. | Families in literature. | Feminist
    theory. | LCGFT: Literary criticism.
Classification: LCC PR858.E6 C36 2023 | DDC 823/.6099287—
    dc23/eng/2022077
LC record available at https://lccn.loc.gov/2022008843

A British Cataloging-in-Publication record for this book is available
from the British Library.

References to internet websites (URLs) were accurate at the time of
writing. Neither the author nor Bucknell University Press is
responsible for URLs that may have expired or changed since the
manuscript was prepared.

♾ The paper used in this publication meets the requirements of the
American National Standard for Information Sciences—
Permanence of Paper for Printed Library Materials, ANSI
Z39.48-1992.

www.bucknelluniversitypress.org

Distributed worldwide by Rutgers University Press

Manufactured in the United States of America

For Robee

CONTENTS

Families of the Heart

THE SUBJECT OF THIS STUDY is a plot convention I define as *surrogate families*: family-like groups of individuals selected by female protagonists to occupy the place vacated by absent or ineffectual parents and kin. I argue that this convention is critical to interpreting eighteenth-century British novelists' depictions of women's choices about marriage. I examine four eighteenth-century authors—Daniel Defoe, Samuel Richardson, Frances Burney, and Eliza Haywood—who published significant and influential novels centered on courtship. All the novels I include also intertwine the theme of marital choice with the plot convention of surrogate families. Although surrogate families take different forms and serve a variety of evolving purposes, they all share the following traits: (1) they are chosen or at least accepted by the protagonist; (2) they share an intimate family-like connection to the protagonist, sometimes even living with her during a developmentally significant stage of her life; (3) they either facilitate courtship and marriage or help the protagonist navigate marital choice and marriage itself; and (4) they help the protagonist improve or learn about herself and the world around her.

My concept of surrogate families draws from historian Naomi Tadmor's and literary scholar Ruth Perry's models of eighteenth-century families while not aligning exactly with either. Tadmor delineates three eighteenth-century conceptions of family: nuclear families, household families, and families of lineage.[1] Nuclear families were created by marriage, and consisted of parents, children, and in-laws.[2] (Sometimes this family model is referred to as the *conjugal family*.) Kinship ties, or the *lineage-family* as Tadmor calls it, extend upward and outward to include relations by blood and marriage across generations. Cousins, uncles, aunts, grandmothers, grandfathers, and even more distant relations belonged to lineage families.[3] The third model was the household family.[4] Household families consisted of "people living under the same roof and under the authority of a householder," including servants, live-in relations, and companions.[5] According to Tadmor, this model is particularly relevant to literary studies because it is "deeply embedded within . . . novels."[6] Perry, on the other hand, classifies family ties based on how they were formed. Consanguineal ties were based on blood relationships, while "conjugal and affinial ties" were created by marriage.[7]

My argument focuses on siblinghood, the relationship most contested between the two models. Perry treats fraternal and sororal ties as consanguineal since siblings are related by blood.[8] Tadmor's model encompasses brotherhood and sisterhood under the umbrella of nuclear families formed by marriage. Both models emphasize origins—siblings share at least one parent, and parents of legitimate children are married to one another—rather than the lived experience of siblings in relation to one another. In contrast, I locate sibling-like relationships at the center of surrogate families: they are its defining feature. Surrogate sisters and brothers choose one another based on affection. Marriage may evolve out of surrogate fraternal or sororal ties, but shared parentage does not create them. Sibling relationships are the paradigm for surrogate family bonds because they are as close to egalitarian as any family ties can be. Despite the different opportunities primogeniture dictated for brothers and sisters, they still occupied the same rung on the family ladder. Surrogate parents also play an important, though often lesser, role in families of the heart. Regardless of whether parenthood is conceived of as control over a household, or over children, it confers power over subordinates. Surrogate parents accrue that power based on choice rather than birth, but the relationship is still hierarchical.

Surrogate family relationships could become more complicated than this straightforward set of parallels initially suggests. This is hardly surprising when you consider how complicated families themselves could be. For example, the status of houseguests in a household family could be ambiguous. They might be considered members of the household, or they might not, depending on factors such as their closeness to family members and the length and reason for their stay. Were long-term guests, like children, "under the authority of a householder," as Tadmor puts it?[9] This is one of many complexities that arise when you apply theory to specific family configurations. Another is the nature of the relationship between household families and lineage families in intergenerational households. Members of household families might live together for periods of time and then join other household families or forge their own nuclear families. Distant relations might reside with members of their lineage family.

Additionally, a person's role in a particular family often changed over time. Mortality rates were high during the eighteenth century, resulting in second or third marriages and consequently nuclear families with complex configurations. Every young adult had a 50 percent chance of losing at least one parent before reaching the age of twenty-one.[10] As Ann Van Sant notes, "families were in continuous formation, changing, sometimes dramatically, over the course of life" as surviving spouses remarried and had additional children.[11] Household families changed regularly. New servants would join a family while others departed. Kin might join a household because of disruptions to their own nuclear or household families: the death of a spouse or changing financial circumstances, for example.

Children might marry, become apprentices, or go into service, leaving their household families to join other households. Even lineage families changed when uncles, aunts, or grandparents died and cousins were born or died. Marriages or remarriages of uncles, aunts, or grandparents could also reshape lineage families. As for household families, they were not always headed by a patriarch. Many household families were presided over by women, including girls' boarding schools, households made up female friends and family members living together, and households headed up by widows and single women.

Household families are particularly significant to my project because they contract and expand to accommodate all kinds of circumstances. They most closely approximate surrogate families because both models evolve over time, often in unpredictable ways. Additionally, members of household families could also become members of one another's surrogate families. The day-to-day intimacy necessary to foster family-like bonds is more likely to emerge when protagonists live for extended periods of time with potential surrogate family members. Young women might leave their own household families and join others for all kinds of reasons. They could go to a boarding school, go into service, move in with members of their lineage families after the death of a parent, or visit friends or kin for months at a time. Each transition into a new household family provides opportunities for casual affinities to develop into surrogate family ties. William Thackeray's tone in *Vanity Fair* is ironic when he describes the family-like connection his two primary female characters form during a weeklong visit: they "loved each other as sisters" because "[y]oung unmarried girls always do, if they are in a house for ten days."[12] Although this passage intends to ridicule the superficiality of young women's friendships, it also unintentionally reinforces the critical role household families play in the formation of young women's surrogate families. As Thackeray's assertion implicitly acknowledges, boarding schools and visits provided young women "liberty of association" their nuclear and lineage families did not offer.[13] The well-known adage that you can pick your friends but not your family does not apply to surrogate families because the potential pool of surrogate family members is limited by opportunity, not by birth. The more household families a young woman lived in, the greater her opportunities for meeting candidates to join her surrogate family. Surrogate ties forged within household families could affect women's lives in numerous ways, the most obvious of which was marriage. Surrogate brothers could become actual husbands. A union based on the ideal of a steady and serene friendship between siblings was perfectly tailored to the concept of what Irene Brown describes as *enlightened domesticity*: the notion that marriage ought to be based on intelligent companionship.[14]

Although surrogate family members in eighteenth-century novels often emerge from household families, surrogate families themselves are more akin to nuclear families. Emotionally and intellectually compatible peers become surrogate brothers and sisters, while elder mentors become surrogate mothers and fathers. Oddly, there are virtually no surrogate uncles and aunts or grandfathers or grandmothers in eighteenth-century novels. Lineage families presumably offered too little in the way of intimacy to be templates for surrogate families. In fact, in Samuel Richardson's *Sir Charles Grandison* (1754), Sir Charles invites his cousin Everard—already a member of his lineage family—into his surrogate family, promising from that moment on they will share "true fraternal love."[15] The love cousins feel for one another is apparently too watered down to express the attachment Sir Charles feels to members of his surrogate family. In some instances, even members of protagonists' nuclear families become part of their surrogate families. For example, Evelina in Frances Burney's *Evelina* (1778) does not know that the virtual stranger (Mr. Macartney) she nominates as her surrogate brother will fortuitously turn out to be her half-brother by the father she has never met.

Surrogate families are not just structurally modeled on nuclear families, but also emulate their affective capacities. Ideally, mothers should be nurturing and supportive guides who prepare daughters to become fulfilled wives and mothers. Fathers should support, cherish, and protect daughters. Brothers and sisters should be friends and confidantes. However, neither in life nor in novels is this *Leave It to Beaver* version of the nuclear family often achieved. Parents might be selfish and authoritarian. Brothers and sisters could be spiteful. For example, the Harlowes in Samuel Richardson's *Clarissa* (1748) are an awful family. Clarissa's parents and siblings are sadistic to her while she lives with them and disown her when she leaves. She replaces her mother with a surrogate mother, her childhood wet nurse and governess Mrs. Norton. Mrs. Norton is suited to this role because she occupied a maternal position in relation to Clarissa during her infancy, and perhaps far longer. On her deathbed, Clarissa addresses the surrogate mother of her childhood as her real mother: "How kindly, my beloved Mrs. Norton, do you sooth the anguish of a bleeding heart! Surely you are my own mamma; and by some unaccountable mistake, I must have been laid to a family that, having newly found out or at least suspected the imposture, cast me from their hearts . . . Oh that I had indeed been your own child, . . . an heiress only to that content in which you are so happy!"[16] Mrs. Norton has behaved during Clarissa's childhood in ways a mother should ideally act, so Clarissa resurrects the relationship. Similarly, Clarissa replaces her malicious sister Arabella with her dear friend Anna with whom she lives during prolonged visits over the course of their youth and adolescence.

Scholars acknowledge how often these sorts of makeshift families appear in eighteenth-century novels, though they use a variety of terms to refer to them. I have chosen to use the term *surrogate family*, following the example of Cheryl Nixon, John Richetti, and several other scholars who also use the same term in a variety of different contexts.[17] Referring specifically to Daniel Defoe's *Moll Flanders* (1722), a novel I examine closely in chapter 1, Richetti defines surrogate

families as "small groups of friends who act as substitute families."[18] Nixon's definition of this plot device mirrors most closely my own meaning. She focuses
specifically on orphaned protagonists, defining surrogate families as family-like
groups that "connec[t] to, replac[e], mimi[c], or eras[e]" defective "biological
famil[ies]."[19] Although Nixon's study of orphans aligns most closely with my own
interests, she focuses almost exclusively on surrogate parents. My argument also
involves surrogate parents, but I posit that relationships between surrogate siblings are more crucial to explicating courtship plots. Shifting my focus from
hierarchical relationships modeled on parenthood to peer relationships modeled
on brotherhood and sisterhood helps explain why, for example, as Janet Todd
observes, eighteenth-century novels feature so many "curiously aimless" relationships between female protagonists and young women with "no blood link" to
them.[20] Many are surrogate sibling relationships, inchoate versions of what Anna
and Clarissa develop in *Clarissa*. Their relationship is the best-known example of
surrogate siblinghood at its most intense. They both lack loving siblings. Anna is
an only child and Clarissa's brother and sister detest her. But they enact ideal
sororal love for one another by adopting one another into what Mark Kinkead-
Weekes refers to as their "family . . . of the heart."[21]

The intensity of Anna's and Clarissa's bond is rare, but its narrative purpose
applies broadly to a wide range of eighteenth-century novels. Not every surrogate
family in every novel qualifies as a family of the heart in the Richardsonian mold.
However, even businesslike protagonists like Moll in *Moll Flanders* rely on surrogate family members to fill in for absent mothers, fathers, sisters, and brothers.
Although Moll seeks pragmatic assistance rather than affection from her surrogate family members, her need for them still brings them back repeatedly to the
forefront of her narrative.

Once you look for them, surrogate families are everywhere in eighteenth-
century novels. For example, Jacqueline Lawson remarks on the significance of a
"family manqué" made up of Roxana and her maid Amy in Defoe's *Roxana*
(1724).[22] She also notes the presence of the "non-sanguineous family unit" that
comforts Clarissa on her deathbed, complete with a fictional mother, father, and
siblings.[23] Van Sant calls attention to Sarah Scott's inclusion of numerous "affective and moral families" in her fiction, and Terri Nickel discerns the same sort of
"imaginary and self-created families" and "affective alliances" in Sarah Fielding's
David Simple and Jane Collier's fiction.[24] According to Jennifer Golightly, surrogate families remain a significant feature of radical fiction published during the
later eighteenth century. She explicates how Mary Hays and Mary Wollstonecraft
incorporate "alternative famil[ies]" into their fiction as a means to "fr[ee] the radical heroines from the constraints imposed upon them by the patriarchal family
and thus allo[w] them more autonomy and independence."[25] The wide selection
of eighteenth-century novels in which surrogate families appear, as well as the critical

consensus of scholars about their importance, attests to the need for the serious and prolonged scrutiny I accord them.

Surrogate families are more important to female than to male protagonists. This is because surrogate family members are one of the very limited means of control they are able to exercise over their circumscribed lives. A male protagonist like Tom in Henry Fielding's *Tom Jones* (1749)—a novel I discuss at more length in the conclusion—joins numerous household family units throughout the course of the novel. He is free to move about from place to place, meet all sorts of people, have love affairs with women, and experiment with multiple identities without requiring anyone's consent or approval. His unknown parentage still limits his opportunities to rise in the world. And his exceptional attractiveness and luck (both good and bad at different moments in the novel) are passkeys to company and places that would be inaccessible to a less agreeable penniless vagrant. Despite the exceptionality of his person and personality, his gender still allows him to do things an equally charming and beautiful young woman could not. For example, while Sophia also elopes from her home and family, she must travel with her maid, avoid associating with travelers at inns, and seek the protection of a (seemingly) respectable chaperone in London. She would endanger her all-important reputation for virtue by gossiping at inns, wandering through the dark woods on foot at night and seeking shelter from a hermit, joining a gypsy gathering, or wandering unaccompanied around London. As a man, Tom gets to make so many decisions that their very multiplicity diminishes the importance of any one. Additionally, he is also allowed to fail at things before he succeeds. His poor decisions might result in temporary financial or personal losses, but he is able to recover from his missteps.

Most female protagonists are not able to "fail upwards" like Tom does. Or if they do, their failures are so insignificant compared to Tom's that they are better described as faux pas. For example, Evelina makes a fool of herself at an exclusive ball, calls her virtue into question by strolling through the dark walks at Vauxhall, and commits a breach of etiquette by writing unsolicited to Lord Orville. These are serious social infractions, but they differ in degree as well as in kind from Tom's transgressions. Linda Bree makes a similar point about David, the protagonist of Fielding's sister Sarah's novel *David Simple* (1744). According to Bree, Sarah had no choice but to make her protagonist a man because her plot required the character to do things that were socially acceptable for men, but not for respectable women. For example, he must have "access to public spaces" and be able to spend a great deal of time "wander[ing] around alone" in places "women would have to chaperoned."[26] Most importantly, David autonomously decides how to spend his time and money. A female protagonist such as Evelina would not be allowed to meander around London at all hours in order to satisfy a "quixotic impulse" to find a real friend.[27] Much less could she have the sorts of casual sexual encounters Tom Jones enjoys with Molly or Mrs. Waters. Her choices are fewer than these male characters' and have greater consequences, so individually they matter more. Thus, decisions about which surrogate family members to accept and which to reject have outsize importance for female protagonists when compared to their male counterparts.

In courtship novels, the most consequential decision for female protagonists is whom to marry. As Helena Kelly argues in relation to Jane Austen's fiction, "[m]arriage mattered because it was the defining action of a woman's life; to accept or refuse a proposal was almost the only decision that a woman could make."[28] In a society in which divorce was exceedingly rare, marriage was, unlike membership in a surrogate family, almost always irrevocable. Novelists' "obsession," as T.G.A. Nelson describes it, with "individual choice in marriage" was one manifestation of larger cultural and historical questions about the effects of gradually shifting marital practices.[29] Young people were increasingly able to choose their spouses, at least within reason.[30] Dynastic arranged marriages were falling out of favor. According to Lawrence Stone in his landmark study *The Family, Sex, and Marriage in England, 1500–1800* (1977), increasing egalitarianism in families and widespread acceptance of the importance of affection in marriage helped children assert their own wishes about the husbands and wives they wanted to marry. While, as Tadmor notes, numerous prominent historians debated up through the 1980s whether families really changed as much as Stone asserted, his larger premise of gradually increasing marital choice for young people over the course of the eighteenth century is generally accepted.[31] He describes the ideal of marriage that emerged during this period as "companionate," meaning spouses were supposed to be intimate friends rather than just partners presiding together over their children and economic affairs.[32] In order to promote this model of marriage, parents had to give up some of their authority and allow their children to make choices that had previously belonged to parents alone.

The advent of the London marriage market and its provincial variants created ideal conditions for marital choice to flourish. The London marriage market consisted of numerous private and public entertainments that were held during the London season, which began late in the fall and ended when summer began. Young men and women met one another at balls, assemblies, and other social functions, exposing daughters and sons to what historian Amanda Vickery describes as a "wide range of socially acceptable potential mates."[33] As Stone notes, the exclusivity of most of these events allowed children "greater freedom of choice, without threatening the long-term interests of the family in the making of a 'suitable' marriage."[34] In addition to the national marriage market in London, regional counterparts emerged in spa towns like Bath where fashionable people spent their summers. The marriage market performed what had previously been the parents' responsibility of selecting and bringing together appropriate potential spouses. Consequently,

the process of courtship became less mediated. Although young women in particular were still escorted to social events by chaperones, once they arrived they
could mingle familiarly with eligible men. As couples danced, conversed, and
played cards, they gauged their emotional and intellectual compatibility. Their
preferences initiated the process of courtship, so parents did not need to become
involved until after couples were already attached to their chosen spouses. As Vickery
observes, "if young people met only suitable companions, they would assuredly
make a suitable, free choice."[35]

The novel is a bellwether of cultural apprehensions about marital choice.
Scholars have long recognized it as the genre most implicated in, as Ruth Perry
argues, a culture's "exigencies," "anxieties," and "pleasures."[36] Courtship novels register
these anxieties through well-recognized conventions such as secret engagements,
elopements, and seductive rakes. Surrogate families also belong on this list. The
insistent repetition of these conventions registers cultural preoccupations about
what might happen if young women abused marital choice or were too naïve to
benefit from it. Recent studies of courtship fiction, Perry's most notably, conclude
that these narratives play central roles in experimenting with, confronting, and in
some cases resisting changes in marital expectations and practices.[37] Novelists
could imagine the most extreme possible consequences of these shifts, which might
be hardly perceptible in the time frame of an actual courtship. Fiction compressed
and exaggerated gradual changes. As Helen Thompson writes, it performed the
"cultural work" of providing "models of choice and expectation" about family and
marriage to a young and largely female readership.[38]

Fiction and historical reality engage in a dynamic relationship, responding
to one another in personally and culturally meaningful ways. As Vickery observed
about letters written by gentry women in the late eighteenth century, "literary
formulae could have a stunning impact on personal expression."[39] The women in
her study expressed personal sympathy for characters like Harriet in *Sir Charles
Grandison* and then, as Vickery notes, "quickly moved from sympathizing with
the novel's characters, to musing on [their] own sensibility."[40] As one reader,
Mary Chorley, wrote to Richardson, "I think if I were to open my heart like
Miss Byron . . . the contents would fill a room."[41] This intense and emotionally
charged language reminds us of fiction's power to enact and interpret cultural
debates about the most personal of choices: how and why to choose one's spouse.
As Thompson observes of courtship novels of this period, while "individual novels
do not answer individual questions of choice—this potential mate versus that
one—they do offer up a general model of courtship, against which the individual
can measure and judge her own circumstances."[42] Though we may not be able to
delineate how the majority of readers responded to these novels, we know from
Chorley's account how deeply felt and personal these reactions could be.[43] It is
not surprising that novels elicited such intimate responses since the novel as a

genre is uniquely suited to depict the progress and outcome of intimacy. Novels absorb and reflect cultural and personal conflict with an immediacy peculiar to themselves. Epistolary novels like *Clarissa* and *Evelina* can describe in detail how companionship or love develops over time from the perspective of characters that join families voluntarily. Those written in the form of a memoir, *Moll Flanders* for example, mimic in the reader's connection to the confessional narrator the familial ties formed by the narrator to other characters. Even omniscient novels like Jane Austen's enjoy through sheer length the leisure to describe in detail how and why chosen personal intimacies thrive or fail.

Translating literary into historical analysis is a thorny proposition at best because it is impossible to make definite conclusions about how literature and life intertwined in the past. With this caveat in mind, it is worth at least speculating about the interrelationship between novels and women's lives because, as readers' accounts in the previous paragraph demonstrate, young women measured their lives against the adventures of the protagonists they read about. As Nixon explains, it is also difficult to calculate to what degree literature provides "evidence of the 'facts'" about "familial attitudes," and equally challenging to determine the role literature played in "circul[ating] . . . ideas about family, domesticity, and gender."[44] Yet, there is widespread consensus that they did. For example, according to Christopher Flint, domestic novels "atomized the family."[45] Mona Scheuermann similarly argues that late-eighteenth-century novels "question the very basis of the parent-child relationship."[46] Groundbreaking studies by literary critics such as Margaret Ezell, Susan Staves, Toni Bowers, Ellen Pollak, and Michael McKeon all offer influential examples of the use of literary materials as evidence for the existence of particular familial structures and of cultural attitudes toward these structures.[47] Many historians also cite novels in their arguments about what actually occurred during this period, including Leonore Davidoff, Catherine Hall, Margaret Hunt, and Amanda Vickery.[48] As Carol Sherman summarizes, "whether artistic representation" is the "cause, effect, or simple co-mingling" of truth and imagination ultimately "cannot be known" with absolute certainty, but that should not discourage us from considering the question of how fiction and culture interrelate.[49]

While the marriage market itself was an experience young men and women shared equally—otherwise it could hardly have resulted in marriages—courtship novels depict much more frequently and with greater attention how women rather than men navigated it. As the supposedly irrational and vain sex, women were thought to be more susceptible than men to poor judgment. Additionally, the consequences of poor matches for women were much more dire than for men because wives became their husbands' property. Consequently, novelists focus more often on women's marital mishaps than on wayward young men. The risks for women were particularly acute during courtship, which usually occurred during an impulsive period of life. Paula Backscheider describes courtship as a "liminal space" between "childhood and adulthood . . . dependency and responsibility" and "autonomy and relationship."[50] What this meant is that young women made adult decisions before possessing adult wisdom or caution. Young women's lives were usually less exciting than the ones depicted in novels. As George Haggerty notes, "courtship and marriage" in novels were often "fraught with seemingly unlikely difficulties."[51] Although these exaggerated plots did not mirror the experiences of most young women, novels and their readers were intertwined imaginatively. Not only did young women look to novels for guidance, but also novelists engaged in a collective thought experiment about how young women might act if they were not subjected to the strict control of guardians and chaperones. What if young women were free to make their own decisions? As Nixon asks, what if they "plott[ed] the self"?[52] How might a female version of Tom Jones behave? Fiction imaginatively enacted these questions.

The unusual and in some cases highly contrived amount of agency female protagonists enjoy to choose surrogate family members and spouses derives from the dearth of effective parents in these novels. As David Paxman bluntly observes, "good parents don't make good stories."[53] Christine Van Boheemen even asserts that parentless children are one of novel's defining characteristics: the "image of the orphan, the foundling or bastard, may well be identified with the genre [of the novel] itself."[54] Protagonists are often either literal orphans or the children of parents or guardians so impotent that they might as well be orphans.[55] Defoe in particular uses "failed parents" as a "plot device to explore pluck of character."[56] For example, the orphaned Moll in *Moll Flanders* becomes involved in numerous rollicking escapades. Even as a child, she enjoys navigating the world according to her wits. In later novels, authors treat the difficulties of orphans or functionally orphaned characters with greater moral seriousness. For example, unlike Moll, Clarissa never takes pleasure in autonomy. But Clarissa's reticence to act on her own behalf is irrelevant given her situation. As much as she would despise Moll's unselfconscious self-sufficiency, she learns to emulate it because after she leaves her parents' house she has to act as "father, mother, [and] uncle to [her]self" (588).

Curiously, men created these strikingly independent female characters, suggesting they were as invested as female novelists in depicting, interpreting, and potentially influencing young women's choices about courtship. However, men's interest in this subject does not mean they came to the same conclusions as women did. Some of the broad distinctions between male and female novelists' depictions of women's marital choices may productively be categorized as gendered. Some caveats apply to this claim, as they always do to assertions about gender. My argument does not apply equally well to every eighteenth-century author and variety of novel. Just as the subject of an impressionistic painting becomes apparent only at a distance, these gendered distinctions work broadly, but not necessarily for each stroke up close. Additionally, there are other forces at work besides gender; one of the most important of these is time. What was considered acceptable for women changes over the course of time, and the novels I examine span almost a century. The particular novels I chose by men were published during the first half of the century, and those by women were from midcentury forward. With these caveats in mind, gender as a category can provide insights into literature that would otherwise be imperceptible or incoherent. The risk of entertaining some degree of essentialism is worth the reward of seeing and being able to interpret the significance of motifs that would otherwise remain unseen.

Chapter by chapter, I trace the depiction of surrogate families through novels by several of the period's most influential novelists: Daniel Defoe, Samuel Richardson, Eliza Haywood, and Frances Burney. My close readings focus on novels that contribute in significant and unique ways to the development of this plot convention. Based on these readings, I detect a pattern in the depiction of surrogate families that begins in Defoe's and Richardson's fiction. While they allow female protagonists some freedom to choose spouses, female authors such as Haywood and Burney are bolder and more explicitly feminist in their use of this plot convention. They realize its potential to offer women autonomy that expands beyond the bounds of courtship. Defoe and Richardson portray surrogate families as a means for female protagonists who either lack families or whose families are so defective as to be effectually absent to advance through society, usually through marriage. Haywood and Burney take this model further, envisioning connections between protagonists and their surrogate sisters and mothers that can substitute for marriage itself. Haywood's and Burney's versions of surrogate families also help protagonists learn, mature, and understand themselves. The goal of this emotional and moral development can be as simple as determining, as Burney puts it in *Evelina*, "to whom" (which is to say, which suitor) a protagonist "most belong[s]."[57] But it can also be used for gynocentric ends. In *Cecilia* (1782), for instance, Cecilia marries her husband to solidify her connection to his mother, who is also her surrogate mother. Cecilia's marriage transforms a mother-daughter relationship that would otherwise be provisional—a step on the way to a desirable marriage— into a permanent bond between members of the same nuclear family.

Gender is one axis by which to measure changes in depictions of surrogate families; time is another. As Backscheider observes, novels always posited family "as a site for dialogic conflict."[58] But female characters who belonged to them were not static over time. Rather, as the novel developed as a genre over the course of the eighteenth century, female protagonists changed with it. As Paxman asserts, until the middle of the century "the term 'development' referred to the opening or unfolding of qualities already inherent in an organism or concept—much as we use the term when we develop a photograph."[59] Early and midcentury novels corroborate Paxman's argument. Defoe's and Richardson's protagonists do not fundamentally change over the course of their novels. Defoe's protagonists learn to perform a variety of personas in order to achieve their ambitions. Richardson's protagonists are far more introspective than Defoe's, but experience still does not alter their personalities or their perspectives on the world. They begin and end their stories as embodiments of virtue. However, as the century progresses, female protagonists become more dynamic. It is likely no coincidence that this shift aligns with an increase in female novelists from midcentury onward. Even Haywood, whose work was popular for decades, shifted her style from romance to domestic realism by midcentury. The characters in her later novels were still not psychologically complex. But they do make practical changes to their conduct. Burney's protagonists go even farther, developing sound judgment and wisdom as they move through the world. While even Burney's protagonists do not demonstrate psychological complexity and plasticity of the sort that would eventually come to be associated with the novel, they are recognizable as early prototypes of characters like Dorothea Brooke and Jane Eyre in ways that Moll and Roxana are not.

I selected authors and novels for this study with the goal of explicating these changes over time, taking gender into account as well as the particular interests of individual authors. I examine two male novelists and two female novelists. Their work spans about sixty years, from the 1720s to the 1780s. Each author contributes substantively to the convention of surrogate families. I argue that there are discernable, coherent changes in depictions of surrogate families during these years. I interpret them broadly as a series of responses to and revisions of a convention that takes on increasingly feminist implications. Some aspects of the individual iterations of surrogate families are best understood as particular to individual authors. My close readings acknowledge these idiosyncrasies. Therefore, to some degree this project constitutes a typology as well as a genealogy of surrogate families in eighteenth-century novels. I focus on novels with female protagonists engaged in courtship since my primary interest is in depictions of young women's choices, and young women's choices in novels are typically limited to courtship and marriage. The particular novels I examine in each chapter pair well while also adhering logically as a group. Each novelist adds something significant to previous authors' depictions of surrogate families by revisiting and critiquing his or her predecessors. In each chapter, I begin with a reading of a novel that establishes a particular author's paradigm for surrogate families. Then I explicate a second, later novel by the same author that complicates or interrogates aspects of that paradigm.

Chapter 1, "Just Business: Surrogate Families as Entrepreneurial Ventures in Daniel Defoe's *Moll Flanders* and *Roxana*," argues surrogate families are the norm in Defoe's novels, while nuclear and conjugal families are aberrations. Defoe's surrogate families are often no more than temporary families of convenience— formed, dissolved, and forgotten in a matter of pages—although a few are nurturing and enriching connections that sustain protagonists for long periods of time. Sometimes this sustenance is emotional; most often it is financial. In *Moll*

Flanders, Moll blithely discards any cumbersome kin she encounters in favor of a series of shifting surrogate ties that offer her mobility, flexibility, and opportunity. In *Roxana*, Defoe complicates the relationship between surrogate ties and marital or biological families in ways that predict the irresolvable conflicts between these family models in Richardson's *Clarissa*. While surrogate family members obligingly come and go according to Moll's strategic preferences in *Moll Flanders*, they "strike back" in *Roxana*, demanding loyalty and exclusivity. Despite the entanglements between family models in *Roxana*, both novels privilege imaginary families over families of origin and families formed by marriage. They also correlate families of choice with entrepreneurship. Later authors reject or conceal the mercenary foundation of Defoe's model of surrogate families while building on its potential to narrate the process of women's self-discovery and social exploration.

Chapter 2, "Building a Foundation for the Family of the Heart: Prototypes of Surrogate Families in Samuel Richardson's *Pamela* and *Pamela in Her Exalted Condition*," argues that Richardson takes up Defoe's convention of surrogate families in his early fiction but uses it to a very different end. Richardson emphasizes moral, intellectual, and emotional compatibility as the qualifications for choosing surrogate families. Although his didacticism minimizes the significance of the social and economic mobility surrogate families promote in Defoe's fiction, telltale traces of this crass aspect of surrogacy remain, particularly in his first two novels, *Pamela* and *Pamela in Her Exalted Condition* (referred to hereafter as *Pamela II*). In *Pamela* and *Pamela II*, Pamela's low status and isolation circumscribe her ability to select aspirational surrogate families. She chooses the most important figures she has access to as her imaginary mothers and fathers. Their acceptance of this familial bond with Pamela provides evidence of her moral and intellectual superiority, helping Mr. B along to his eventual decision to marry her. However, in *Pamela II*, Pamela's elevated status allows her to select Polly Darnford, a wealthy member of the gentry, as her surrogate sister. She gains another sister, Mr. B's sister Lady Davers, through marriage.

Chapter 3, "Perfecting the Family of the Heart: Relationship Remembered in Samuel Richardson's *Clarissa* and *Sir Charles Grandison*," argues that Richardson's vision of surrogate families matures in *Clarissa* and *Sir Charles Grandison*. In these later novels, he places surrogate families in direct competition with biological ties, in contrast to their formulation in *Pamela* and *Pamela II*. In the two *Pamela* novels, Pamela's biological family is absent and ineffectual, providing no meaningful obstruction to the formation of surrogate ties that displace it. In *Clarissa*, however, Clarissa's biological family actively disputes Clarissa's right to form and maintain surrogate connections. Surrogate ties cannot naturally develop in these circumstances, but instead must be deliberately forged by Clarissa as a means to resist the claims of her nuclear and lineage families. The novel's macabre conclusion in which Clarissa's corpse returns to Harlowe Place demonstrates that the

Harlowes own Clarissa's body, but her affections belong entirely to the surrogate family members she keeps close to her person and heart on her deathbed. In *Sir Charles Grandison*, Richardson imagines a utopian means of resolving the conflict between surrogate families and families of origin; they will merge into a hybrid Grandison clan that is anchored by marriage but expands outward as it welcomes every worthy person to join it as a surrogate mother, father, brother, or sister.

Chapter 4, "An Affinity for Learning: Eliza Haywood's *The History of Miss Betsy Thoughtless* and *The History of Jemmy and Jenny Jessamy*," argues that Haywood's last novels *The History of Miss Betsy Thoughtless* (1751) and *The History of Jemmy and Jenny Jessamy* (1753), both of which were published roughly during the same years as Richardson's mature fiction, steer the narrative convention of surrogate families as they are introduced in *Pamela* and *Pamela II* between the Scylla of tragedy in *Clarissa* and the Charybdis of utopia in *Sir Charles Grandison*. For Haywood's pragmatic protagonists Betsy and Jenny, surrogate families become a means to experiment with multiple identities distinct from their nuclear or lineage families. They select a variety of surrogate family members based on transitory desires, interests, and aspirations. As they learn about themselves and the world, they discard deleterious surrogate relations such as Miss Forward in *The History of Miss Betsy Thoughtless* and Sophia in *The History of Jemmy and Jenny Jessamy* and in doing so "shed the skin" of immature versions of themselves. As this process repeats itself over time, both protagonists mature into the sort of self-knowledge necessary to make rational decisions about marriage. Even when Betsy accedes to a poor marriage, her moral and intellectual growth allows her to select a better match the second time around. In Jenny's case, though her parents arrange her marriage, their death allows her to wait until she has engaged with the world before deciding whether to enact their wishes. Her experiences before she agrees to marry Jemmy consist largely of experimenting with a variety of surrogate connections that help her understand her own preferences and recognize that they align perfectly with those of her original fiancé.

Chapter 5, "Adopting to Change: Choosing Family in Frances Burney's *Evelina* and *Cecilia*," argues that Frances Burney in *Evelina* and *Cecilia* merges Haywood's and Richardson's later versions of the convention of surrogate families. She borrows from Haywood the optimistic notion that surrogate families allow women to learn about themselves and the world, enabling them to select appropriate spouses. She takes from Richardson's *Clarissa* the potential for surrogate families to replace deficient families of origin. Burney's hybrid version of surrogate families is better than the sum of its parts for her female protagonists. For example, they are more able than Haywood's Betsy to discard undesirable families of origin. Though they exercise the same sort of prerogative as Richardson's Clarissa to cobble together families for themselves, they are not forced to suffer as she does. In *Evelina*, Burney directly opposes blood ties to surrogate relations, with surrogacy proving the more significant predictor of what sort of match Evelina is able to make. In *Cecilia*, the orphaned Cecilia is left solely responsible for the disposal of herself, her uncle's fortune, and her family estate. Only by rejecting this vestige of her nuclear and lineage family is she able to free herself fully to pursue the life and husband of her own choice.

Since the parameters of my study exclude some potentially instructive novels, I address two of these illuminating outliers in the conclusion. The first is Sarah Scott's *Millenium Hall* (1762), which comprises multiple histories of women who live together in a communal household family. Since this novel is focused on multiple protagonists whose courtship narratives are inset into a larger frame narrative describing their community, it does not fit into this project. Nevertheless, it is worth briefly addressing because it is by a female author and about failed courtships and marriages that lead to the formation of a household family made up of chosen surrogate family members. The other novel I consider is *Tom Jones*. Its male protagonist excludes it from consideration. However, its subject is relevant. Tom joins numerous surrogate families and makes decisions about courtship and marriage. His chosen wife, Sophia, does the same thing although with less freedom because her gender constrains her actions. Thus, Fielding's novel provides an opportunity to compare and contrast a young man's and young woman's experiences with surrogate families. Together, these novels demarcate the narrative limits of surrogate families from its most conservative to its most radical iterations. In *Tom Jones*, Tom transforms surrogate families rather than the other way around. He is an object lesson in why surrogate families play a much less significant role in novels about men than about women. However, in *Millenium Hall*, women create an Amazonian version of surrogate families that excludes men altogether. The women who live in this utopian community become one another's mothers, fathers, brothers, and sisters. This all-female surrogate family provides an alternative, and in some cases even an escape, from marriage rather than a means to achieve it.

JUST BUSINESS

Surrogate Families as Entrepreneurial

Ventures in Daniel Defoe's

Moll Flanders and *Roxana*

IN DANIEL DEFOE'S NOVELS, SURROGATE families, or as John Richetti calls them, "small groups of friends who act as substitute families," are the norm, while nuclear families are aberrations.[1] Defoe's plots veer toward the picaresque, which means the household and nuclear families he depicts are often transitory: formed, dissolved, and forgotten in a matter of pages.[2] Surrogate families are often protagonists' only nurturing and enriching connections. Sometimes the help they provide is emotional; most often it is financial. Defoe privileges surrogate families over nuclear or household families because he correlates choice with entrepreneurship.

Surrogate families in Defoe's novels supplement and sometimes even substitute for marriage. Marriage takes many forms in Defoe's novels, including bigamy and liaisons that resemble marriage. In his novels, marriage is just one of many adventures and it may be embarked on repeatedly and coincide with all sorts of other significant relationships. This permissive depiction of marriage is not only unusual for the period, but also directly contradictory to his own advice about it in didactic texts. As David Blewett points out, "between 1715 and 1727 alone" Defoe "produced six books dealing with various aspects of family relationships—courtship, marriage, the bringing up of children, and the treatment of servants," all with an emphasis on "the new morality of family life."[3] The new morality to which Blewett refers idealizes domesticity and endorses companionable unions between loving spouses. Defoe's didactic texts such as *The Family Instructor* (1715) and *Religious Courtship* (1722) popularized the harmonious family life Lawrence Stone associates with the eighteenth century in *The Family, Sex, and Marriage in England, 1500–1800*.[4] As I mention in the introduction, Stone claims that companionate marriage—marriages based on "emotional satisfaction" rather than "ambition for increased income or status"—became more widely accepted over the course of the eighteenth century.[5] Laura Curtis argues that Defoe's families in his didactic works such as *The Family Instructor* and *Religious Courtship* "clearly belon[g] to the category of affective individualism."[6] In other words, they promote the happy, loving vision of marriage and family Stone describes. In contrast, Defoe's novels depict marriage in primarily economic terms. This discrepancy requires explanation.

Paula Backscheider's explanation of the purpose of travel in Defoe's novels, that it "express[es] a deep desire and realistic need to survey the world" and prioritizes the "quest for personal as opposed to social and family identity," also helps explicate the purpose of surrogate families in his fiction.[7] As Hal Gladfelder similarly argues, Defoe's protagonists "embody" an "enterprising" energy that "tends . . . to set the self against all others."[8] However, even the most self-interested protagonists occasionally need friends, though of a particular type. Moll in *Moll Flanders* (1722) describes the sort of friend best suited to an enterprising body like herself as someone who will faithfully "advise" and "assist" her and to whom she can "commit the Secret of any Circumstance."[9] While spouses, parents, or children would seem to be the most obvious and reliable sort of "friends," Defoe's protagonists prefer flexible and opportune intimacies tailored to their own momentary needs and circumstances. Surrogate families offer the best of both worlds. Neither mere friends nor blood relations, they are dedicated but disposable. Nuclear families may outlast their usefulness or demand more than they are able to reciprocate. Loyal attachments to spouses, fathers, mothers, and children are not merely cumbersome, but also in the case of Defoe's highly adaptable protagonists actually signify a deficiency of ambition.

Even the most atomistic of Defoe's protagonists still contend with an amorphous force propelling them back to their origins despite their efforts to remain autonomous. In *Colonel Jack* (1722), for instance, Jacobite rebels beside whom Jack fights reappear in Virginia as transported felons. Unlooked for reappearances of jettisoned kin and spouses occur in *Moll Flanders* and *Roxana* (1724) as well. The tension between the desire of Defoe's protagonists to plot their own courses— represented by surrogate families—and the manacles that shackle them to a single identity or destiny—represented by ties to nuclear family members—is so integral to his novels that Klaus Jochum does not even differentiate the two. He notes that the "relationship between parents or substitute parents and grown-up children is very important in Defoe's novels," unconsciously registering the equal significance of both models of family.[10] Understanding Defoe's larger fictional project, and by extension the history of the genre he helps create, necessitates equal attention to and analysis of his depiction of surrogate and nuclear families.

The tension between these family models is most pronounced in Defoe's novels featuring female protagonists, *Moll Flanders* and *Roxana*. In these novels, the strain Jochum describes determines the trajectory and outcomes of their narratives. The contention for precedence between nuclear and surrogate families is still present in novels like *Robinson Crusoe* (1719) and *Colonel Jack*, but only peripherally.

For example, while Robinson Crusoe attributes his shipwrecks to his father's curse, no family member returns to upbraid him with his disobedience or upset his good fortune. Although he marries and has children when he returns to England, family life is a mere afterthought for him. Defoe kills off Crusoe's wife in one sentence. In comparison, he devotes whole pages to descriptions of Crusoe's attempts to bake bread, construct furniture, and grow crops on his island.

However, in *Moll Flanders* and *Roxana*, the tension between nuclear, surrogate, and household families is exigent to the novels' thematic developments and conclusions. As Ellen Pollak observes, for "both these women, the stakes of fleeing family ties are much higher than for the sometime father and husband, Robinson Crusoe."[11] She argues that because "female agency will inevitably be delimited by the demands of kinship," the "class ascent" of Defoe's heroines along with their other "transgressions," particularly their promiscuity, "trigger . . . a menacing confrontation with their own familial pasts."[12] Toni Bowers also notes the intensity of the conflict between self-seeking and obligations to nuclear families in *Moll Flanders* and *Roxana* versus Defoe's novels about men. Moll and Roxana "abandon and defraud others who threaten their security," just like Robinson Crusoe.[13] But Roxana's daughter returns like a specter and destroys her happiness. One of Moll's sons reappears too. He poses no threat to Moll, but his presence reminds readers of all the other children she has left abandoned in her wake. Additionally, Bowers interprets Moll's and Roxana's rejection of their children as a sort of self-loathing they must expiate. Crusoe, on the other hand, never seems to feel much emotion at all. Because they are women, Moll and Roxana have to face up to the nuclear families they reject. This is true even though they are not typical heroines of eighteenth-century novels. Psychologically, they differ little from Defoe's male protagonists and partake very little in the cult of virtue that would come to be associated with female protagonists such as Clarissa in Samuel Richardson's *Clarissa* (1748).

Moll's own words, excerpted from a passage I quote earlier, provide a complementary explanation for the centrality of surrogate families to eighteenth-century fiction about women. She states that surrogate families, or friends as she calls them, are far more important to women than men because to be "Friendless is the worst Condition, next to being in want, that a Woman can be reduc'd to: I say a Woman, because 'tis evident Men can be their own Advisers, and their own Directors, and know how to work themselves out of Difficulties and into Business better than Women; but if a Woman has no Friend to Communicate her Affairs to, and to advise and assist her, 'tis ten to one but she is undone" (116). Although Moll's resiliency makes it difficult to imagine her being undone by any sort of adversity, she and Roxana must depend on others to help them accumulate and invest money. They cannot go to sea or engage in trade. For them, surrogate families are not just a luxury to help them advance socially and economically, but also a necessary means of survival in a world in which other types of families may at any moment disintegrate or become burdens rather than assets.

Moll Flanders and *Roxana* share numerous other similarities. Two fairly representative readings of the novels emphasize their shared fixation on two themes: money and family. Ann Kibbie describes them as "companion pieces," a "comedy and a tragedy of capital."[14] Spiro Peterson characterizes them, in strikingly similar terms, as "essentially companion studies in the domestic relation."[15] While some scholars focus their attention on Defoe's depiction of love and money in both novels, a focus on finance predominates. It is remarkable how often scholars describe Moll and Roxana as aspiring businesswomen although neither engages in any legitimate business enterprises other than purchasing and selling financial instruments. For example, Michael Shinagel describes Moll Flanders as the "incarnation of the commercial spirit" and Jacqueline Lawson calls Roxana the "ultimate 'She-Merchant,'" a "feminine embodiment of Defoe's 'Complete English Tradesman.'"[16] The two dominant readings of the novels—that they are either about money or family—intersect at the point of surrogate families because Moll and Roxana seek their fortunes and their husbands in the surrogate families they join.

Other similarities between the two novels derive from their shared focus on female protagonists. They share themes of botched maternity, femininity, and domesticity. Bowers's observation that in *Moll Flanders* "good motherhood and economic autonomy are pitted against one another as if they really were mutually exclusive possibilities" applies equally to *Roxana*.[17] Both characters abandon numerous children in their quest for financial security. Marriages are equally disposable, formed far more frequently based on calculation than on attraction or affection. Though Moll and Roxana both describe themselves as whores, they rarely make decisions based on sexual desire.[18] Neither passion nor the desire for domesticity motivate their actions. Instead, as Srividhya Swaminathan suggests, their connections to female friends and mentors help them navigate the world.[19] Marilyn Francus even argues that these connections to other women displace maternity, since in the two novels there is "no replication of, or extension of, nurturing beyond the pairs of women."[20] I agree with both Swaminathan and Francus, but would add that these nurturing female friendships are better understood as surrogate families.

In Moll's case, her ambition pushes her toward other people because she needs them to achieve success. She is not really social by nature but knows that a woman cannot go it alone like Crusoe does. Scholars sometimes overlook or underrate Moll's connections to other people on the basis of assumptions that, as Tina Kuhlisch argues, "Moll never establishes true relationships with the many people she meets."[21] However, just because Moll chooses friends for financial rather than emotional reasons does not make them any less meaningful to her, or less significant to the trajectory of the narrative itself.[22] As James Thompson notes, for Defoe "friendlessness is presented fundamentally as a financial problem."[23] Moll asserts that social connections are particularly important for women because they need friends to get out of "Difficulties and into Business" (116). Despite her atomistic impulses, Moll must seek through others the means of making, growing, and safeguarding a fortune.

Defoe's apparent acceptance of Moll's preference for surrogate ties formed exclusively to promote her economic advancement demonstrates a moral flexibility on his part about marriage and family not only unusual for the period, but also directly contradictory to his own advice about these topics in *The Family Instructor* and *Religious Courtship*. None of his protagonists crave the stability of hearth and home that is the foundation of a life well lived in these didactic texts. Scholars offer numerous explanations for Defoe's protagonists' cavalier attitudes toward ties Defoe himself apparently held sacred. Most of their arguments focus on the difference between what is right in theory and what is realistic to do in particular circumstances. Shirlene Mason argues that in "his didactic works Defoe concentrates on the sin and its dire consequences. In his fiction he puts the sin in context of an evil situation in which sin is unavoidable if the person involved is to survive."[24] Juliet McMaster makes a similar claim, noting *Moll Flanders* deals with actual difficulties women faced because society's "operative standard" was the "displacement of love by money."[25] Other scholars go further, claiming that in *Moll Flanders* Defoe in some sense debunks his own theories, demonstrating, as Austin Flanders writes in reference to the novel's incest incident, the "irrelevance of conventional codes of moral judgment for his rootless characters."[26] While these arguments are all insightful, they are not collectively satisfying. The incongruity they attempt to explain, particularly glaring in *Moll Flanders*, is what interests me. This dissonance is most obvious in Moll's violation of her duties as a wife and mother. Although much less widely noted, her preference for surrogate families united by temporary financial advantages over other family models is also a significant and insufficiently understood manifestation of this discrepancy.

Moll exhibits an entrepreneurial desire to advance herself that her two first families, the parish orphanage, and the group she refers to as gypsies, impede.[27] I define these two groups as nuclear families since birth is supposed to determine whether you belong to them. Both fit Samuel Johnson's definition of *family* as a "household," "generation," or "race."[28] The group Moll refers to as gypsies and "Egyptians" are racially segregated in England, accepting new members based only on birth or adoption (28). Similarly, membership in a parish is determined by place of birth. Neither of these families allows outsiders to voluntarily join or leave them. Authorities in both types of families police membership. According to Moll, the gypsies "discolor" or "blacken" their adopted children's skin (28). Magistrates established formal procedures to determine who belonged to eighteenth-century parishes. It is almost impossible to believe a three-year-old child such as Moll would be capable of prevailing over the legal and conventional barriers erected to keep her in one of these insular families and exclude her from the other. However, according to her recollection, or "Notion in my Head" as she calls it, she does exactly this, hiding from the gypsies and refusing to "go any farther with them" and then engaging the "Compassion" of the parish magistrates to designate her "one of their own, as much as if [she] had been born in the Place" (28–29). It is impossible to know for certain whether Moll actually abandons the gypsies intentionally, as she believes she does, or whether she imposes this interpretation retroactively based on the mature version of herself who tells the story. However, in either case her account demonstrates two significant things about Moll's conception of herself and her evolving understanding of how families affect her ability to pursue her ambitions: she aspires to improve her situation, whatever the circumstances, and is able to do so with more success if she trades up to families with increased promotional opportunities. The inert structures of families whose membership is determined by birth stymie her self-advancement.

Moll tries to hone her self-promotional skills while she lives at the parish orphanage but runs up against the limitations imposed by a rigid family model based on birth rather than choice. By manipulating her nurse, the head of the household family she belongs to, Moll is able to exert some control over her prospects. Her skill, charm, and beauty make her the nurse's favorite child, a privileged status that ultimately allows her to avoid the magistrates' requirement that she go into service when she turns eight. Moll's greatest fear about becoming a servant is being placed as a "Drudge to some Cook-Maid" and thus becoming vulnerable to beatings by "the Maids" in an unknown master's household (29). Her comments reveal that the prospect of social demotion scares her more than corporal punishment. It is not so much that she will be beaten, but rather that the maids will be allowed to beat her that bothers her. The primary symptom of Moll's anxiety about this transition—she is "always Crying"—is overt and tailored to exploit the tenderness of her "good Motherly Nurse" (30). Moll explicitly claims she "Ha[s] no Policy in all this [crying]" and that her response is "all Nature" (31). Even if this ostentatious grief is actually unintentional, at the very least its effectiveness teaches her how to exploit the status she enjoys as the favorite daughter in her household family.

Moll self-consciously enacts this knowledge when she starts performing the role of aspiring gentlewoman to neighborhood ladies for tips, even parlaying the jest into a week as a companion to the daughters of one her admiring audience members. Moll states that the "Taste of Genteel living" she gets during this stay makes her "not so easie in [her] old Quarters" (34). Instead, she wishes to remain "among Gentlewomen" (34). I would argue that it is not just the parish orphanage to which she refers in this instance, but rather, more broadly, the inflexible family it represents, which she views as constraining rather than enabling. It is worth observing in this context that Moll expresses virtually no curiosity about her own mother or her other relatives despite being told that "some Relation of my Mothers took me away for a while as a Nurse" (28). It is not just the impracticality of finding her relations or making claims on them that dictates this indifference. Moll is willing to take risks of all sorts if she thinks there will be a reasonable chance of reward, and her exigent circumstances should make her desperate enough to at least make inquiries. Rather, I interpret Moll's lack of interest in her own family as recognition that there is little to be gained by anchoring herself to a lowly nuclear family such as hers is likely to be. She is better off seeking household families with better promotional opportunities, which her nurse's death gives her immediate occasion to do.

Moll interprets the time she spends as a member of her next family as a cautionary tale against marrying for love or domesticity. This gentlewoman's family, as Moll refers to it, is one of the only intact nuclear families that merit more than passing mention in any of Defoe's novels. His unusual and prolonged narrative attention to it indicates how important Moll's experience in this household is to her development. Moll occupies a strange role in the gentlewoman's household family as a sort of amphibious (to use one of Defoe's favorite terms) land-water creature: both a companion to the daughters and a family servant. From her perch on its periphery she observes its members, studying their behavior anthropologically. It becomes for her a sort of exemplary *everyfamily*, one that inverts all of the domestic ideals advocated by Defoe in his didactic works such as *Religious Courtship* and *The Family Instructor*. In these texts Defoe explicitly rejects mercenary matches and recommends women instead marry religious husbands who will morally guide their households. In contrast, Moll learns to marry for wealth and status and to view family members as competitors in the Hobbesian war of one against all.

The very name Moll uses to refer to this family—the gentlewoman's family—denotes its lack of guidance by a strong father, a serious fault according to Defoe's didactic writing. Moll describes the father in passing as a "man in a hurry of publick Affairs, and getting Money, seldom at Home, thoughtful of the main Chance," but unconcerned about family matters, which he delegates entirely "to his Wife" (62). It is particularly telling that the father is missing during two episodes that determine the future composition of his nuclear family. One occurs at the dinner table. The younger son announces his intention to marry Moll, provoking an "Uproar" from his brothers, sisters, and mother (53). In another scene, the mother unilaterally consents to his marriage, informing her husband after the fact "by Post" (64). In contrast, the father in *The Family Instructor* spends so much time talking with his wife and children that the series of dialogues between them takes up more than 400 pages.[29] His moral directives about when they should pray, what they are allowed to read, and where they may go enforce a corporate moral as well as social identity on their family. This is the opposite of the laissez-faire gentlewoman's family.

Not only the father, but also the gentlewoman and her daughters model the mercenary attitudes about marriage Moll later adopts as her own. The sisters are quarrelsome and vain, educated in social graces meant to impress suitors rather than religious principles intended to prepare them to nurture families. Their attitude toward marriage is consistent with their overall worldview: wholly pragmatic. One sister explicitly states that "nothing but Money now recommends a Woman" to a potential husband (37). Though largely undeveloped as characters, they resemble somewhat the frivolous elder sister in *The Family Instructor* who protests when her father burns her playbooks, novels, and ballads. Their mother, who ought in their father's absence to educate her children religiously, instead focuses only on maintaining the family's "very good" and, if the lessons in *The Family Instructor* are seriously intended, unearned reputation "for Vertue and Sobriety, and every valuable Thing" (92). Her worldly view of marriage is apparent in her mournful response, "there's one Son lost," to hearing about her son's intention to marry Moll (56).

While the parents and sisters in the gentlewoman's family stoke Moll's matrimonial aspirations, the brothers provide her with tutorials in how to achieve them. The younger brother would seem to be the sort of husband Defoe would recommend to any young woman. He has strong earning potential and is willing to defy his family for her sake. He wants to marry her, not seduce her. What is missing is religion. Unlike the prophet-like younger son in *The Family Instructor*, this younger brother never seems to think about God at all. Even his romantic desire to marry for love is a manifestation of the selfishness characteristic of his entire family. He coerces Moll into marriage by courting her so persistently and publicly that even if she turns him down she will still be ejected from the house. His aggressive courtship forces Moll to the altar "like a bear to the stake," and his lack of ready money leaves her dependent on earnings that dry up when he dies five years later (48). From this younger brother Moll learns she must assess and manipulate potential suitors before they have any opportunity to pursue her. She also makes certain to carefully scrutinize their fortunes, understanding through experience the advantages of ready money over contingent revenue.

From the elder brother Moll learns that if she allows herself to love and trust a suitor, she is likely to become a disposable mistress rather than a wife. Moll believes the attractive, wealthy elder brother's promises to eventually marry her. She engages in a monthslong affair with him based on that assumption. However, he is a canny and experienced rake who, like Mr. Elton in Jane Austen's *Emma* (1815), talks "sentimentally" about marriage, but "act[s] rationally."[30] Moll's poverty makes her an undesirable spouse, but a perfectly acceptable mistress. Far more depraved than the elder brother in *The Family Instructor*, whose greatest fault is petulance, this brother avoids his counterpart's comeuppance by deceiving rather than defying his family. He acts parts to everyone, playing a dutiful son and brother to his family and a passionate lover to Moll. It is ironic that this self-indulgent sensualist supposedly discontinues his affair with Moll for the sake of family honor, after learning she might marry his brother and "become my Sister" (62). His renunciation burlesques the family loyalty and moral probity it is supposed to signify. The more likely explanation for his sacrifice is a selfish one; he performs ardor in order to engage her affections, and then remorse in order to conveniently dispose of her. Moll learns from her apprenticeship as this brother's mistress that courtship itself is a performance, and in order to obtain an advantageous match she must occupy the stage rather than observe from the gallery. "LOVE," she determines as a discarded mistress, is a *"Cheat"* and a "Game," and in order to procure a desirable husband she must act her part based on rational self-interest rather than emotion (66).

Based on these paradigmatic relationships with the brothers and the mercenary ideals of marriage she adopts while living in the gentlewoman's family, Moll develops principles of courtship meant to maximize her marital profits and minimize the risks she takes to achieve them. Melissa Mowry interprets Moll's intentions to become "part of [this] prosperous family" by marrying the elder brother as arising not just from ambition, but also "desire to belong to a greater whole."[31] However, it is hard to believe Moll cares much about contributing to a stable community. Instead, I agree with Gladfelder, who emphasizes Moll's "irremediable sense of apartness" which frees her to engage in the "relentless pursuit" of profit.[32] The marriage market is driven by competition, and any woman who succumbs to the romantic notion of belonging to a "greater whole" is vulnerable to becoming a mistress. The marital axioms Moll develops based on her experiences in this family constitute a sort of business plan intended to woo investors without exposing herself to the attendant risks of speculation. She begins to use explicitly commercial language to describe marriage, repeatedly conflating faulty spouses with dangerous business "ventures," good husbands to revenue or "prize[s]," and marriage to a "Lottery" (77).

Moll's increasingly cynical views about marriage directly contradict Defoe's own advice to courting couples in *Religious Courtship*, which was published, as Blewett notes, within a month of *Moll Flanders*.[33] In *Religious Courtship*, Defoe cautions young people not to "act an unwise Part for both Time and Eternity" by ignoring the "religious Principles and Temper" of suitors in order to pursue anyone who is "Rich and Handsome."[34] Moll learns when her first lover spurns her not to fall prey to a handsome face, but according to Defoe's assessment of marriage she becomes shrewder rather than wiser. He states unequivocally in *Conjugal Lewdness; or Matrimonial Whoredom* (1727) "Love is the only Pilot of a married State; without it there is nothing but Danger in the Attempt; nothing but Ruin in the Consequence."[35] Moll understands danger and ruin only in economic terms.

She is the very definition of the "matrimonial whore" Defoe derides in his pamphlet, described by Blewett succinctly as "one who uses the institution of marriage improperly for gain."[36] The affectionate companionship Defoe recommends elsewhere appears only as cessations in Moll's story when she claims she is "landed in a safe Harbour, after the Stormy Voyage of Life" (161). These periods are typically brief, and her safe harbors often prove to be floodplains. As Mona Scheuermann observes, money, not marriage is the real "source of security for Moll."[37]

The most erotic scenes in the novel, consequently, are about accumulating money rather than having sex. Several representative scenes occur between Moll and men she either marries or with whom she has long-term marriage-like relationships. These scenes stand in for courtship and consummation. The most obvious of these is when Moll's married friend forces one of her hands into his "Drawer" of gold coins, demands she take a handful of them and "put them into [her] Lap" and then "[pours] out all [her] own Money among his" (105). The double entendres continue as she carries the loot "into [her] own Chamber" (105). The series of scenes in which Moll brings gold, linen, and cash to her half-brother/husband are less explicit but equally playful. For Moll, mingling money signifies marital commitment more than consummation because she considers her goods more valuable than access to her body. Even the least libidinous union, her marriage to her banker husband, commences with a flirtatious exchange about money. She comes to him for advice on how to invest her money and he responds with a proposal that she solve her economic problems by marrying him (121). In each case, marriage or at least long-term commitment is cemented not by a ceremony or by sex, but by uniting funds. When those funds fail, Moll considers the business venture of marriage concluded and reenters the market as a free agent. For example, her second husband, the draper, may well be alive when Moll marries many, if not all, of her future husbands. But she considers him "effectually dead in Law" because he is bankrupt and absent (91). Despite the probable bigamy she repeatedly commits, Moll continues to pursue for-profit matches because financial prospects are better for a pretended wife than an avowed mistress.

Although Moll continues as long as possible to pursue social and economic advancement through marriage, she cannot entirely avoid becoming entangled by family ties. Motherhood, a likely outcome of marriage, repeatedly threatens to tie her down. She also unexpectedly becomes trapped by her nuclear family. Her mother and half-brother emerge unexpectedly in the persons of her husband and mother-in-law. Her incestuous relationship with her half-brother/husband exacerbates her already marked aversion to nuclear families. In fact, incest becomes for Moll an exaggerated version of kinship itself, insular and stifling to her entrepreneurial instincts. Since Moll's hostility to nuclear families only increases over the course of her lengthy marital career, she repudiates her newborn and newfound relations with all possible expediency.

Children are the most obvious example of nuclear family members Moll rejects. She raises most of them with apparent competence and affection as long as the marriage that produced them lasts. However, once it ends she disposes of them. When possible, she leaves them with members of their fathers' lineage families. For example, she gives custody of the children by her first husband to their grandparents. When linear families or nuclear families are unavailable to raise her children she pays other people to take them off her hands. Only one of Moll's sons reappears later in the novel, and she seeks him out for primarily mercenary reasons. There are two possible interpretations of the novel that would hold Moll blameless for this behavior. Perhaps financial exigency necessitates Moll's business-like disposal of her children. However, David Spielman's analysis of money in the novel implicitly refutes this interpretation. He concludes based on calculations about the present-day value of Moll's wealth that "at no point in the course of [her] relationships does Moll experience anything like poverty," and that even at what she claims is one of her lowest points she still possesses a fortune equivalent in today's money to about £50,000.[38] Even when she does have enough money to keep her children, she doesn't. Another possible explanation for Moll's detachment from her children is that her attitude toward them was culturally normative during the eighteenth century. Childhood mortality was high and children often lived apart from their parents for long periods of time. Babies and young children were often cared for by nurses. Older children often left their nuclear families to join differently configured household families as apprentices or domestic servants or to attend boarding school. However, Ashley Marshall's findings about abridgements of *Roxana* and *Moll Flanders* suggest most eighteenth-century readers probably did not find Moll's indifference to her children acceptable. She observes that "one of the major problems" readers had with Roxana, who also disposed of numerous children, was her "poor treatment of her children."[39]

Although *Roxana* is not *Moll Flanders* and what was true of the second half of the century may not have been equally true of the first half, it is still reasonable to conclude based on Marshall's findings that Moll's nonchalance about her children would have been considered unusual and inappropriate and thus requires explanation. I posit that the reason for her dislike of motherhood is because children are antithetical to ambition. Moll has an especial dislike for the expensiveness of motherhood. As infants and young children, they are certain to be costly and troublesome. As young adults they must be educated and placed in some sort of apprenticeship or service. As adults they are far more likely to expect an inheritance than to provide one. For Moll, who is wary of acknowledging even fairly profitable blood ties, children have no charms.

Moll's treatment of her children still elicits condemnation from modern scholars. Shinagel denounces her as an "unnatural mother who steadfastly rejects her moral—and natural—responsibility as a parent," and Jochum describes Moll as an "utter failure" as a mother.[40] David Paxman claims that she has "sincere feelings" for her children, but that she nevertheless "brushes them aside" when necessary "as impediments in her quest for economic and romantic security."[41] Going even further, Francus accuses Moll of "consciously choos[ing] . . . infanticide" in certain instances over the wearisome self-sacrifice associated with motherhood.[42] Though Moll never actually murders any of her children, Francus's point is well taken. Moll's experience with her own nurse aside, orphans left in group homes with professional nurses were notoriously prone to disease, neglect, and abuse. Moll's refusal to raise these children manifests her larger animosity toward being tied down by kinship. Unlike marriages, which she screens for profitability, children always take rather than give; they are the opposite of productive investments.

Moll's disrelish for immutable family ties of any sort is also evident in the deterioration of her relationships with her mother and half-brother after she discovers they are kin. Moll appreciates the financial security her position in a prominent Virginia family provides her, so she cleaves to the source of their wealth: her mother-in-law. This relationship cools significantly, however, when Moll learns her mother-in-law is actually her mother. Moll explains the alienation from her mother as a symptom of her overriding disgust with her incestuous marriage to her half-brother (87). However, it is surprising that her horror is not mitigated at all by excitement over a reunion with her family. Defoe emphasizes Moll's coldness by contrasting it with her mother's passionate display of emotion, "kiss[ing]" her daughter through her tears despite the devastating implications of this revelation (92). Lois Chaber explains Moll's unkindness toward her mother by interpreting it as a sign that Moll never fully acknowledges their kinship since her mother "seemed [to be] only a surrogate mother—a mother-in-law—for so long."[43] Rather, I would argue that far from "leveling," as Chaber asserts, ties by blood with surrogate ties such as Moll's connection to her nurse and governess, Moll's realization that she has committed incest amplifies her qualms about kinship itself.[44] While Moll's relationship to her mother becomes more detached after learning they are related, her bond to her brother ruptures entirely. Her instinctive repugnance at having sex with him explains her "provoking" behavior to him while she remains in Virginia (90). However, it does not account for the enduring bitterness apparent in her pronouncement many years later when she returns to the American colonies that "the old Wretch, my Brother (Husband) was dead" (274).

This incest episode only intensifies Moll's desire to act as a free agent. Katerina Kitsi-Mitakou argues that the ultimate "object of Moll's desire" when she commits incest "is the mother, or even [Moll's] 'self'" (since Moll resembles her mother so much).[45] I agree with Kitsi-Mitakou that discovering a biological family nested like a Russian doll inside a conjugal family is a form of self-discovery, and would expand her claims to include Moll's half-brother/husband as well. However, if Moll sees herself reflected in her newfound relations, she proves to be no

Narcissus. Far from falling in love with these images of herself, she becomes "uneasie" and "restless" to separate herself fully from them by returning to England (99). Moll experiences the forced intimacy of discovering they are connected inextricably to her as a form of entrapment. After leaving, she returns to her earlier practice of marital entrepreneurship, a "Scene of Life" she is qualified to succeed at since she is "still far from being old" (100).

While serial matrimony remains profitable for quite a long time for Moll, her governess introduces her to a more abiding and remunerative family model: the surrogate family. Moll meets her governess, or Mother Midnight (an ambiguous term meaning midwife, bawd, and abortionist) as Moll initially calls her, while she is seeking out new marital opportunities. Their bond is much more immediate and emotionally intense than Moll's connection to her biological mother, so much so that it constitutes what I call surrogate motherhood. Inconveniently pregnant by her husband Jemy who has now abandoned her, Moll becomes ill with worry about how to safely give birth to and then dispose of their child. By helping Moll out of her difficulties, the governess "births" Moll back to life again, or as Moll phrases it, "put[s] new Life and new Spirit into my very Heart" (141). Defoe turns what is typically a simple metaphor signifying invigoration into a literal physiological phenomenon when he writes that Moll's "Blood began to circulate immediately" upon speaking to the governess (141). Before Moll even becomes an inmate of the governess's lying-in hospital, she has already become her surrogate daughter. The unusual degree of intimacy between Moll and her governess leads Robert Erickson to a similar conclusion about the maternal nature of their bond.[46]

The governess intensifies this maternal connection with Moll by redefining Moll's view of motherhood itself. In a scene that is often viewed as ironic, Moll confesses to her governess her qualms of conscience about abandoning her infant son. The episode consists of a lengthy conversation (spanning three pages) positing alternative theories of motherhood and child-rearing. Moll, an admittedly unlikely proponent for her own position, argues that mothers must raise their own children because "Affection was plac'd by Nature in the Hearts of Mothers" by God (150). According to Moll, relying on paid surrogates to "take the Child off" a mother's hands for as "long as it lives" is a form of infanticide because their "Gain consists in being quit of the Charge" (152). The governess counters Moll's argument by portraying motherhood as one of many "Trades." Any woman can learn to perform a mother's duties and will perform them well because she is paid to do them. According to this logic, foster mothers may even be superior to biological mothers because they "get their Bread by it," while biological mothers must act out of instinctual altruism (151).

Although Moll initially appears skeptical of the governess's economic vision of motherhood, over the course of the novel she comes to endorse it and to adopt it as her own. Even as Moll appears to doubt the equation between profit and conscientiousness espoused by the governess, she cannot help but respect the simple pragmatism of the governess's final defense of paid surrogates. The governess reminds Moll she cannot afford to enact the lofty ideals of motherhood she advocates and needs to instead "be contented with things as they must be, tho' they are not as [she] wish[es]" (152). Despite her reservations, Moll follows the governess's advice and spends ten pounds to hire a "Country Woman" to "take the Child off our Hands entirely" (153). The linguistic markers in the conversation suggest that Moll's acceptance of the governess's vision of motherhood is personally as well as philosophically significant. As Moll's use of "our" rather than "my" in reference to her own child indicates, Moll now sees herself as a member of the governess's family. This family is defined not by birth or by marriage. It is forged while Moll is a patient in the governess's lying-in hospital, which is a sort of household family. What bonds them most closely, though, is their shared economic vision. Defoe clarifies the nature of this familial connection through his use of the term *mother* more than thirteen times during the course of the conversation, at least five of which are direct addresses by Moll to the governess, whom she "had now learn'd to call Mother" (151). The relationship between Moll and her new economic mother is cemented by mutual self-interest, a stronger foundation than blood in Moll's view for an enduring connection.

The surrogate mother/daughter relationship formed between Moll and the governess continues to thrive over time because it fulfills their mutual expectations of profitability. When Moll and the governess reconnect after the death of Moll's banker husband, they are both in reduced circumstances: Moll has no income to support herself, and the governess has become a pawnbroker. The governess assists Moll by fencing her stolen goods and acting as a liaison between Moll and other members of London's criminal underworld. The governess also arranges for Moll's education as a thief by locating an expert "School-Mistress" for Moll to apprentice under as a pickpocket "just as a Deputy attends a Midwife without any Pay" (171). The governess even masterminds one of Moll's most lucrative schemes, the mercer's cash settlement for falsely detaining and defaming Moll. She directs her to numerous profitable ventures, such as stealing from a family whose house is on fire. Over the course of her lengthy criminal career Moll accumulates £700 as well as many stolen goods, making her, according to the governess, the "richest of the Trade in *England*" (209). If the economic advantages Moll reaps from her connection to the governess are fairly obvious, the benefits the governess enjoys are even more overt since she takes a "Share of the Gain" of Moll's exploits with "no Share in the hazard" (181). Moll's surrogate mother is perfectly matched to her, as both share a spirit of entrepreneurship, a delight in conning the credulous, an unscrupulous willingness to exploit any situation, and an insatiable ambition for profit.

More surprisingly, the relationship between Moll and her surrogate mother also develops many aspects of the selfless love Moll asserts mothers instinctually feel for their children. The favoritism the governess displays for Moll in giving her the "full value" for any stolen plate she smelts, something Moll knows the governess does not do for other "Customers," hints early on at the increasing exclusivity of their attachment to each other (170–171). Later, the governess not only protects Moll, but also places herself at risk for her sake, hiding Moll in her house when an angry mob tries to seize her for theft. In contrast, she does nothing to intervene when numerous of her other associates hang for their crimes. The intimacy that develops between them becomes so marked that the governess actually refers to herself and Moll as a unit, advising Moll to "[leave] off while *we* were well" and be "satisfy'd with what *we* had got" (emphasis mine) (216). Her sentiments as much as her phrasing signify that this relationship is not just transactional for the governess. While economic opportunism would dictate that the governess encourage Moll to keep stealing, she instead proposes to forgo any further profits merely for the sake of protecting her surrogate daughter.

The nurturing relationship between Moll and her governess becomes even more pronounced after Moll is caught stealing and sent to Newgate. The governess apparently has access to all of Moll's money and stolen goods, so it is in her interest to let Moll hang. Instead, she attempts repeatedly and at some expense (though the bribes she offers would be paid for with Moll's own money) to free Moll. After Moll is condemned, the governess continues to "[act] a true Mother to [her]," coming to her surrogate daughter's aid emotionally and pragmatically (231). She tends to Moll's spiritual health by encouraging her to repent. She also provides Moll with invaluable practical services: arranging Jemy's passage on the ship that transports Moll to America, purchasing the necessary items they need to settle there, and negotiating the terms of their freedom once they arrive. It is telling that the boatswain who carries a letter to the governess from Moll mistakes her for Moll's "Sister" and is surprised to learn she is "no Relation" of Moll's, but rather a "dear Friend" (250). He assumes that only a relation would display such empathy and offer so much help since "there are few such Friends in the World" (250). Even though Moll ultimately reunites with one of her sons and never sees her governess again, the boatswain's casual observation is far more insightful about the nature of Moll's relationship to the governess than he is capable of knowing. For Moll, this friend is the only relation, according to his understanding of the word (which mirrors Moll's in her earlier conversation about motherhood with the governess), Moll ever really has.

Although Moll is ultimately forced to leave her governess for a new life in the American colonies, she imposes desirable aspects of her former surrogate family on the remaining members of her two nuclear families: Jemy and Humphry. Moll is accustomed, after her many years partnering with the governess in their criminal enterprises, to accumulating her own capital. Rather than depend on another potentially hapless husband, Moll refashions her marriage to Jemy to exercise financial free will. This final marriage is the only one Moll enters into knowing she is richer than her husband. It is not mercenary motives or the desire for status that drive their union. Moll needs a spouse for practical reasons. Since it would be difficult for her to transact business independently in the colonies, she marries a man who allows her to control their accounts. Jemy resembles the sort of wife Moll was formerly consigned to being. He allows her to decide which plantation to buy and how to invest their money. He reveals how little he knows about any of these transactions when the goods purchased with Moll's ill-gotten gains arrive from England. He worries Moll has run them "too deep in Debt," a response that reveals the extent of his ignorance about their finances (273). He is the matrimonial whore Moll once was, thanking providence that he "married a Fortune, and a very good Fortune too," and leaving the rest to his spouse (274). This inverted spousal relationship is the closest approximation Moll can achieve in marriage to the financial autonomy she experienced in her surrogate family.

Moll also transforms her relationship to her son Humphry into a profitable connection founded on principles she forms and capital she accumulates as the governess's surrogate daughter. When Moll returns to the colonies she seeks out her kin in order to claim an inheritance. The sight of her son Humphry walking around their plantation sends her into a state of emotional rapture similar to the one she experienced when the governess explained how to dispose of a different child. The scene is overwrought and sentimental, recounting how Moll's "very Bowels mov'd" at the sight of him, leaving her exhausted by her paroxysm of emotion, "we[eping], and kiss[ing]" the ground on which he stood (260). This agitation also characterizes a letter Moll sends, ostensibly to her half-brother/husband but really to her son (who Moll knows reads all the family correspondence). It is full of "Passionate" outpourings of a tormented heart to "[see] my one, and only Child" (267).[47] These two passages forge a stylistic connection between Moll's relationships with her son and her governess. Defoe further reinforces this association through Moll's gift of a stolen watch to Humphry, who she tells to "now and then kiss" it for her sake (271). This relic of Moll's surrogate family embodies her connection to the governess, who funded the training that made Moll an expert watch-puller. Humphry construes the watch just as Moll would wish, as a "Debt upon him, that he would be paying, as long as [he] liv'd" (271). Typically, motherhood is conceived of as a lifelong debt to one's children, but through the watch Moll upends the conventional terms of this relationship. The watch that becomes the emblem for this unorthodox model of parenthood is best interpreted not as a gift from Moll to her son, but instead from the governess to Moll. It is a lasting memorial to surrogate parenthood, a tribute that pays regular dividends, and thus reflects the values of the surrogate family in which it originates.

Moll's straightforward, future-oriented, and practical worldview allows her to jettison husbands, children, and even her mother without remorse. She retains

Jemy and Humphry only because they are willing to conform to the surrogate family model rather than expect her to adopt a woman's conventional role in a nuclear family: serving her children and obeying her husband. Moll requires them to grant her the authority and autonomy she learns to exercise as the governess's surrogate daughter. Her casual ruthlessness about discarding unprofitable or unco-operative family members is a necessary precondition for her consolidating these two-family models. Defoe's later novel, *Roxana*, begins similarly to *Moll Flanders* and its trajectory appears to move toward *Moll Flanders*'s harmonious synthesis of different family models. However, the narrative veers away from *Moll Flanders*'s narrative trajectory once family models begin to compete with one another.

Every aspect of *Roxana* is more complicated and exaggerated than *Moll Flanders*. For example, Roxana's greed is much more insatiable than Moll's. Several of Moll's marriages are marginally profitable, but Roxana's marriages and marriage-like relationships are so lucrative and her investment strategies so effective she describes herself as "wallowing in Wealth," accumulating a fortune of nearly £60,000.[48] Unlike the blithe Moll, Roxana feels remorse about her self-indulgence and attempts to take responsibility for children she abandons. One of these children becomes so obsessed with Roxana that she compares her to a "*Plague*" and an "Evil Spirit" (246, 252). Moll does not have this problem because she never contacts any of her children who might still need things from her: only the one who has something to give. Additionally, while Moll enjoys a playful, affectionate, and comparatively uncomplicated relationship with her surrogate mother, Roxana's connection to her surrogate relation, Amy, is the reverse: complex, passionate, violent, and destructive.

Lawson attributes the explosiveness of Roxana's relationships to the novel's uneasy blend of multiple types of family models: "Roxana contains no integrated or well-defined family unit. Instead, Defoe presents an extended and amorphous domestic network consisting of Roxana, her legal husband and numerous illicit lovers (including, it is hinted, the Restoration monarch himself), the assorted off-spring of these holy and unholy alliances, and, finally, the maidservant Amy, no blood-relation to Roxana though surely her kinswoman in blood. This strange and aberrant family configuration—this family manqué—is denied from the outset the possibility of domestic stability and coherence."[49] Lawson's observation is astute, though I interpret this lack of "stability" and "coherence" differently. Though Roxana tries at times to adopt the simple for-profit worldview displayed by Moll, she is unable to successfully overcome her emotions. Neither can her daughter Susan, nor her surrogate relation Amy. Emotion and excess—both in terms of extravagant feelings and extraordinary sums of money—disrupt each of her families and place them in competition with one another.

Roxana's marriages are fewer and farther between than Moll's because she determines that marriage is inimical to enterprise. Roxana's conclusions about marriage are the antithesis of Moll's creed that a "Woman should never be kept for a

Mistress, that had Money to keep her self" (67). Moll perceives marriage as more financially secure than being a mistress because while a husband has a legal obligation to support his wife, the maintenance a kept mistress enjoys is always precarious. Essentially, Moll is more risk averse than Roxana, at least to a particular type of risk. Rather than fearing abandonment by a bored lover, Roxana fears marriage to a "Fool," her memorable description of her first husband who closely resembles the elder brother Moll wishes to marry in *Moll Flanders* (25). Although Moll and Roxana are both abandoned at some point by worthless husbands (the draper and the fool), they come to contrary conclusions about what these desertions reveal about marriage. Moll blames herself for choosing the wrong sort of husband, while Roxana decides marriage itself is faulty. Husbands, she determines, are as prone as lovers to abscond, and are apt to bankrupt their wives before leaving.

Roxana's desire to maintain control over her wealth is the basis for her famous attack on women's subjection in marriage. Having accumulated an impressive fortune as the mistress of a jeweler and a prince, Roxana is unwilling to relinquish control over it. She rejects outright a wealthy, agreeable, and companionable merchant (though she later marries him anyway), supposedly because she objects to marriage for feminist reasons. She characterizes marriage for women as "nothing but giving up Liberty, Estate, Authority, and every-thing, to the Man" and becoming "a meer Woman ever after, that is to say, a Slave" (130). She confides to readers, though, that these ideals conceal her real motive for refusing the match, equally feminist in its own way. She is willing to "give up [her] Virtue" but not her "Money" (130). Moll expresses concern occasionally about joining fortunes with her husbands, but never very forcefully because she has far less to lose than does Roxana.

Although Roxana is ultimately reunited with and marries the discarded merchant, the fruits of her excessive wealth and avarice prevent her from enjoying the happy ending experienced by Moll in parallel circumstances. It is telling that Roxana celebrates her marriage by securing a settlement for her friend the Quaker "distinct from any of the Effects" belonging to her husband (208). The gift itself acknowledges the reality that not every marriage is like the one depicted in *The Family Instructor*. Some husbands take family responsibilities seriously, but others exploit their power over their wives and children. Roxana's qualms about marriage become a self-fulfilling prophecy, ultimately poisoning her relationship with her new husband. In Roxana's case, it is the wife rather than the husband who is to blame for their distresses. The merchant proves to be a model husband: wealthy, agreeable in temperament, and desirous that Roxana should "[settle] in Trustees Hands, for [her] own Use" her substantial fortune (214). However, Roxana is unable to enjoy her marital tranquility.

Although time and mutual affection might bring about a sea change in Roxana's cynical views of marriage, motherhood is another matter. She feels guilty for abandoning her children in the same measure as she resents them simply for existing. At first, this attitude appears to be just an exaggerated version of Moll's distaste for expense and trouble. After Roxana's husband abandons her, she must dispose of their five children. Expressing much the same sentiment as Moll's governess, who advises Moll to adapt her expectations about motherhood to fit the reality of her impoverished situation, Roxana states that her "Circumstances hardened my Heart against my own Flesh and Blood" (34). Consequently, she forces some of them on her husband's relations (literally leaving them on their doorstep) and gives at least one to the parish: both actions with clear precedents in *Moll Flanders*. Roxana sometimes appears more callous even than Moll, especially when it comes to the fate of her illegitimate children. For example, when Roxana's infant son by the prince dies during their travels in Italy, she is not "sorry the Child did not live, the necessary Difficulties attending it on our travelling, being consider'd" (98). Moll expresses horror when the governess suggests she might abort an unwanted child, but Roxana "would willingly . . . [give] ten Thousand Pounds" to be "rid of" her illegitimate pregnancy by the merchant (142). She later admits she does not love the resulting son, who she "scarce [sees] . . . four times in the first four Years of its Life" (217). Roxana's continued references to her son as "it" even after her marriage to the merchant provide further evidence of antipathy to her illegitimate children. The intensity of her feelings about her children and her past makes her vulnerable to their intrusion into her present.

Roxana's susceptibility to the backward-looking emotions of regret and shame also distinguishes her from Moll. Unlike Moll, Roxana feels enough remorse for deserting her legitimate children that she eventually seeks them out in order to provide for them. In a peculiar scene, Roxana interrupts a long description of the wealth she accumulates as a mistress with the sudden "remember[ance]" that fifteen years ago she had "left five little Children, turn'd out, as it were, to the wide World" (161). Moll reunites with Humphry for purely circumstantial and opportunistic reasons, neither of which explain Roxana's quest for her lost children. Roxana seeks out her son by her first husband to give him money, not to take it from him. Justifying her generosity based on his legitimacy—he is the "only Son [she] had left, that" she has a "legal Right to call Son"—Roxana anonymously spends thousands of pounds establishing him as a merchant (172). She cannot reveal herself to him since she does not want him to "know what a Mother he had, and what a Life she liv'd" (172). Consequently, she cannot expect to receive any recognition of her bounty. She does not invest money in his business prospects in order to reap future profits. As contradictory as it seems for a woman who repeatedly describes herself as a "Whore" and an unnatural mother to behave selflessly for the sake of her son, self-interest cannot account for her actions (54). Love, duty, guilt, or some combination of the three are the only plausible explanations for her behavior. These emotional motivations disrupt the straightforward and economically driven vision of motherhood depicted in *Moll Flanders*.

Not only does Roxana act against her self-interest in seeking out and offering money to her children, but one of her children, Susan, also acts against her self-interest in demanding Roxana acknowledge her. Roxana's perverse and destructive relationship with Susan is the catastrophe at the center of Defoe's novel. As Kibbie notes, it is also a "nightmare version of the happy mother-child reunion in *Moll Flanders*," and thus thematically connects the two novels.[50] The relationship between Roxana and Susan becomes increasingly adversarial because Susan will not accept an anonymous "buyout" from Roxana in lieu of acknowledgment as Roxana's daughter. As Jochum observes, Susan is "motivated by claims of kinship and by an inextinguishable desire to be recognized" as Roxana's daughter, not by social or economic ambition.[51] These primal desires stake claims on Roxana that do not align with her obligations to her husband and her surrogate family member, Amy. In the absence of the rational coolness promoted by unmitigated economic self-interest, these competing models cannot coexist. Amy's probable murder of Susan provides the strongest evidence for this incompatibility.

Susan's demands to be acknowledged by Roxana become so shrill and insistent they force Roxana and Amy to retaliate. Initially, Susan seems to accept Amy's offer to simply provide her the means to "appear as a Gentlewoman" without revealing anything about her parents (173). However, Susan wants her mother more than her mother's money, and fixates on the possibility that Amy "was really her Mother; and that she had for some particular Reasons, conceal'd it" (219). Language itself repeatedly proves inadequate to express the primal nature of Susan's desire to be recognized as a daughter, and she responds to Amy's rebuttals with violent fits and tears, at one point "crying . . . as if she wou'd kill herself" (221). Amy attempts to force Susan to accept her mother's bounty and not ask for anything more. She threatens that she will "leave [Susan] to the World, as she found her" and let her "go a-begging" or into "Service again, and be a Drudge, as she was before" unless she stops hounding Roxana (221–222). Rather than rationally deciding that money and no mother is a better outcome than no money and no mother, as Moll would undoubtedly have done, Susan becomes even more obsessed with Roxana. She investigates her movements, pursues her across England, and harasses her friends. Susan's passion forces Amy and Roxana to respond in anger rather than act in a calculated fashion. By provoking this panicked and angry response, Susan does arguably "kill herself"; she upsets the precarious balance Roxana establishes between her marriage to the merchant, her perceived duty to her legitimate but abandoned children, and her connection to her surrogate relation Amy, and thus instigates her own murder, presumably at Amy's hands.

Susan's ambush of Roxana threatens to breach the barriers Roxana and Susan erect to prevent Roxana's husband from learning about the other families Roxana belonged to before she married him. Consequently, Roxana is forced to prioritize the family members she cares about most and to protect them by dispossessing others. Her emotions and behavior become increasingly erratic as she attempts to make this difficult choice. Although Roxana's relationship with her husband would seem to be most vulnerable to Susan's interference, the contest for Roxana's loyalty is enacted between Susan and Amy. They deliberately and viciously compete with one another for primacy, assuming Roxana's husband will be less dear to her than either of them. Amy goes so far as to tell Roxana she might murder Susan if it is the only way to keep her away. Roxana responds to this threat "*in a Rage*," promising to retaliate by "cut[ting]" Amy's Throat with [her] own Hand." Even as Roxana appears to embrace Susan at Amy's expense, she forgives Amy's aggression because she believes it is the product of "Affection and Fidelity" (223). The incoherence of Roxana's feelings when confronted with inescapable choices about which family member she will cleave to is also evident in her conflicted feelings about Susan. Although Roxana attempts to help Susan financially and protect her from Amy, she also admits she would welcome Susan's death as long as she "dropp'd into the Grave by any fair Way" (246). In fact, Roxana's conflicted feelings toward her namesake are so acute that when social niceties require her to kiss Susan, she feels at the same moment both "Horror" and "inconceivable Pleasure" (227).

Defoe metaphorically represents the intensity of this conflict through an imaginary pregnancy Roxana invents in order to avoid a lengthy boat trip with Susan, Amy, and her spouse. Roxana's supposed pregnancy imaginatively combines all her families: it is attributed to her husband; it stands in for her daughter, Susan; and it is reminiscent of Roxana's and Amy's consecutive pregnancies and the daughters they subsequently produce fathered by the same man (the jeweler). The novel's prolonged references to this fictitious pregnancy emphasize its thematic importance. First, Roxana's husband misinterprets a reference by the ship's captain to Susan— "I hear your Lady has got a Daughter more than she expected"—as an allusion to his own unborn child (242). Roxana also expresses a longing to be "deliver'd" from Susan, a suggestive choice of words since it combines two opposite and equally applicable meanings: to give birth and to murder (246). It is ultimately Roxana's surrogate family member Amy who carries out Roxana's unspeakable (except through innuendo) wish, to "murther [her] own Child," and thus finally resolve the rivalry between Roxana's different models of family (246).

Amy's connection to Roxana is characterized by the same passionate, irrational, and jealous attachment Susan feels for Roxana. Amy initially acts as Roxana's surrogate mother, protecting and mentoring her, introducing her to wealthy "suitors," and arranging her financial affairs. Tellingly, Roxana's first mention of Amy by name occurs when Roxana's husband has abandoned her and she despairs of supporting herself and her children. Amy, who Roxana describes as a "resolute Girl," not only encourages Roxana to abandon her children, but also actually formulates and carries out the means to force the parish and their paternal relations to care for them (34). Once Amy establishes this precedent, she continues to make decisions for Roxana for much of the novel. Although the control Amy exercises over the passive Roxana identifies her as Roxana's surrogate mother, Amy is still a maid in Roxana's household family, which relegates her structurally to the role of a daughter. Just as Pamela in *Pamela* (1740) identifies herself as her mistress's surrogate daughter, Amy is in a daughter-like position in relation to Roxana. Additionally, Amy sometimes acts more like Roxana's surrogate sister than her mother or daughter. She experiences courtships and pregnancies alongside Roxana, acts as her confidante and companion while they live together, and is close enough to Roxana's age to be her peer. While Amy officially remains Roxana's maid for a long time, she receives no pay after Roxana's husband leaves. It is significant that Amy does not seem to regret losing her earnings. If anything, she seems pleased that her relationship with Roxana is no longer transactional. Not being paid by Roxana helps establish her as Roxana's surrogate family member. Once Amy joins this surrogate family, she becomes jealous of any woman who tries to displace her. She is not threatened by Roxana's husbands or lovers because she never aspires to occupy a masculine role in Roxana's surrogate family. However, Susan's determination to claim Roxana as her mother is an exigent threat to Amy, who refuses to relinquish her primacy in Roxana's surrogate family. This bizarre affiliation between Roxana and Amy becomes less pragmatic and more violent over the course of the novel.

The connection between Amy and Roxana is far more intense than the one Moll forms with her governess. Roxana describes Amy as "faithful to me, as the Skin to my back," a metaphor that articulates their indivisibility as a sort of physical union (38). Roxana's dependence on Amy becomes so acute because Roxana relinquishes to Amy her capacity to think and act whenever she is confronted with difficulties. As Terry Castle explains, Amy becomes Roxana's "alternate self . . . act[ing] out her mistress's fantasies."[52] Roxana appears oddly unconscious of this process. She does not question why Amy is willing to arrange her affairs, run the household, and help her dispose of her children. Insofar as she analyzes Amy's complex feelings for her at all, she puts them down to loyalty. She praises Amy's "violent Affection for her Mistress, in which no Servant ever went beyond her" (43). The closest she ever comes to reflecting on the reasons for Amy's obsessive devotion to her is when she explains that Amy's behavior "amounted to no more than this . . . *like* Mistress, *like* Maid" (82). As the novel proceeds, Roxana and Amy share a lover (the jeweler) who fathers daughters by both of them. Prophetically, Roxana's daughter dies. Amy also acts as head of the "little Family" Roxana leaves behind to guard her wealth while she travels with the prince (98). Amy continues in this role for most of the novel, becoming so necessary to Roxana that after she leaves Roxana describes herself as "destitute" without her (258). Roxana concedes how inextricable the two of them have become when she contemplates murdering Amy to protect Susan but knows she cannot enact her threat because "to have falln' upon Amy, had been to have murther'd myself" (246).

Roxana's conclusion demonstrates how much more powerful the bond between Amy and Roxana has become than Roxana's connections to her children, former spouses, and lovers. Like Moll, Roxana marries happily, reconciles with at least one of her children, and enjoys a prosperous life outside of England. Susan is no longer a threat since she is presumed to be dead, and Amy disappears. Roxana learns to manage her own money, so "notwithstanding the Absence of [her] old Agent *Amy*" she is able to retain her wealth (267). Her now-legitimized son by the merchant even accompanies his newly married parents to Holland, uniting Roxana's nuclear families in a manner similar to Moll's eventual reunion with Humphry and marriage to Jemy. However, the last few sentences of the novel unravel all this wish fulfillment. Despite Roxana's claims that she will not reconcile with Amy unless Amy proves herself innocent of Susan's murder, Amy joins Roxana in Holland anyway "without giving" any such "Satisfaction" (267). The final paragraph of the novel is worth quoting in full, as it mysteriously implicates Amy for the subsequent dismantling of Roxana's nuclear family and prosperity: "after some few Years of flourishing, and outwardly happy Circumstances, I fell into a dreadful Course of Calamities, and Amy also; the very Reverse of our former Good Days; the Blast of Heaven seem'd to follow the Injury done the poor Girl, by us both; and I was brought so low again, that my Repentance seem'd to be only the Consequence of my Misery, as my Misery was of my Crime" (267). What happens to Roxana's husband and child? What happens to Roxana herself? Is Amy in some way responsible for the "dreadful Course of Calamaties" Roxana describes, or is her presence merely incidental? The questions raised by the novel's conclusion are numerous, but for my own purposes what is most important is that Roxana's husband and child simply fall out of the narrative, displaced by Amy and the apparition of Susan (the "poor Girl" to whom the passage refers).

The conclusion of *Roxana* demonstrates that Roxana's surrogate family cannot coexist peacefully with her nuclear family. Neither will Amy relinquish Roxana, as the governess does Moll when Moll and Jemy are transported to the colonies. Amy's desire to control Roxana outweighs even rational self-interest, negating the primary advantage of surrogate families—that they are provisional and thus severable—in *Moll Flanders*. As Defoe illustrates in *Roxana*, the drive for material gain and individual freedom that prompts protagonists to form surrogate families also has the potential to perversely distort them.

BUILDING A FOUNDATION FOR THE
FAMILY OF THE HEART

Prototypes of Surrogate Families
in Samuel Richardson's *Pamela*
and *Pamela in Her Exalted Condition*

S AMUEL RICHARDSON DEVELOPS A DISTINCT version of the novelistic convention of surrogate families that first appears in Defoe's *Moll Flanders* (1722) and *Roxana* (1724). In his earliest novels, *Pamela* (1740) and *Pamela in Her Exalted Condition* (1741, hereafter referred to as *Pamela II*), Richardson incorporates aspects of Defoe's model of surrogate families but reimagines their purpose. Richardson's novels conclude with marriage and domesticity, which are just steps along the way to prosperity in Defoe's novels. Consequently, Richardson's surrogate families play roles related specifically to these outcomes. Moll's governess mentors her in thieving and scheming as much as she does courtship. However, surrogate family members in Richardson's first two novels serve a less capacious function. They demonstrate Pamela's moral worth. Pamela's decisions about surrogate family members are limited because as Mr. B's servant, captive, and eventually wife, she only has access to members of his hand-picked household families. Despite these constraints, her principled decisions about whom to accept and reject testify to her virtue. Just as Defoe's depiction of family was more complex and unsettled in his later novel *Roxana* than in the earlier *Moll Flanders*, *Pamela II* complicates *Pamela*'s premise that different family models can peacefully coexist.

Richardson's two Pamela novels experiment with the narrative possibilities of surrogate families. As his storytelling matures, these surrogate family prototypes also evolve. They eventually become the fully developed surrogate families at the center of his later novels, *Clarissa* (1748) and *Sir Charles Grandison* (1754). But while Pamela's surrogate families are inchoate compared to Clarissa's or Harriet's, they are important because they lay bare the most fundamental narrative purpose of surrogate families. A surrogate family is, as Mark Kinkead-Weekes calls it, a "family of the heart."[1] Although the term he uses is singular—family—its implications ought to be understood as plural because a family of the heart "exten[ds] . . . into a model of community."[2] According to Weekes's argument, Richardson's vision of marriage is outward facing. This is subtle but discernible in the two Pamela novels, particularly in the second half of *Pamela*. Pamela models her perfections to her neighbors. Their admiration of her becomes a vector spreading goodness outward into the whole community. If her Lincolnshire friends follow her example, the entire countryside can become an "extended brotherhood, sisterhood, fatherhood and childhood of the heart."[3]

Since Richardson is a moralist, his surrogate families look different than Defoe's. Richardsonian heroines would never adopt slippery figures like the governess in *Moll Flanders* or Amy in *Roxana* into their surrogate families. Defoe's protagonists prefer shrewd surrogate family members rather than upright ones because they want to know how to get ahead, not how to be good. Marriage is just one of many means to achieve that end. On the other hand, Richardson's protagonists are truly virtuous. For them, the only acceptable method to improve their lives is to marry a good man like Sir Charles in *Sir Charles Grandison*. Consequently, surrogate families look different in Richardson's novels than Defoe's. Moll seeks out surrogate family members who will "advise and assist" her financially, while Richardson's protagonists only accept surrogate family members who provide sound and compassionate moral guidance.[4] By attaching themselves to scrupulous surrogate families, Richardson's protagonists attract (or, in Pamela's case, create) reputable husbands.

Pamela does not have to go far to find a future husband to reform; he is the head of her household family. He takes on this role after his mother, who had been Pamela's mistress for several years, dies. All servants belonging to a household were structurally subordinate to their masters, occupying the legal position of dependents or wards. Thus, they were all in the position of the head-of-household's children. However, few would have been treated as surrogate daughters or sons. Pamela was in that privileged position because Mr. B's mother mentored her, superintending her moral and intellectual education as well as teaching her how to dress and act like a member of the gentry. Pamela was accustomed to wearing her mistress's cast-off clothes and shoes, dancing with her, reading to her, and participating in her social gatherings. Their connection is so intense and intimate that her dying command to her son is to "Remember my poor *Pamela!*"[5] Mr. B interprets his mother's words in a perverse manner, abusing the authority she confers on him. He treats Pamela as his property rather than his responsibility, even referring to her as his "Child" as he attempts to rape her (69).[6]

Pamela is not a literal orphan, but she may as well be one because her parents cannot protect her from Mr. B. As Naomi Tadmor observes in her reading of *Pamela*, Pamela is "friendless" despite having loving parents because they "cannot, or are unwilling to, come to [her] help."[7] They offer only one practical admonition to their daughter: return home if Mr. B continues to molest her. They do nothing to help her follow their advice. The one action her father takes to protect Pamela fails so abysmally it only underscores his impotence. Mr. Andrews walks all night to Mr. B's estate in order to demand Pamela's safe return. He arrives so disheveled that when the grooms find him in the morning they mistake him for a "crasy" beggar (87). As far as Mr. B is concerned, he might as well be a beggar. When Mr. B tires of Mr. Andrews's complaints, he silences him with the implicit threat to remember "who I am" (89). He is invincible, able to kidnap Pamela, eject her father from his house, and leave her parents with no recourse to recover her other than appealing to God. Their "Prayers for their poor Daughter, and for a happy Issue to an Affair that almost distracted them" are all they can offer to counter Mr. B's complete jurisdiction over Pamela (90).

As an orphan in situation if not in fact, Pamela must construct a surrogate family to protect her. Given her isolation and status as a servant, her potential surrogate family members already belong to another family: Mr. B's household. She strategically cultivates a daughter-like relationship with its most important members, including Mr. Longman the steward, Mr. Jonathan the butler, and Mrs. Jervis the housekeeper. Christopher Flint asserts the importance of these surrogate ties, arguing that Pamela's "easy assimilation into Mr. B's household stems from the way in which others quickly adopt her," with Mrs. Jervis acting as her "mother" while "Jonathan and Mr. Longman treat her as a daughter."[8] All Pamela's fellow servants apparently love her (except Jane the kitchen maid, and Pamela "seldom" descends to the kitchen), but she cultivates relationships only with the ones who have the most authority, and thus the greatest ability to shame Mr. B and undermine his stratagems (40).

Mr. Jonathan and Mr. Longman are important members of Mr. B's household family. Their paternal connection to Pamela elevates her status in the household and reinforces her reputation as a virtuous young woman. Their favor becomes increasingly significant as Mr. B appears to withdraw his. Pamela's stature in the household would plummet if these influential father figures did not counterbalance Mr. B's overt and frequent complaints about Pamela's insubordination. Mr. Jonathan even prioritizes supporting Pamela over his duty to Mr. B, confiding that he "will sooner believe any body in Fault" than Pamela, presumably including Mr. B (46). As head of the household staff and a man of independent means, Mr. Longman has the stature not just to speak on his own behalf, but also to act as a proxy for the servants below him. As their representative, he pleads to Mr. B to "relent a little" and forgive and reinstate Pamela (69). Mr. B resents this meddling, viewing their advocacy as insurrection. He blames Pamela for the "Hornet's Nest" she has raised in his household family and worries it "may have stung" his "Reputation . . . to Death" (61). From his perspective, all his employees are in the same childlike position in relation to him. By protecting Pamela from him they usurp the parental authority he is supposed to exercise over all of them as master of the house.

Mrs. Jervis is the maternal counterpart to Pamela's surrogate fathers. As housekeeper, she oversees the other servants. Although all the servants are subordinate to Mr. B, she would be the equivalent of an elder sister in Mr. B's household family. She is more than Pamela's ally; she is also her surrogate mother. There are numerous instances of Jervis avowing motherly feelings for Pamela and Pamela reciprocating them. Jervis wishes she was wealthy enough to live independently and keep Pamela "like a Daughter" (23). Pamela writes to her parents that Mrs. Jervis "uses" her "as if [she] were her own Daughter" (14). She also tells Jervis she loves her more than anyone except her "own Father and Mother" (36). Jervis's wish to live with Pamela even suggests that her love for her surrogate daughter is more important than Pamela's duty to her parents because Pamela would presumably live with them, not with Jervis, if she left Mr. B's household. Pamela cultivates this daughterly role so earnestly that it sometimes displaces her duty to her parents. Though Pamela consistently signs her letters to her parents as their "*dutiful daughter*," she does not actually do as they ask and leave Mr. B's service after he attempts to seduce her (17). Rather, she keeps close to Jervis, seeking her protection from his increasingly aggressive attacks. It is telling that later in the novel when Pamela is imprisoned by Mr. B at his Lincolnshire estate, she wishes impulsively for the protection of "my dear Mrs. *Jervis!*" and only afterward corrects herself, adding as a sort of afterthought "or rather, to be safe with my dear Father and Mother!" (106). Pamela and Jervis isolate themselves from the rest of the household staff as if they were a sort of household within Mr. B's household. They spend their leisure time alone together. Pamela reads Jervis "good Books . . . whenever [they] are alone," just as she had read to Mr. B's mother (15). Additionally, Jervis and Pamela "breakfast, dine, and sup" together, apart from the other servants. They even sleep together. Mr. B acknowledges the depth of Jervis's loyalty to Pamela, "fleeringly" describing Pamela as telling "a Tale every Day" to "good Mother *Jervis*" about his attacks on her (64).

If Jervis is Pamela's chosen surrogate mother, then Mrs. Jewkes is her doppelgänger: a Joan Crawford–style "Mommie Dearest" who tries to force Pamela to accept her as a mother figure. The two housekeepers have similar names and both attempt to advise and chaperone Pamela as a mother would. However, these similarities only serve to emphasize their more significant differences. Although Flint describes Jewkes as a "female surrogat[e]" for Mr. B, embodying his "anti-family, antifeminine qualities," Pamela interprets Jewkes in relation to Jervis, not Mr. B.[9] As Pamela writes to her parents, Jewkes is "unlike" the "good Mrs Jervis in every thing" (181). Pamela prefaces almost every reference to Jewkes with an insulting epithet. Among many other unflattering monikers, Pamela calls her a "wicked Creature," an "inhuman Tygress," a "Wretch" and a "vile Procuress" (99, 163, 105, 187). In contrast, Pamela makes blandly positive observations about Jervis. She is always "good Mrs. Jervis" or simply Mrs. Jervis. Pamela's invective against

Jewkes gives her moral authority over her captor, the only form of authority she is able to exercise.

Pamela's exaggerated descriptions of Jewkes's ugliness and depravity can be interpreted as her way of rejecting her as a surrogate mother. These grotesque physical descriptions make Jewkes sound like a monster. She is a giantess with thick arms, a face "flat and broad" with a color so unhealthy it looks "as if it had been pickled a Month in Salt-petre," and "dead, spiteful, grey goggling" eyes (105). Considering how repellant this portrait of Jewkes is, it is significant that Pamela follows it with the clarification that her "Heart" is "more ugly than her Face" (105). Sometimes Jewkes is a devil, sometimes a creature, and at one point Pamela even describes her as the mythological beast "*Argus*" with "an hundred Eyes" (113). All these descriptions seek to dissociate Pamela from Jewkes, implying that they are not merely dissimilar, but in fact belong to different species. Just as *Pamela* is, as Terry Eagleton observes, a sort of "cartoon version of *Clarissa*, simplified, stereotyped and comic in outcome," Jewkes is an evil stepmother out of a fairy tale.[10] By extension, Jervis occupies the role of a mother whose absence forces her daughter into the evil stepmother's clutches.

Pamela's forced captivity at Mr. B's Lincolnshire estate recreates in an exaggerated manner the conditions that foster her daughter-like intimacy with Jervis in Bedfordshire. Pamela is forced into constant physical proximity to Jewkes. Mr. B commands Jewkes "not to trust [Pamela] out of her Sight," so the two of them are always together (116). Although Pamela could try to cultivate a close relationship with Jewkes and exploit it to improve her own situation, she refuses to do so. Her criteria for selecting surrogate family members are antithetical to mere opportunism. Rejecting Jewkes as a surrogate mother is the inverse moral equivalent of nurturing the same bond with Jervis. Both decisions demonstrate Pamela's upright morality. Richardson implicitly contrasts Pamela's responses to these two similar situations. For example, Pamela asks Jervis to sleep beside her while she tries to refuse sharing a bed with Jewkes. She even attempts to justify her protest with a transparent fib that reminds the reader of her attachment to Jervis. She tells Jewkes "I love to lie by myself" even though Jewkes is aware "Mrs. Jervis was [her] Bed-fellow at t'other House" (102). Pamela calls Jewkes a "Jezebel" and "*London* Prostitute" even though these insults result in what Pamela considers to be severe beatings (117, 165). She also frequently upbraids Jewkes for immorality. These affronts goad the irascible Jewkes into acting like the evil stepmother Pamela believes her to be. Pamela seems to revel in her martyrdom when her defiance leads to predictable consequences such as Jewkes taking away her shoes or tricking her out of her money. She frequently describes herself as so "frighten'd" by Jewkes that she is powerless "even to relieve [her] Mind by . . . Tears" (105). Pamela's consistent and largely futile defiance of Jewkes's authority enacts a narrative that relegates Jewkes to the role of evil stepmother and preserves Jervis's status as her only surrogate mother.

By choosing Jervis as her surrogate mother and rejecting Jewkes, Pamela demonstrates her strong moral character and suitability to become Mr. B's wife. Mr. B is able to see Pamela's relationship with Jewkes and Jervis through Pamela's eyes because he reads about it in her letters. These letters portray Jervis as a fairy godmother character and Jewkes as an evil stepmother. In most of the novel's episodes, Jewkes even appears more nefarious than Mr. B. The best example of this dynamic is Pamela's account of the attempted rape at the Lincolnshire estate. She focuses more on Jewkes's role as accessory to the assault than on Mr. B's culpability as its agent, blaming "this most wicked Woman, this vile Mrs Jewkes" for urging him on (189). When she awakes after her fit, she is more scared of Jewkes than of Mr. B, pleading to the man who just tried to rape her to "take from me this most wicked Woman, this vile Mrs Jewkes" (189). She repeats this same scapegoating pattern whenever Mr. B abuses her. According to Pamela, no matter what Mr. B does he "is not half so bad as this Woman" (227).

Paradoxically, Pamela's exaggerated account of Jewkes's depravity becomes the foundation for the happy conclusion to her own story. Since Jewkes represents and enacts Mr. B's worst impulses, rejecting her as a surrogate mother indirectly rebuffs Mr. B's attempts to exploit his authority as head of the household family. Just because all his servants are structurally subservient to him does not make them equal to one another. The distinction Pamela draws between Jewkes and Jervis demonstrates Pamela's superior discernment. She is, after all, his mother's surrogate daughter and thus connected to him in a manner far more significant than their hierarchal relationship in his household family would suggest. In a sense, Pamela is Mr. B's surrogate sister, and sororal and fraternal relationships often anticipate marriage in courtship novels. But it takes Pamela's rejection of Jewkes to make him recognize her as a potential partner and peer. Her contemptuous characterization of Jewkes as a prostitute, jezebel, and "abominable Designer" implicitly asserts that she is Jewkes's opposite: a princess rather than a prostitute; a potential wife rather than a jezebel; and an innocent victim instead of a schemer (187). Her account of Jewkes convinces Mr. B that she is not the vixen disguised in country attire he frequently accuses her of being.

Pamela's marriage to Mr. B not only completes his nuclear family (he gains a wife and eventually an heir), but also restores order to his household family. Pamela hires back the servants who acted as her surrogate parents when she lived at the Bedfordshire estate. Mr. B dismissed them because they helped her; after his marriage, they are reinstated for the same reason. Pamela's marriage also reconciles their conflicted loyalties to Pamela and Mr. B. To obey one is to obey the other once they preside together over the same household family. Pamela's parents share in the bounty and goodwill created by their daughter's marriage, accepting Mr. B's offer to manage his Kentish estate. Her marriage even heals the breach in Mr. B's nuclear family. Pamela smooths over the conflicts between Mr. B and his equally hot-headed sibling Lady Davers. As Mr. B's wife and Lady Davers's sister-in-law, it is no longer appropriate for Pamela to remain close to the servants she previously accepted as surrogate parents. She now favors them as trusted inferiors rather than seeking mentorship or protection from them. When Jervis dies in *Pamela II*, Pamela describes her as her "other Mother" who watched over her as she remained in her "single State" (558). By implication, Jervis's parental role ends with Pamela's marriage. Not only does Pamela discard surrogate family members after she marries, but she also distances herself from her parents. As Mr. B's wife, she inherits an elite nuclear family that is incompatible with the one into which she is born.

Pamela II chronicles Pamela's first years as a wife and mother. The marriage recalibrates her nuclear family by making Lady Davers her sister. This change is beyond her control, but she is able to reconfigure her surrogate family based on her own preferences. She does not need practical help from surrogate family members any longer. As long as they are high enough in the class hierarchy to be appropriate companions for her, she can pick and choose them based on her own interests and affinities. Consequently, her decisions about which to select reveals more about her as an individual than her acceptance or rejection of the few servants she has access to in *Pamela*.

The grace and ease with which Pamela wins over her new sister Lady Davers demonstrate how successful she is in her new role. Lady Davers's abusive behavior to Pamela before and immediately after her marriage is an exaggerated version of the contempt all Mr. B's gentry friends express for her. Lady Towers and her companions poke and prod Pamela, joking about how likely Mr. B is to seduce her. Sir Simon expresses the same sentiments when Mr. Williams tries to enlist his aid in helping Pamela escape from Mr. B. He scolds Williams for interfering with Mr. B's concerns and then dismisses the issue out of hand because Mr. B "hurts no Family" by kidnapping Pamela. Even a well-respected clergyman (Mr. Peters) refuses to help Pamela because her predicament is too commonplace. Lady Davers's violent treatment of Pamela—verbally abusing her and even boxing her ears—differs in degree but not in kind from these other responses. Just as Lady Davers "can't bear" the thought that Mr. B's marriage authorizes a former servant to "*think*" of her as a "Sister," Mr. B's neighbors cannot imagine her belonging to the gentry (365). However, Lady Davers ultimately becomes so attached to Pamela that she insists Pamela address her as "*your* Sister," the very thought of which had once provoked her to beat Pamela (30–31). The increasingly intimate relationship between Lady Davers and Pamela demonstrates Pamela's acceptance into Mr. B's world of wealth and leisure. It is as significant a right of passage for her as the neighborhood gathering in which the neighbors who ridiculed her before now compete with one another to praise most superlatively the ladylike way she slices a cake, serves cordials, and walks down a garden path.

Pamela bolsters her connection to Lady Davers through correspondence. Lady Davers encourages Pamela to write to her "in the same manner [she] did with [her] Parents."[11] This offer formalizes Pamela's acceptance into the B family. She demands Pamela "divest [herself] of all Restraints" in the letters she sends her, prioritizing "Truth and Nature" over formality and decorum (29–30). While Lady Davers appears to encourage Pamela to share her thoughts and feelings, the content of their letters is formal, not egalitarian. Lady Davers's request is paradoxical. On the one hand, she asks Pamela to write to her as a sister; on the other, she explicitly describes herself as Pamela's elder sister, and as such "intitled to expect . . . Duty, in [that] degree" (30–31). Their hierarchical relationship is also evident in Lady Davers's breezy remark that she expects to "receive six, seven, eight or ten Letters, as it may happen" for every one she sends Pamela (31). The reason Lady Davers gives for this discrepancy also prohibits mutual confidence from developing between them. She informs Pamela that the purpose of their correspondence is to entertain Lady Davers and to improve Pamela. Lady Davers promises to scrutinize Pamela's behavior as a wife and as a debutante in society in order to "[find] fault" with it, and then advise Pamela, though "not in a splenetic or ill-natur'd way," how to correct it (31). She even shares Pamela's letters with her friend Lady Betty so they can collaborate in their critiques of Pamela and "freely" let her "know [their] Minds" if they find anything "censurable" in her conduct (31). Lady Davers does not seem to realize that ganging up with Lady Betty to bully Pamela will have a chilling effect on their correspondence. In the same letter, Lady Davers asserts with no apparent irony that assessing Pamela's letters will help the two of them become "more and more acquainted" (31). These strictures preclude familiarity from developing between Pamela and her sister-in-law. However, the very existence of their correspondence signals Pamela's unequivocal acceptance by Mr. B's family.

The closings and forms of address in the letters Lady Davers and Pamela exchange signify the intimacy their banal content fails to convey. It is only in *Clarissa* that Richardson matures enough as a novelist to envision the sort of letters sisters of the heart like Anna Howe and Clarissa Harlowe might really exchange. Pamela's and Lady Davers's letters remain static, but their form of address shifts from formality to familiarity. This transformation commences when they start to regularly address one another as sister rather than "Your Affectionate Davers" and "Your Ladyship's most Humble and obliged Servant, P[amela] B" (25, 28). Pamela begins signing her letters to Lady Davers as "Your obliged Sister, and Servant" and Lady Davers signs hers to Pamela "Your Affectionate Sister and Admirer" (364, 439). Lady Davers courts this familiarity so actively that she becomes concerned when Pamela at one point omits to "subscribe Sister, as usual" (396). Remarkably, the same Lady Davers who beats Pamela for marrying into the B family now blames Mr. B, who Lady Davers suspects of having a dalliance with a widowed countess,

for alienating her from her "*only* Sister" (406). She begs her sister-in-law's forgive-
ness for "my Brother's Faults," promising "He shall be none of my Brother" if he
is cruel to Pamela (396–397). She even offers to raise a "Hurricane" much greater
than the "Storm" she unleashed on Pamela in the previous novel, this time to punish her brother for his infidelity. Even though Lady Davers eventually reconciles
with her brother, he is no longer important to her in his own right, but rather as a
means to spending more time with Pamela. She moves in with her brother after
her husband dies not to be close to him, but in order to "enjoy the Company and
Conversation of her excellent Sister" (602). Not only Lady Davers's affection for
her brother, but also her high valuation of her pedigree (which she originally claims
Pamela pollutes through her marriage to Mr. B) become eclipsed by her all-
consuming loyalty to her sister Pamela.

Pamela's connection to her surrogate sister Polly Darnford, unlike her relationship with Lady Davers, is based only on mutual affection. Polly (one of Sir
Simon's daughters) initiates a correspondence with Pamela so they can share their
experiences as young married women. They choose one another as companions
because they are intellectually and temperamentally compatible. Although they
do not live together in a household family, they are constantly brought together
by living in the same country neighborhood. Their intimacy blossoms through letters, predicting the surrogate sister relationship between Anna and Clarissa in
Clarissa.[12] Unlike the dry letters Pamela exchanges with Lady Davers, the correspondence between Pamela and Polly is affectionate, playful, and instructive. They
moralize to one another over the course of the novel on subjects such as marriage,
death, and wives' religious and family obligations. They are social equals. Their
relationship advances neither of them in society, unlike Pamela's connection to
Lady Davers. Pamela and Polly's correspondence invigorates them intellectually
and teaches them to enact philosophical and moral standards through their daily
domestic responsibilities.

Polly is a prototype of Anna Howe in *Clarissa*, drawing Pamela out through
her playful style and humorous anecdotes. Polly is more exuberant and expressive
than Pamela, confiding to Pamela "I love you" in her first letter before even request-
ing Pamela engage in an "ample Correspondence" with her (58). Her style is spir-
ited and even at times satiric. The comic portrait she draws in a number of her
letters of her peevish sister and her marriage to a preening husband culminates in
an amusing passage in which she predicts both spouses will "jangle on," learning
to avoid one another rather than improving themselves for the other's sake (478).
Such observations foreshadow Anna's dismissive sallies about marriage in *Clarissa*.
Pamela's feelings for Polly are also tender, with Pamela confiding to her parents
that she "loved [Polly] from the Moment I first saw her" (100). Pamela's letters are
more meditative and morally reflective than Polly's, previewing Clarissa's sedate
style. For example, her request that Polly visit the dying Jewkes becomes a sermon

on death, employing conventional rather than personal language. Jewkes is now just another "poor Soul . . . shivering . . . on the Edge of Life" in need of "God's Mercies," hardly recognizable any longer as the comically monstrous evil stepmother described in the previous novel (468). Richardson informs his readers in *Pamela II*'s conclusion that Pamela and Polly maintain their surrogate sisterhood through letters until Polly dies in childbirth. Just like Anna and Clarissa, their intimacy endures until death parts them.

Pamela's loyalty to her sister Lady Davers and her surrogate sister Polly supersede her fidelity to her parents. Although Lady Davers's relationship to Pamela is too formal for candidness and intimacy to develop between them, it still displaces Pamela's ties to her parents. In *Pamela II*, Pamela becomes the Andrews's patroness. They manage Mr. B's Kentish estate, making them her employees. Her style of addressing them in letters remains sentimental, and she tells them "I am no Lady to you" (14). The content of her letters, however, contradicts this promise. For example, in one early letter Pamela advises—which as their benefactor is the same thing as demanding—her parents not hire their relatives to work on the Kentish estate. This is exclusively her decision. Far from dictating it, Mr. B tells Pamela "Your Father is his own Master: He may employ whom he pleases" and states that their relations in all fairness "should . . . have the Preference" over strangers (17). However, Pamela believes "it would be better to have *any body* other than Relations" as employees because they might exploit her parents' kindness and cheat Mr. B (18). Her indifference to her extended family's difficulties and her highhandedness with her own parents demonstrates how much her new nuclear and surrogate families have eroded her connection to them. The paucity of letters directed exclusively to the Andrewses in contrast to the numerous letters Pamela writes to Lady Davers and Polly reinforces this interpretation. The few letters she does exchange with her parents focus largely on Pamela's attempts to get them to support her in her desire to breastfeed her child against Mr. B's wishes. She stops writing to them when they instead side with Mr. B, reminding her that "the Duty of every good Wife" is to "acquiesce" to her husband (317). She turns to Davers for practical advice about acclimating herself to her new station. When she wants to confide personal concerns and seek moral guidance she writes to her surrogate sister Polly. Thus, Pamela's parents gradually become afterthoughts in her affections. Her request to Polly to send her letters to her parents after she has read them only confirms their secondary status (227). In fact, her parents virtually drop out of the novel as it progresses.

While Pamela's parents seem to fade away, her role in her family and community solidifies. Pamela's influence extends beyond the B family and her surrogate sister Polly and into the surrounding countryside. As Kinkead-Weekes observes, Pamela's marriage "liberate[s]" her "truer self," establishing her in "a widening circle of community" maintained through letter writing and hospitality.[13] This extended community foreshadows Richardson's mature vision of surrogate families in his later fiction. According to Margaret Doody, Pamela's influence over her neighborhood anticipates the family of the heart in *Sir Charles Grandison*, a novel in which the "the greatest compliment that can be given to the outsider is a welcome into the unit, and the sign of the generous heart is its perfecting and widening of family ties."[14] She further argues that the harmonious effects of belonging to the right surrogate family "radiat[e] . . . outwards to society at large. In the best kind of family, and the best kind of society, both variety and harmony are possible, and different personalities can develop most fully by acting within the atmosphere of a refined and sensitive community."[15] In *Sir Charles Grandison*, the community is even more far-reaching. The "large harmonious group" with its nucleus in the Grandisons' ideal nuclear family extends internationally "all the way from Northamptonshire to Grandison Hall to Colenbrook to London and several cities in Italy" (45).[16] I address Richardson's mature depictions of surrogate families in *Clarissa* and *Sir Charles Grandison* in the following chapter.

PERFECTING THE FAMILY OF THE HEART

Relationship Remembered in Samuel

Richardson's *Clarissa* and

Sir Charles Grandison

RICHARDSON'S FINAL NOVELS, *CLARISSA* (1748) and *Sir Charles Grandison* (1754), take the moral, emotional, and practical consequences of cultivating surrogate families more seriously than *Pamela* (1740) or *Pamela in Her Exalted Condition* (1741).[1] Surrogate families are no longer just a means to marry well, or to augment married life. In *Clarissa*, Richardson places surrogate families and nuclear families into direct and consistent conflict. The competition between them outlives even Clarissa, who dies because she will not submit to demands made by her nuclear and lineage families. In contrast, *Sir Charles Grandison* merges nuclear families, household families, and surrogate families through the protagonist's marriage. Together, the two novels offer hyperbolic but antithetical visions of what family means. Just as *Moll Flanders* (1722) and *Roxana* (1724) enact a surrogate family utopia and dystopia, *Clarissa* and *Sir Charles Grandison* are a tragedy and comedy of surrogate families.

Surrogate families are based on the premise that affinity, not birth, should determine who belongs to a particular family. Clarissa asserts as much in different terms when she writes to her surrogate sister Anna Howe that the world is "one great family" connected through "relationship forgot": our common ancestry through Adam and Eve.[2] According to this biblical model, any worthy person is a potential relation since everyone is related. However, for the Harlowes—Clarissa's nuclear and lineage family—the only criterion for claiming family membership is consanguinity, or "relationship remembered" (62). As David Paxman observes, the Harlowes' "brand of generational thinking conceives of the family as an institution with prior claims over the people born into it."[3] They are a more menacing version of the Hobbesian family Moll lives with in *Moll Flanders*. In pursuit of their corporate goal to "*rais[e] a family*" economically and socially, they not only deny their obligations to anyone unrelated to them, but also sacrifice Clarissa (77). Inversely, Sir Charles in *Sir Charles Grandison* enacts Clarissa's ideal of the great family by annexing seemingly every worthy person he meets into his extended surrogate family. Sir Charles's Harlowe-like father Sir Thomas dies before the novel even begins, leaving his heir Sir Charles to freely exercise his generosity of spirit as paterfamilias of the Grandison clan. He marries his surrogate sister Harriet and adopts every worthy person he meets into their surrogate family. In doing so, he achieves Clarissa's vision of a great family, creating a modern-day Eden that extends limitlessly outward from Grandison Hall.

Female protagonists Clarissa and Harriet resemble Pamela in *Pamela* and *Pamela II* in at least one significant way: their choices about surrogate family members signify their virtue and predict the sort of husbands they will select. They also differ from Pamela in significant ways. Unlike Clarissa and Harriet, Pamela is isolated. Her surrogate family members are all employed by, related to, or are longtime neighbors of Mr. B. Her choices about whom to invite into her surrogate family are extremely limited. Clarissa and Harriet (the female protagonist of *Sir Charles Grandison*) meet numerous people unconnected to their nuclear or lineage families. Their choices are more varied and circumstantial than Pamela's, but so are their possibilities to fail. In Clarissa's case, none of the suitors she encounters are worthy of her so in order to maintain her integrity she must remain single. Instead of selecting a suitor, she dies and "marries" Jesus. Her surrogate parents and siblings, Anna in particular, help her understand herself sufficiently to make this decision and support her as she enacts it. Rather than help her find the right suitor, her surrogate family members give her the "moral and emotional nourishment," as Hina Nazar puts it, to die.[4] The connection between marriage, female morality, and surrogate families is more straightforward in *Sir Charles Grandison*. As Bonnie Latimer points out, Richardson spends "seven volumes detailing Harriet Byron's preference for Sir Charles."[5] Surrogate family members act as advisers, confidants, and moral counselors as Harriet navigates a lengthy and complicated courtship.

Clarissa and *Sir Charles Grandison* envision marriage as an intensified type of surrogate siblinghood. Richardson chooses the relationship between siblings as his model for marriage because it is egalitarian rather than hierarchical. Children are supposed to be dutiful to their parents. Even Anna, who defies her mother in large and small ways throughout *Clarissa*, asserts without any apparent irony that "*parental* authority" ought to be held "sacred" (85). Marrying a father figure would inscribe this unequal dynamic on the union. Siblings may have different levels of status within a particular family, but they are all equally subject to their parents' authority. Their relative equality with one another offers the potential for mutuality, warmth, intimacy, and candor. Sir Charles is Richardson's exemplar of how a brother should treat his siblings. He benevolently supports and guides his sisters before and after their marriages. He also bestows this brotherly concern and affection on surrogate brothers and sisters he adopts based on moral, intellectual, and emotional compatibility. His chosen wife Harriet spends the majority of the novel as one of his surrogate sisters, and their married life will presumably be a continuation of the intimacy they develop as surrogate siblings. Clarissa develops a correspondingly intense sororal closeness to her surrogate sister, Anna.

Even surrogate family ties that do not perform an obvious function such as helping land a desirable husband are more binding than ties to nuclear or lineage families in *Clarissa* and *Sir Charles Grandison*. In *Clarissa*, the novel's macabre conclusion demonstrates that while the Harlowes may own Clarissa's body, her affections belong entirely to the surrogate family members she lives and corresponds with before she dies. Her surrogate family members are the brothers, sisters, mothers, and fathers she deserves, not the ones accidents of birth impose on her. She chooses them based on their upright characters, empathy, and decency: all traits the Harlowes conspicuously lack. Her surrogate family members become her "family of the heart," as Mark Kinkead-Weekes calls the self-authored families that occur so frequently in Richardson's fiction.[6] While Clarissa's surrogate family replaces the Harlowes in *Clarissa*, Harriet's marriage melds her lineage (she is an orphan raised by her aunt and uncle so she does not have a nuclear family) and surrogate families with Sir Charles's surrogate, nuclear, and lineage families to create an all-embracing blended family. Snowball-like, this intermingled family gathers up and incorporates into itself seemingly every worthy person Harriet and Sir Charles meet.

Paradoxically, protagonists' intense connections to surrogate family members not only attach them to the wider community of the "great family," but also enable them to individuate. In Clarissa's case, the letters she exchanges with her surrogate sister Anna hone her mind and scrutinize her most deeply held beliefs. Their wide-ranging exchanges about family and marriage branch into tributaries of philosophy, introspection, and meditation. As Clarissa attempts to justify her beliefs and actions to Anna, she tacitly undermines her allegiance to the Harlowes. She is not supposed to write to Anna at all, so the very act of exchanging letters with her defies her family's authority. Additionally, even when she endorses the conventional notion that daughters should obey their parents, she ultimately veers into explanations of why she refuses to do so. As Latimer notes, all Richardson's female protagonists are "marked out by their ability to understand and to make choices, a quality crucial to individuality."[7] The selfhood they assert through their correspondence is, as she also points out, often ineffectual because it is constantly "pitted against the legally and socially sanctioned expectations of others who will not honour those claims."[8] Nevertheless, the epistolary form of his novels implicitly aligns readers with protagonists' points of view, not the perspective of the powerful figures who oppress them.

Richardson's own epistolary exchanges at the time he was writing *Clarissa* and *Sir Charles Grandison* mirror the surrogate families he depicts in them. As Donatella Montini observes, Richardson's correspondence became increasingly voluminous while he was writing his final novels.[9] During this period he increasingly cultivated what Terry Eagleton describes as a "female coterie" of correspondents who became his "extended family."[10] He maintained numerous correspondences with female admirers, many of whom began writing to him because of their intense emotional and moral responses to *Clarissa*, and to a lesser degree *Sir Charles Grandison*.[11] Some of these correspondents included Hester Chapone (neé Mulso), Lady Bradshaigh, Lady Echlin, Sarah Wescomb, Mary Delany (neé Granville), and Sarah Fielding.[12] Richardson referred to his closest female correspondents in familial terms that positioned him as an "ensconced patriarch" addressing beloved but occasionally wayward daughters.[13] As Sylvia Marks observes, "[m]any of Richardson's female correspondents" explicitly "asked to become his 'adopted' daughters, and they in turn addressed him as 'Papa.'"[14] In his correspondence with Chapone, for example, she often referred to him as "my adopted papa," and "my dear papa Richardson," while describing herself as "your Miss Mulso, your child."[15] He sometimes referred to them as sisters.[16] Even when he adopted the posture of a brother instead of a father, he most likely viewed himself, as Lady Davers explicitly does when she writes to Pamela, as an eldest sibling.[17] While his novels extol the virtues of egalitarian relationships between surrogate siblings, he probably did not intend for his own correspondents to presume they were his equals. In fact, Sören Hammerschmidt interprets Richardson's urgent and frequent reminders to female "correspondents [of] their or his own iterations of their familial relationship" as a rhetorical technique meant to assert patriarchal authority.[18]

Richardson further extended his intellectual reach over his imagined daughters and sisters by incorporating some of them into his daily domestic routine, or in some cases, his household family. A few of his correspondents stayed at his house for long periods of time. When they were not staying with him, they visited so often they might as well have belonged to his household family. His daily life resembled the extended families of the heart he depicts in his novels. Anna Letitia Barbauld memorably and in distinctly eighteenth-century terms described the aging Richardson as living "in a kind of flower-garden of ladies" who were his "inspirers, his critics" and his "applauders."[19]

It is a testament to the emotional intimacy fostered through the exchange of letters that some of Richardson's closest relationships—his connection to Lady Bradshaigh and Lady Echlin in particular—were exclusively epistolary. This was possible because, for Richardson, familiar letters were, as he described them, the "cement of friendship, . . . more pure, yet more ardent, and less broken in upon, than personal conversation can be even amongst the most pure."[20] Much of Richardson's correspondence with his female readers probed, analyzed, and debated the same moral questions he addresses in his fiction: women's education, status, and marital responsibilities. For example, he famously engaged in an epistolary debate with Hester

Chapone about marital choice and filial obedience in *Clarissa*. The exchange was so lively that she eventually published her side of a correspondence.[21]

Not just the content, but also the form of Richardson's letters resembled his novels. Both intersperse personal revelation with description and analysis of domestic events. They also focus less on reporting than on expressing feelings. Richardson's female protagonists value the qualities Richardson sought out in his correspondents: complete sincerity and emotional transparency. In his letters to his female correspondents it was not unusual for him to compare them to characters in his novels. For example, one of his letters to Lady Bradshaigh describes her as the "Twin-sister" of Anna Howe because of her "Spirit and Earnestness."[22] Familiar letters of the type Richardson pioneered candidly revealed the writer's whole heart and mind. In fact, Richardson even described Lady Bradshaigh as a "daughter of [his] own mind."[23]

Although the intellectually stimulating correspondence Richardson engaged in with his surrogate daughters encouraged them to think critically about their subordination to men, he did not tolerate any direct criticism of patriarchy. He consistently endorsed the submission of daughters to fathers and wives to husbands. He described parents as "Soverigns" who "must in general be left for God to Punish."[24] In an exchange with Chapone, he specifically argued that even a paragon of virtue such as Clarissa was not fit "to be judge of the reasonableness or unreasonableness" of parents' orders, going so far as to describe disobedient children as "Levellers."[25] Only in the exceptional case that obeying one's parents meant disobeying the higher authority of God was there any legitimate excuse for defiance. As Paula Backscheider concludes of *Clarissa*, "Richardson inscribed the patriarchy approvingly on Clarissa's death," asserting through the novel's dire conclusion the importance of maintaining patriarchal authority even if it cost daughters their lives.[26] According to this logic, Clarissa should have married Solmes.

However, even Richardson recognized the contradiction between his adamantine didacticism and the complex moral questions about family authority raised by his novels. For example, as Tom Keymer notes of the aforementioned exchange between Richardson and Chapone about *Clarissa*, while Richardson manifested an "evident horror at the implications of Clarissa's transgression" in disobeying her parents' demand to marry Solmes, he also maintained an "idolatrous attachment" to her.[27] Keymer concludes that Richardson ultimately "found her [Clarissa's] case simply insoluble."[28] As Keymer points out, Richardson consistently avoided answering the question of whether Clarissa should have married Solmes by stating that her case "stands by itself" and concluding that no real daughter familiar with the novel ought to "plead" Clarissa's "example for *noncompliance*" unless she shares "*her* [Clarissa's] *reasons*."[29]

Clarissa has a lot of reasons, and all of them originate with her nuclear and lineage families. The different branches of the Harlowe family are united, at least until Clarissa's grandfather's death, by their quest for status and money. This is the opposite of the shared humanity and morality Clarissa believes should connect worthy members of the "great family." The first volumes of the novel focus on what Anna describes as the "disturbances" that erupt in Clarissa's family (39).[30] Clarissa laments the loss of a prelapsarian period before the novel begins when all the "different branches" of the Harlowe family were in sync (56). They worked in concert to enrich Clarissa's elder brother James so he would be able to achieve their collective ambitions. (I will refer to Clarissa's brother as James and her father as Mr. Harlowe) As Cynthia Wolff notes, as the future patriarch of the Harlowe family, James is at "the center of their interests" to such a degree that he even gains "complete domination over his father."[31] When Clarissa's grandfather deviates from this plan by giving Clarissa property, he drives a wedge between Clarissa and her relations. They hatch "intrigues and plots" worthy of "undermining courtiers" to restore the patriarchal family structure undermined by her grandfather's will (82). By forcing Clarissa to marry Solmes they restore the possibility of order since her inherited property will revert to them if she dies without children. Being reunited with their property is the Harlowes' version of paradise regained. They hoard, while Clarissa shares. Their mercenary understanding of family as a united front in a war for status and power is antithetical to Clarissa's desire to affiliate with others who share her altruistic worldview.

Clarissa is too good for her worldly nuclear and lineage families. As obvious as this is to everyone except her family members, her refusal to acknowledge it is one of her best qualities. For Richardson, her loyalty to the other Harlowes demonstrates her superiority over them. In reality, her brother, sister, and parents resemble the Hobbesian family Moll resides with for a time in Daniel Defoe's *Moll Flanders* rather than the orderly and loving family in Defoe's *The Family Instructor* (1715). James has all the selfishness and none of the breezy charm of the rakish elder brother who seduces Moll. However low Moll's lover's opinion may be of his parents and siblings, he never explicitly insults them. On the other hand, James refers to his grandfather and uncles as his "stewards" and dismisses his sisters as "chickens brought up for the tables of other men" (77). Clarissa's sister Arabella is an exaggerated version of the petty sisters in *Moll Flanders*. As for Clarissa's parents, they are crueler, more manipulative, and more unreasonable than the wary mother and absent father in Defoe's novel. Clarissa's father is a sickly and inaccessible patriarch referred to by everyone except Clarissa as a "gloomy tyrant" (426). Clarissa's mother is weak and passive, acting against her own judgment in order to appease the "ungovernable spirits" of her husband and son to preserve an illusory appearance of "peace and union" in her family (189). Her willingness to do what her husband wants is not portrayed as a virtue, but rather a form of selfishness; her ruling passion is avoiding conflict, and she is willing to sacrifice her favorite daughter to appease it. The members of Clarissa's lineage family are equally ungenerous. Her uncles are self-satisfied, insular single men unaccustomed to opposition.

Clarissa is the only member of her nuclear family who really subscribes to the patriarchal family model the Harlowes use to try to browbeat her into submission. Clarissa only demonstrates how unlike them she is when she repeatedly protests in her letters to Anna that she will never "suffer [her] interests to be separated from the interests of [her] family" (99). Her siblings try to outplay their elders, who they view as opponents, in order to better their own fortunes. They turn against Clarissa because they view her as a competitor who will "*out-uncle* as well as *out-grandfather* [them] both" unless they find a way to keep her from inheriting more of the family's wealth (80). Mr. Harlowe is supposed to exercise authority over his wife and children, but instead he obliges James and Arabella in order to "prevent all occasions of disunion and animosity in his family" (45). The Harlowe uncles join this "*embattled phalanx*" of family members attacking Clarissa (150). No one but Clarissa lives up to the values they espouse.

Mr. Harlowe is a caricature of a patriarch. He is absent for so many important family scenes that T. C. Eaves and Ben Kimpel call him a "cipher."[32] In the rare instances he speaks or writes to Clarissa directly, he addresses her almost exclusively in short declarative sentences that express his will, or in phrases such as "No expostulations!" and "No qualifyings," that deny her the opportunity to respond (64). He is forever gazing at her so "stern[ly]" that she is "unable to say one word to him," or "banish[ing]" her from his presence if she does speak (93). He interprets any resistance on Clarissa's part as a declaration of secession from the family, telling her several times "I will have no child, but an obedient one" (64). Kathryn Steele interprets Clarissa's "sullen" silence in the face of her father's demands as a strategy allowing her to "remain a dutiful daughter" by "refrain[ing] from voicing . . . opposition."[33] I disagree with this reading because Clarissa's father never allows her the opportunity to respond to him other than by silence or assent, so her choice is between silence and consent, not silence and dissent. Mr. Harlowe views Clarissa as *a* daughter, an abstraction whose role is to act according to his wishes. Rather than offer her the "mercy and indulgence" she explicitly begs of him, he enacts through writing the same silence he imposes on her in person, demanding she "write no more" unless she conforms to his will (125–126). Every letter he sends includes injunctions against Clarissa writing or speaking, and when his letter requires a response he demands she answer "directly to the point" without any "evasion" (267). When she ceases to obey, according to this logic, she stops being a daughter. He is a straw man representing the worst aspects of patriarchal authority, repeatedly pronouncing his will and then disappearing from the stage. He even seems to endorse this view of himself when he signs his final letter to Clarissa as "a justly incensed Father" rather than *your* justly incensed father (126).

Mr. Harlowe's letters to Clarissa perform the opposite function of friendly letters as described in Richardson's correspondence, which was to foster an intimate and ongoing conversation of like minds. It also supports Jerry Beasley's claim that Clarissa's father embodies *Clarissa*'s central themes of "law and duty," particularly human duty to obey the "law of God the Father."[34] Just as God does not have to justify his edicts, neither do fathers, who reign over their families by divine right. Although Richardson refuses to attack or even undermine the patriarchal family order exemplified by Mr. Harlowe, he illustrates quite graphically its shortcomings by implicitly contrasting Clarissa's static and impersonal awe for her distant father with the organic and dynamic process by which her family of the heart evolves. Mr. Harlowe renders Clarissa essentially lifeless by silencing her. This is the opposite of the ideal of the family of the heart, in which members enliven one another through conversation, confidence, and compassion.

Charlotte's way of speaking to Clarissa is just as unsympathetic as Mr. Harlowe's, though her approach is different. She exploits her daughter emotionally in order to achieve through solicitation the same ends her husband pursues through intimidation. Scholars often justify Charlotte's inaction because she lacks the power to defend Clarissa against her irascible husband.[35] But she is more inert than impotent. As Paxman observes, she is "passive, indolent, narrow of mind and weak-willed."[36] For example, while Charlotte frequently encourages Clarissa to confide in her, she promotes these confidences not to understand Clarissa, but rather to enforce her submission as payment for the supposed "*generosity*" she shows in permitting them (92). In these emotionally charged conversations Charlotte frequently adopts the rhetorical posture of a "friend" offering to "advise" rather than "command" her daughter (97). In this Charlotte is like Anna, who devotes letter after letter to advising Clarissa about minute particulars of her behavior. However, while Anna's guidance is intended to achieve the best outcome for Clarissa, Charlotte's counsel is focused on improving her own situation. Rather than sympathize with Clarissa as a victim, she blames her for acting selfishly and pleads, often with tears in her eyes, for Clarissa to marry Solmes and restore the "peace which costs" Charlotte so "much to preserve" (89). Clarissa is moved by these episodes. Though she does not accede to her mother's wishes, she admits to Anna that her "mamma's condescension distressed" her "Infinitely more . . . than rigour could have done" (96). While neither of Clarissa's parents is ultimately able to force her to marry Solmes, the futility of their efforts is less important than recognizing their methods as complementary means of achieving the same purpose: to kick or kiss Clarissa into obedience.

Charlotte's letters to Clarissa are equally self-serving. The only lengthy letter she writes to Clarissa during the entire first section of the novel reveals the extent of her egocentrism. She complains "I am as much blamed and as much punished as you are; yet I am more innocent," and laments that Clarissa, her favored child who once was "all [her] comfort" and "made all [her] hardships tolerable" now perpetuates them (124). She signs another letter "Your *more* unhappy mother" in order to surpass Clarissa's claims to victimization in subscribing herself "Your *very* unhappy child" in a previous letter (230–231). She asks Clarissa to burn a letter she sends to her in order to avoid conflict with her husband or other children. She fears they will think it is too empathetic to Clarissa, but in reality it is abrupt and selfish. Far from showing "too much of the *mother* in it," it just provides further evidence that she is too little of a mother to Clarissa (125). After Clarissa leaves Harlowe Place, Judith Norton—Clarissa's wet nurse and "surrogate mother" as Katherine Binhammer describes her—writes clandestinely to Charlotte to ask her to reconcile with Clarissa.[37] Assuming that any mother would want to believe the best of her child, she hints at extenuating circumstances justifying Clarissa's apparent elopement. But Charlotte expresses no interest in hearing them, responding instead with her own grievances at losing in Clarissa a sympathetic ear to her complaints. She also blames Clarissa for the Harlowes' public humiliation of being "stripped of [their] ornament" (584). It is apparently Clarissa's fault that without her they are now viewed by others as "but a common family" (584). The letters Judith and Clarissa exchange are far warmer and more affectionate than the ones Charlotte sends to her daughter. It is telling that Clarissa seeks solace from Judith rather than Charlotte after Lovelace rapes her. She writes to Judith, "[s]urely you are my own mamma" and wishes she "had indeed been your own child, born to partake of your humble fortunes, an heiress only to that content in which you are so happy!" (986).

Surrogate sisters and brothers are generally more important than surrogate mothers or fathers in courtship novels, and *Clarissa* is no exception. While Clarissa loves Judith, they are too far removed in age and situation to become one another's confidantes. Instead, Clarissa's pent-up tenderness is redirected to her surrogate sister Anna. Anna and Clarissa become surrogate sisters when they are young. They grow up together, visiting each other daily and often staying at each other's houses. This connection actually intensifies after Clarissa's parents forbid her from seeing or exchanging letters with Anna. Although Clarissa remains at Harlowe Place for several hundred more pages after she and Anna begin exchanging letters secretly, their lover-like clandestine correspondence is a spiritual elopement. While Clarissa could theoretically return to her family after she absconds with Lovelace, her prioritizing of Anna over her parents proves irrevocable. Every time Clarissa absconds from her house to secretly deposit a letter for Anna, she metaphorically leaves behind her family. Her emotional lodestone becomes the chicken house where she hides these letters, not Harlowe Place. While it is unclear whether Clarissa deliberately departs with Lovelace, her correspondence with Anna is undeniably voluntary and defiant. Clarissa implicitly acknowledges this when she asks Anna to "condescend to carry on a private correspondence" (66). Clarissa acknowledges how "undutiful" this request is, but follows her heart anyway, explaining she "cannot bear the thought of being deprived of the principal pleasure of [her] life," Anna's "conversation by person and by letter" (66). Implicit in this statement is the fact that her family is no longer Clarissa's principal pleasure.

Anna's and Clarissa's letters to one another are written in what Kinkead-Weekes describes as a "language stronger than friendship: the language of the family."[38] Clarissa's parents and siblings rebuff her when she tries to confide in them, but Anna invites her to correspond with complete sincerity: a "friendship like ours admits of no reserves" (67). Although Clarissa continues to profess loyalty to her family until she dies, her letters to Anna belie her claims. They frequently "expose" her family's "failings" in sarcastic and bitter passages (82). This is only one of the symptoms of the displacement of Clarissa's ties to her nuclear family by her connection to Anna.[39] Clarissa craves the sort of guidance her family will not give her, so she deputizes Anna to provide it. She specifically asks Anna to "observe anything in me . . . faulty" and "acquaint me with it" so she can attempt to reform (73). Their connection is so profound they sometimes even refer to one another not just as surrogate family members, but also as second selves. Anna describes the two of them as one person—"You are me"—implicitly asserting that Clarissa belongs to her rather than to the Harlowes (69). Her assertion is reminiscent of Roxana's description of Amy as "faithful to me, as the Skin to my back."[40] Both sets of surrogate sisters are alter egos, so inseparable that to sever their connection would be a sort of suicide. What Roxana says of Amy, that "to have falln' upon Amy, had been to have murther'd myself," is equally true of Anna and Clarissa (246). Even though Anna and Clarissa are not connected to one another by blood or marriage, they understand themselves to be indissolubly related. Clarissa's willingness to embrace the relationship on these terms anticipates her eventual division from the Harlowes.

In contrast, Clarissa's brother and sister speak and write to her in ways that push her away rather than encourage communication. James speaks in outbursts, just as his father does. For example, when asked to explain his objections to Lovelace, James does not speak rationally or persuasively. Instead, he indulges in a tantrum about how he had "ever hated" Lovelace, "ever should hate him," and therefore "would never own him for a brother, or [Clarissa] for a sister, if [she] marrie[s] him" (49). Just as Mr. B in *Pamela* developed into an irascible adult because he was never restrained as a child, James becomes increasingly querulous throughout the first section of the novel as his outbursts go unchecked by his parents. Only Clarissa refuses to comply with his vision of himself as the sun around which the rest of the Harlowes ought to revolve.[41]

James's correspondence also repulses rather than invites intimacy. His letters to Clarissa are sarcastic and mean-spirited. For example, a letter he writes to her conveying their parents' decision to disallow Clarissa to attend church is inflammatory. He insultingly addresses her as "miss" and suggests her real motive for wanting to attend services is to enlist public sympathy at her family's expense (119). He italicizes parts of words Clarissa typically uses in her letters to him—"in-*ten*-tion" is a good example of this—in a typographical version of schoolboy taunts aimed at overly grave schoolfellows (119).[42] In other letters he contemptuously refers to her as "Miss Pert" and "Miss Cunning-ones" and describes her letters as "impertinent scribble," "quaint nonsense," and "nothing-meaning vocatives" (138, 257, 161). He dismisses her complaints as tiresome sermons delivered by a "pert preacher" (221). The Harlowes isolate Clarissa from her friends and neighbors in order to "mortify [her] into a sense of [her] duty" (119). However, James is more interested in the spectacle of her abasement than in forcing her to marry Solmes. He takes lurid pleasure in imagining Solmes raping Clarissa at their uncle's isolated estate (218). He also encourages his father to publicly eject Clarissa from Harlowe Place, a scene he hopes to bring about in order to dramatize her degradation (121).

Arabella behaves and speaks to Clarissa in a manner antithetical to Clarissa's concept of sisterhood. Spurned by Lovelace, who orchestrates a proposal so insulting Arabella is forced to turn it down, Arabella becomes "inflamed by disappointed love and revenge" so that she "forget[s] to be a sister" (85). Appropriately for a character of this type whose ruling passion is vanity, Arabella's first appearance in the novel is before a mirror, posing and inviting Clarissa to compliment the beauty that supposedly attracts Lovelace (42). This episode pointedly contrasts with Clarissa's later description of Anna as a "looking-glass" set before her to "let [her] see [her] imperfections" (73). Their differences ensure Clarissa will never find "a friend in [her] sister" (113). Arabella prefers unburdening herself to her chambermaid, Betty Barnes, who will flatter rather than advise her (264). Arabella's only other close companion is her brother, who joins forces with her to despoil Clarissa, their "common enemy" (80). Richardson suggests in several passages that the connection between these siblings has incestuous overtones, with Clarissa more than once describing their bond as "lover-like" (294). This sinister couple becomes increasingly menacing as Charlotte and Mr. Harlowe retreat from the family's conflicts. In this vacuum of authority, James and Arabella become their parents' proxies. They perform intimacy in front of Clarissa in order to emphasize her exclusion from the family circle. Clarissa discovers them walking "hand in hand" in the garden (294). She proffers her hand to "dear Bella" in hopes of being acknowledged as a sister, but Arabella spurns her, forcing Clarissa to "withdr[aw]" her hand "as hastily" as if it had "been bit by a viper" (294–295). They now pose as Adam and Eve in the garden, relegating Clarissa to the exiled status of the envious serpent unable to share in their companionship.

Arabella's letters to Clarissa enforce this ostracism. The persona Arabella adopts in them is comparable to that of *Pamela*'s Mrs. Jewkes, whom

Arabella resembles physically and psychologically. Arabella is less exaggeratedly grotesque than Jewkes, but still "masculine in her air, and in her spirit," with a "plump, high-fed face" often seen "foaming with passion" (309, 60, 229). Arabella relishes the opportunity to amplify and aggravate reports of her family's renunciation of Clarissa. This is especially pronounced in a letter she sends in response to Clarissa's request to reconcile with her family after leaving with Lovelace. Arabella torments her absent sister by protractedly describing their father's curse, their mother's tears, and Clarissa's boarded-off room. Her letters to Clarissa are all conclusive in tone and content, foreclosing rather than inviting a response. They also abjure in different ways and to different degrees Clarissa as a member of the Harlowes. For example, a letter sent to Clarissa while she is still secluded in her room at Harlowe Place concludes "Adieu, mamma Norton's sweet child" (230). It is significant that Arabella does not identify herself in her closure as a friend or a sister, titles that would allow Clarissa to stake an ongoing claim on her attention. Instead, she refers to Clarissa as "mamma Norton's sweet child." (Judith Norton, as I mention earlier, is Clarissa's wet nurse.) This rhetorical gesture casts Clarissa out of the Harlowes and inserts her into a family that serves them. It is the equivalent of Lady Davers insisting her brother is a member of the Andrews rather than the B family. She also expels Clarissa from the Harlowe family through her closure, "adieu." By writing "goodbye," she precludes a response.

As cruel as Arabella's early letters to Clarissa are, they become even more sadistic after Clarissa's departure with Lovelace from Harlowe Place. Arabella now refers to Clarissa as "Sister that was," an unequivocal declaration of divorce (509). She also becomes more aggressive about denigrating Clarissa's status. She no longer refers to Clarissa as Judith Norton's child, which would at least accord her some relationship to the Harlowes since as a servant Judith would have belonged to their household family. Now she intimates that as an unmarried single woman in ambiguous circumstances, Clarissa is no one's child, a bastard without any surname she is "*permitted* . . . to go by" (509). She even calls Clarissa a "common creature," or prostitute (509). This insult has significant connotations beyond its obvious effrontery. It implies that Clarissa has lost the status she was accorded as a Harlowe and has now become just another member of the indistinguishable masses of "common" people.

Arabella regards anyone other than her family and friends as a nonentity; Clarissa sees them as members of the "great family" made up of all of humanity and universally connected through "relationship forgot" (62). As Alex Hernandez notes, "from the beginning of the novel" Clarissa's Christian concept of family "extend[s]" via her charitable projects "to the wider boundaries of the parish" and beyond.[43] This family expands outward as the novel progresses. Clarissa envisions a Christian utopia where obligations are based on shared human bonds that transcend kinship. In contrast, Arabella's notion of the world outside Harlowe Place is of a Hobbesian dystopia in which an unprotected woman must engage alone in the war of one against all, inevitably becoming, as she predicts Clarissa will, "a beggar along London streets" (510). As distant as the streets of London are both socially and geographically from Harlowe Place, they are apparently not far enough away to satisfy Arabella. In a letter Clarissa receives from Arabella on her death-bed, Arabella suggests Clarissa travel to the American colonies and live obscurely in Philadelphia (1256). This particular letter exemplifies the purpose of all Arabella's letters to Clarissa. It seeks to enforce not only social distance between Clarissa and the Harlowes, but also unbridgeable physical distance. Further, it implies that Clarissa's elopement is a criminal act meriting the same punishment Moll Flanders suffers for theft: transportation.

Clarissa must not only choose the right surrogate family members to replace her faulty nuclear and lineage family, but she must also reject the nefarious surrogate family Lovelace tries to force on her. Lovelace assumes he will be able to change Clarissa by controlling her environment. By tricking her into living in a household family made up of prostitutes posing as ladies he hopes to transfigure her into a member of their degraded sisterhood. However, even at her most vulnerable, Clarissa is selective about who she invites into her surrogate family. She adopts surrogate family members based on their kindness, generosity, and virtue, not exigency, convenience, or status. Stranded, with a known libertine as her only protector, Clarissa has to act as "father, mother and uncle for [he]rself," deciding which surrogate family members to spurn (588).

Clarissa's captivity in the brothel is similar to Pamela's at Mr. B's Lincoln-shire estate, except that Clarissa does not know she is a prisoner. Instead, she believes she is joining a ready-made respectable household family complete with the maternal and sororal ties she has lost. Other fraudulent surrogate family members employed by Lovelace to delude Clarissa include two courtesans who assume the characters of his aunts and Captain Tomlinson, a pretended friend of one of her uncles. Anna refers to these surrogate family members Lovelace tries to impose on Clarissa as his "familiar[s]" because they are like evil spirits controlled by a conjurer (1015). However, another related meaning of "familiar," a member of a family or household, is more relevant in this instance. Captain Tomlinson, Mrs. Sinclair (the brothel's madame), and the prostitutes are members of Lovelace's moral and spiritual family.

Numerous scholars have remarked on the significance of this household made up of, as John Dussinger describes it, "misplaced surrogates" who "lay claim" to Clarissa.[44] Margaret Doody notes that this family with its morally grotesque members posing as reputable women is itself a "parody of the house of Harlowe, and a reflection of it."[45] Similarly, Kathleen Oliver describes it as a "masquerade version of Harlowe Place" in which Lovelace's "various minions play the roles of Harlowe and Lovelace family members."[46] Mrs. Sinclair, known as "mother Sinclair," focuses exclusively on the status and reputation of her house, just as Clarissa's mother Charlotte does (522). Arabella and James savor the spectacle of Clarissa's abasement in more subtle but no less vicious ways than do their doubles, Sally and Polly, the prostitute "daughters" of Sinclair's family. Finally, Lovelace is the brother who runs the family (in this case literally, because he employs them), just as James is the Harlowes' de facto patriarch. By confronting the faults of her own family in the guise of the inhabitants of mother Sinclair's house, Clarissa answers a question Lovelace poses about her: "[w]hose daughter is she?" (426). He intends the question to be rhetorical, reminding his correspondent Mr. Belford that Clarissa is only a daughter of a self-aggrandizing family whose status is inferior to his own. As just another of his conquests, many of whom were also from respected families, he believes she will fall and prove to him that all women are rakes at heart, true daughters of mother Sinclair.

Clarissa must reject Lovelace's spies without knowing anything about their connection to him, making her "trial" a test of her fundamental nature rather than, as he views it, of her susceptibility to seduction. In *Pamela*, Pamela knows Jewkes is Mr. B's agent. Resisting her requires only that she adhere to prescriptive ideals of virtue. This is not the case in *Clarissa*. Clarissa's entrapment resembles the fairy tale of the princess and the pea, a story in which the princess reveals her lineage through a somatic and instinctual detection of a pea buried beneath layers of mattresses. Similarly, Clarissa reacts with instinctual aversion to corruption and perversion, though she does not consciously recognize them. She has no apparent basis for her dislike of Sinclair, who appears to be "courteous and obliging," or her "kinswomen" who "seem to be genteel young women" (524). Their veneer of respectability has been constructed so thoroughly that even their library, purchased secondhand by Lovelace for exactly this purpose, provides evidence of their piety and taste (525). Clarissa wants to trust them because she deeply misses belonging to a family. As she writes, it "is natural . . . for a person to be the more desirous of making new friends in proportion as she loses the favour of old ones" (126–127). Despite all this, Clarissa distrusts them. She refuses to regularly eat or converse with any of them and will not sleep beside a supposed guest of Sinclair's even though her refusal appears unjustified and rude. She later defends this refusal to integrate into Sinclair's household in terms that reveal she intuitively "want[ed] not to establish [her]self" with this family (690). As for Captain Tomlinson, she tells him she is suspicious that he belongs to the "*confederacy of his [Lovelace's] creatures*" (834). Clarissa's recognition of the nefarious powers at work to deceive her seems to create a sort of magical outcome, as the false surrogate family members resume their true forms. For example, the scenes surrounding Clarissa's rape portray Sinclair as a monster "foaming at the mouth" with "blubber lips," "arms kemboed," and "eyebrows erect, like the bristles upon a hog's back . . . over her half-hid ferret eyes" (967–968, 883).

Although Lovelace orchestrates Clarissa's placement in Sinclair's household family, Clarissa's prospective "sisters" have their own reasons to degrade her. Polly and Sally aggressively try to force Clarissa to become Lovelace's mistress because, like Arabella, they resent being looked down on. Repeatedly, when Lovelace wishes to retreat from his escalating cruelty to Clarissa, "these creatures," as he calls them in a letter to Belford, "endeavour to stimulate" him to "treat [Clarissa] as flesh and blood" (535). Their desire to witness the degradation of a superior sibling "alien" to their family (Anna's apt description of Clarissa in the Harlowe household) explains why they continuously pressure Lovelace to "make a point of conquering" Clarissa (247, 634). As this last phrase indicates, Sinclair and her prostitute daughters construe Lovelace's actual rape of Clarissa not as his victory over her virtue, but rather as their own triumph over a resistant family member (675). This is especially evident when they "offer their helping hands" to assist the rape, "rejoic[ing]" over the prospect of an act they believe will "reduc[e]" Clarissa "to their level" (702, 729). They are involved in the preparations for Lovelace's rape of Clarissa (they advise him to drug her with opiates) as well as its enactment (1011). The extent to which Lovelace's agents dominate the household family he establishes for his own purposes becomes even more apparent after the rape. In Lovelace's temporary absence, Sinclair, Polly, and Sally try "*breaking*" Clarissa to their will (906). Clarissa tries to escape. Without Lovelace's direction or even his permission, Sinclair has Clarissa arrested for debt to force her wayward daughter to return to their household family. However, Clarissa refuses their offers to pay her bail on the condition that she return to their house. Literal imprisonment in a sponging house is preferable to the spiritual and moral degradation of belonging to Sinclair's household family.

After Clarissa decisively rejects Sinclair's household family, she constructs her own surrogate family of the heart. The Harlowes also fade into the background. As she informs the officer in the sponging house, she now "ha[s] no friends" of any sort (1054). According to Wendy Lee, Clarissa's isolation is a necessary condition for her to begin to construct a surrogate family. Only through the "total relinquishment" of all her attachments to her nuclear and household families is she able to forge purposeful bonds.[47] As Ewha Chung argues, Clarissa selects surrogate family "members based on acquired merit and virtue rather than blood ties."[48] These "ties of pure friendship" based on a "union of like minds," Clarissa's description of her connection to her surrogate family members, prove "much more binding and tender" than "the ties of nature" (1114).

Unlike Pamela, Clarissa does not select surrogate family members for the purpose of helping her achieve a companionable marriage. This is evident because she determines against marriage before she even chooses many of her surrogate family members. However, in a more abstract sense, Clarissa's chosen surrogate family does testify to her worthiness to marry an ideal husband. That

PERFECTING THE FAMILY OF THE HEART

husband is not a man, though; he is far better than any man, even one as godlike as Sir Charles. Her romanticized, prolonged, and deliberate death functions as a Christian courtship preparing her for a union with Jesus. She even describes herself on her deathbed as a "bridal maiden" awaiting the opportunity to put on her "wedding garments" (the white nightgown she intends to wear after death) before she goes to live in her last "house" (a coffin) (1339). She dies with a sort of "I do" on her lips as she walks down the aisle to her waiting bridegroom, "come—Oh come—blessed Lord—JESUS!" (1362). The "honest strangers" who make up her surrogate family ease her into death (1272).

In the middle-class boarding house Clarissa lodges in until she dies, she adopts surrogate parents whose kindness and warmth contrast with the meanness of the Harlowes as well as the sadism of mother Sinclair. Her chosen surrogate fathers are an apothecary and a doctor who help her during her illness. As healers, they provide benevolent patriarchal guidance of the sort that Defoe recommends in *The Family Instructor*. These surrogate family members are never members of Clarissa's household family. Living in a house with her would be inappropriate given their status and her unmarried and unprotected state. However, his privileged access to her on her deathbed creates the sort of intense intimacy that would otherwise take much longer to form. They become the heads of a surrogate family made up of members Derek Taylor understatedly describes as "truly decent."[49] While this description may sound like it damns the doctor and apothecary with faint praise, the Harlowes' total lack of decency makes it a genuine commendation. Richardson heavy-handedly emphasizes their fatherly roles, referring repeatedly to their affection for Clarissa as paternal or "filial" (1082, 1351, 1090). She signifies her willingness to adopt them into her surrogate family by discontinuing her payments to them. She explains her decision to her doctor as a desire to "no more affront" him with "tenders that have pained you for some time past" since she now "look[s] upon" him "only as a friend" (1277). This concession on her part is extraordinary, since she sells her own clothing rather than be financially obliged even to her surrogate sister Anna. The only people she is willing to accept money from are the Harlowes (who refuse to send her any). As her illness progresses, her attachment to her parents becomes just another of the many "old" ties that have now "fall[en] off" (1248). When the doctor writes to Clarissa's "implacable father" to apprise him of his daughter's impending death, he asserts his status as Clarissa's new parent by taking it on himself to reproach him for his "unforgiving" behavior (1277, 1153).

While Clarissa's surrogate fathers give her the patriarchal recognition she longs for, her surrogate mother Mrs. Lovick nurtures and loves her. Charlotte is too self-pitying and self-regarding to comfort her daughter. However, the widow lodger who replaces her loves Clarissa in the way she always wanted to be loved by Charlotte. She is, as Belford observes, "as careful of" Clarissa "as if she were her mother" (1350).[50] While Richardson does not draw Lovick finely, he does focus a great deal of attention on the ways Clarissa displaces her unreciprocated love for Charlotte onto this surrogate mother. Consequently, her presence at Clarissa's deathbed becomes a constant reminder of Charlotte's absence. For example, when Clarissa's doctor reprimands Lovick and Mrs. Smith (the landlord's wife) for allowing Clarissa to indulge her "solemn whimsy" of placing a coffin next to her sickbed, they remind him of the "*little authority*" they are able to exercise as "strangers about her" (1316, 1352).[51] Most poignantly, Clarissa must call on Lovick to pray for her in her last days because she has "[n]o dear mother . . . to pray by me and bless me!" (1272). Lovick even metamorphoses at times into Charlotte in Clarissa's imagination, as she "delights[s] herself in thinking she was in her mama's arms" (1351). This scene starkly contrasts with the few instances in which Charlotte embraces her daughter, which all turn out to be attempts to manipulate her into complying with the family's plans.

Clarissa completes her surrogate family with Belford, a brother figure who treats her with the fraternal tenderness she craves, but never receives, from James. As is the case with Clarissa's surrogate fathers, Belford is never a member of her household family. The social prohibitions that prevent them from residing with her apply doubly to him since he is an unmarried man reputed to be a libertine. Instead, he becomes her advocate and admirer at a distance. Lovelace allows him to read Clarissa's letters and visit her when she lives with Lovelace in the brothel. Instead of praising Lovelace's ingenuity, Belford castigates him for abusing the trust of the finest "lady in the world" (555). He pledges to become "a means of saving this excellent creature," a truly brotherly impulse (555). Belford ultimately transfers his loyalty from his brother rake Lovelace to his surrogate sister Clarissa. He informs Lovelace that if he is forced to choose between him and Clarissa, he will choose Clarissa: "I had rather lose all the friends I have in the world (yourself included) than this divine lady" (1357). After Lovelace rapes Clarissa, Belford makes good on this ultimatum. Clarissa formally signifies her privileged relationship to her surrogate brother by inviting him to become her executor, a role she acknowledges is typically reserved for family members. By accepting her offer, he becomes her defender even after her death, enforcing her wishes when the Harlowes would prefer to ignore them. However, Belford's remarkable attachment is also evident in less dramatic ways throughout the correspondence between Belford and Lovelace. After the rape, for example, Belford warns Lovelace that if he were Clarissa's biological "brother, her violation must have been followed by the blood of one of us" (884). In reality, Belford's forbearance demonstrates that he is a better brother than James. However reluctantly, Belford respects Clarissa's injunction that she not become the occasion for more violence between men. On the other hand, James uses Clarissa as an excuse to duel with Lovelace, a rival "he had ever hated" (49). The public mortification James suffers when he acquits himself poorly in this contest extends to his whole family, adding insult to injury.

Richardson implicitly contrasts Belford with James. Clarissa's surrogate brother proves to be better than her actual brother in every respect. James resents Clarissa's intellectual and moral superiority, but Belford reveres and is ultimately reformed by her "superior excellence" (1128).[52] His connection to Clarissa cultivates the "humane qualities" she recognizes in him and encourages him to better himself (1164). Clarissa is able to inspire in Belford the reformation she hoped to bring about in Lovelace. Belford undergoes a Christian conversion, not only amending his attitudes toward women, but also promising to "desert" his libertine companions since, as Clarissa teaches him, "nothing is worthy" of the "sacred name" of friendship "THAT HAS NOT VIRTUE FOR ITS BASE" (1090, 1126). Belford provides the most convincing evidence of his transformation in his letters to Lovelace. He tries to accomplish what Clarissa could not, urging Lovelace to give up his libertine ways and "live a life of reason rather than a life of a brute, for the time to come" (1090). Through Belford, Clarissa is able to enact the feminine ideal of radiating goodness outward through her family into the world, something she was unable to accomplish with her nuclear family or Sinclair's household family.

Clarissa's surrogate sister Anna likewise surpasses Arabella, her counterpart in Clarissa's nuclear family. Anna takes pride in the distinction she enjoys as Clarissa's surrogate sister. She willingly takes "a second place" in company because she wishes to emulate Clarissa's morals and manners, referring to Clarissa as her "monitoress" who "direct[s] me in everything" (1114, 1348). Whereas Clarissa's fallen status incites ridicule from Arabella, who calls her an "undone creature," Anna, a much more gifted satirist than Arabella and therefore far more capable of crafting stinging witticisms, shows only compassion for Clarissa's inadvertent faults (1160).[53] Anna and Clarissa enact Richardson's ideal of friendship cultivated through correspondence. Their connection intensifies even as they are forcibly separated and their relationship becomes exclusively epistolary. The tone of their letters becomes increasingly informal and lover-like. For example, Anna tells Clarissa she loves her as "never woman loved another," a love so exclusive "no *third* love can come in between" (40, 131). She refers to Clarissa as the "true partner of my heart" whom she loves "*more* than *myself*" (1114, 356). She is even willing to abandon her own family and prospects in order to "go off privately" with Clarissa and "live and die together" (331). Clarissa's feelings for Anna are no less intense or romantic. Shortly before she dies, Clarissa offers Anna's future husband Mr. Hickman the miniature of Anna she always wore around her neck, but only after she kisses the image several times and laments losing her "*Sweet and ever-amiable friend—companion*—sister" and "lover!" (1357).[54] Significantly, as James Reeves remarks, Clarissa leaves all her most personal bequests, including clothing and her book of meditations, to surrogate family members such as Judith and Anna rather than to the Harlowes.[55]

Anna's and Clarissa's lover-like style provides evidence of their perfect intellectual pairing: a disinterested love that allows them to write to one another from the heart. An ideal surrogate family connection like theirs must be based on a sort of intellectual and moral compatibility that neither one achieves with any member of her nuclear or lineage family. It fosters a sense of equality that allows them to correct each other's faults without asperity and to accept criticism graciously. The complete candor they share requires absolute trust, as Clarissa acknowledges when she writes to Anna that "each should say or write to the other whatever was upon her mind, without any offense to be taken; a condition that is indeed indispensable in all friendship" (135). The intellectual basis for this union with her surrogate sister is particularly suited to Clarissa, who as Belford observes is "all mind" (555). It is ironic that Lovelace, who fails to understand the nature of Clarissa's mind until it is too late, makes the most trenchant observation about the necessary interconnectedness between surrogate ties and intellectual compatibility, observing that "[g]enerous minds are always of kin" (1093).

The kinship of generous minds is robust enough to permit correction as well as approbation. Anna and Clarissa frequently offer each other advice and criticism of the sort neither welcomes from their parents. They become one another's conscience, facilitating moral growth and thoughtful judgment. The seriousness with which they regard one another's good opinion is most evident in Clarissa's appeal to Anna after her rape. She writes, "[n]obody but Miss Howe, to whom, next to the Almighty, and my own mother, I wish to stand acquitted of willful error, shall know the whole of what has passed" (853). As Clarissa writes to Anna, their surrogate sisterhood requires honest expostulations about one another's beliefs and actions: "Spare me not therefore, because I am your *friend*. For *that* very reason spare me not. I may *feel* your edge, fine as it is; I may be pained: you would lose your end if I were not: but after the first sensibility (as I have said more than once before), I will love you the better, and my amended heart shall be all yours; and it will then be more worthy to be yours" (280). Their loving sisterhood allows them to criticize without offending one another. As Anna writes, she is more receptive to Clarissa's "reproofs" than to her mother's because they are "accompanied with love" and "calculated to improve, and not to provoke" (432).

Although Clarissa never marries, her correspondence with Anna prefigures Harriet's with Charlotte in *Sir Charles Grandison* by focusing largely on moral questions related to courtship. In Anna's case, she is culpable for toying with Hickman. She amends this behavior based on her correspondence with Clarissa. Clarissa's final letter to Anna, delivered after her death, begs her friend to "not suspend the day" of her marriage, a directive Anna agrees to in a letter to Belford, though she regrets the loss of her "monitoress" whose "advice and instructions" she predicted she would need in order to "acquit [herself] tolerably" as a wife (1377, 1457). Clarissa's situation is more complex because her mercurial suitor and precarious situation circumscribe her choices about courtship while at the same time making them more exigent than Anna's. By recounting in minute detail every meeting with Lovelace and asking Anna to interpret his passing remarks and smallest actions, she fulfills Anna's request to "inform me of everything that passes" (407). Together, they are able to pass moral judgment on him and to come to the decision that regardless of the consequences he is unworthy of marrying Clarissa. By writing to one another about their trials during courtship they amend their own character flaws, with Anna gradually learning to "subdue [her] own passions" and Clarissa attempting through her Christian submission to death to "amend" in herself what "has been amiss" (550, 578). After Clarissa dies and Anna takes her surrogate sister's advice to marry Hickman, she names her firstborn daughter Clarissa. It was tradition for mothers to give eldest daughters their own names. By naming her daughter Clarissa, Anna implicitly identifies Clarissa, even after death, as a beloved family member.

Surrogate, nuclear, and lineage families are often at odds in *Clarissa*, but in *Sir Charles Grandison* they merge to such an extent they become indistinguishable. Courtship and marriage synthesize these family models. Richardson frustrates every attempt to reconcile nuclear and lineage families with surrogate families in *Clarissa*. On the other hand, in *Sir Charles Grandison* they align so often and in so many ways it becomes almost ludicrous. In *Clarissa*, Richardson dangles before readers the possibility of matches between Anna and Clarissa's brother and Anna's mother and Clarissa's uncle Anthony. Either marriage would formalize Anna's and Clarissa's surrogate sisterhood. They would become members of one another's nuclear families. Then, as Clarissa poignantly writes to Anna, she would have "a friend in a sister" (55). However, nothing comes of either potential match. Harriet, on the other hand, marries her surrogate brother Charles, thus forming a nuclear family that extends outward to his sisters Charlotte and Lady L, who have already adopted Harriet as surrogate sisters. This is only one of the many hybrid family models envisioned by Richardson in his final novel.

The number of surrogate ties proliferates in *Sir Charles Grandison* so exponentially that the world seems to become the "one great family" Clarissa hoped to replicate. As Betty Schellenberg argues, Richardson expands the scope of Sir Charles's influence through a "redefinition of 'family' not as blood kinship but as a fraternity of sentiment and sensibility."[56] Every kind person Harriet meets, and every worthy suitor she rejects in Sir Charles's favor, becomes a surrogate brother or parent. Although Sir Charles and Harriet marry each other, their marriage unifies this vast surrogate family they collectively acquire rather than excluding rejected suitors. Rebecca Barr interprets this phenomenon as a grand metaphor at the center of the novel. Sir Charles and Harriet's "union is a symbolic consolidation of" the novel's larger "moral family."[57] In *Clarissa*, Clarissa ultimately comes to the Hobbesian conclusion that "*innocent* and *benevolent* spirits are sure to be considered as *aliens*, and to be made sufferers by the *genuine sons* and *daughters* of [the] *earth*" (1020). In *Sir Charles Grandison*, morally upright members of the great family band together in a combined surrogate and biological family modeled on the great family Clarissa aspires to but never achieves.

In *Sir Charles Grandison*, the Clarissas of the world are the rule, not the exception. Virtuous characters recognize one another instantly, with surrogate families forming almost instantaneously. As Sir Charles states with so much certainty that he must believe it to be self-evident, "like minds will be intimate at first sight."[58] As these ties multiply, they spread through ever-expanding networks that move outward throughout England and even abroad. Potential conflicts, most notably those presented by the numerous suitors Harriet and Sir Charles must reject in order to eventually marry one another, are warded off by forming surrogate ties to those they spurn. Nuclear and lineage families do not threaten this utopian concord. All of the selfish and tyrannical family members are either dead before the novel commences, as in the case of Sir Charles's father Sir Thomas, or reformed by surrogate family members, as occurs to Sir Charles's maternal uncle Lord W and his rakish cousin Everard. Even the major conflict of the novel, which is supposed to be the possibility that this "Prince of the Almighty's creation," Sir Charles, might marry an Italian Catholic instead of an English protestant, is glossed over when Clementina becomes just another of his many surrogate sisters (3: 236).

Surrogate families are so important in *Sir Charles Grandison* that even members of nuclear or linear families aspire to be adopted into them. Uncles, aunts, cousins, and even grandparents are reconfigured as surrogate family members, as these are the only ties deemed by Richardson to be intimate enough to be significant. This has the peculiar effect of both denigrating and reifying the value of kinship at the same time. For example, Sir Charles advises his cousin Everard to act morally rather than try to evade the consequences of one of his many scrapes because doing so will earn Sir Charles's "true fraternal love" (5: 514). It is apparently irrelevant to Sir Charles that Everard already merits familial status by virtue of being his relation. On the other hand, Sir Charles invites virtual strangers such as Harriet and Jeronymo to become his sisters and brothers; they are promoted instantly to the status of family members, while his cousin is put on familial "probation" until he proves he is truly rehabilitated.

Harriet and Sir Charles are so prodigal with their offers to adopt friends and relations into their surrogate families that at times it is farcical. Numerous potential suitors grow weary with their provisional status as what Charlotte terms "nominal" brothers and sisters (2: 441). Indeed, surrogacy is often connected to the possibility of marriage: surrogate parents or grandparents might become in-laws, and surrogate brothers, sisters, or children might become spouses. Not every suitor is content with the consolation prize of being adopted into the hero's or heroine's surrogate families. In some inadvertently comic scenes a few openly express frustration at being classed among the numerous imagined brothers and sisters Sir Charles and Harriet accumulate throughout the novel.

The orphaned Sir Charles and Harriet attract numerous surrogate parents. Just as jilted suitors populate the ranks of their surrogate brothers and sisters, most of their surrogate parents were these suitors' relations. For Harriet, the most important surrogate parent figures are Sir Rowland and Lady D, both close relations of suitors she rejects. Sir Rowland takes his role as surrogate father so seriously that Harriet and Sir Charles must ultimately remind him of his obligations to his actual kin. When he tries to include her in his will as an heir, she refuses his offer because doing so would "deprive . . . those who have more than a stranger's claim" to his fortune (4: 405). However, it is only in instances such as this one, when the assertion of surrogacy threatens the integrity of nuclear or lineage families, that Harriet or Sir Charles admit there is any meaningful distinction between different family models. Surrogate ties are otherwise treated with great solemnity. For example, when Sir Rowland and Lady D visit their "daughter" Harriet after her marriage to Sir Charles, she introduces Sir Rowland to Sir Charles as "my father" and Sir Charles asks Lady D to "look upon him as her son" (7: 299, 7: 301–302). Sir Charles adds these surrogate parents to those who have a prior claim to him, including his tutor Dr. Bartlett, his potential parents-in-law the della Portas, and his uncle Lord W. Just as Everard is supposed to regard Sir Charles's invitation to become his surrogate brother as a promotion over his actual status as Sir Charles's cousin, Lord W is ecstatic when Sir Charles acknowledges Lord W's wedding gifts not out of the "duty" to which he is "intitled . . . by the ties of blood" but because Lord W's graciousness forges a "bond of gratitude that never can be broken" (4: 343). Sir Charles asserts straightforwardly to Lord W that kinship is less durable than their newfound alliance "of the mind" (4: 343).

Sir Charles and Harriet also act as surrogate parents to Emily Jervois, Sir Charles's ward. Becoming Emily's surrogate mother redirects the competition between them for Sir Charles's attention into nurturing on Harriet's part and deference on Emily's. Emily becomes so attached to Harriet as a maternal figure that she chooses to "love" and "obey" Harriet in preference to her wayward mother who is not "as good as [Harriet]" (3: 26). This particular adoption into the Grandisons' surrogate family presents unique difficulties because Emily's continuing sexual attraction to Sir Charles threatens the foundations of their nuclear family. This "daughter's" overt desire to replace Harriet as the object of Sir Charles's affection exposes how implicitly incestuous this surrogate family model is. Most of the "brothers" and "sisters" invited into the Grandisons' surrogate family, including Mr. Fowler, Mr. Orme, Clementina, and Mr. Greville, are former suitors that are now supposed to have become surrogate siblings. Thus, the basis of many of the

Grandisons' surrogate connections is sublimated sexual attraction expressed as familial love. Richardson is not squeamish, particularly in Clementina's case, about the way unfulfilled desire cements this family of the heart. However, Emily's inability to transform her passion into daughterly affection makes her difficult to incorporate into the Grandison household. She is evicted, though Richardson characterizes this removal in softer terms as an adoption into Harriet's lineage family. Harriet's grandmother upon first meeting Emily invites her to come live with her as "a second Harriet" who will "supply the place" of her absent granddaughter in their household (7: 321, 6: 227). Thus, the most problematic of Harriet's and Sir Charles's surrogate ties becomes the means to fixedly attach Harriet's lineage family to her nuclear and household family at Grandison Hall.

As in *Clarissa*, surrogate siblings rank higher in emotional status than surrogate parents or children. Richardson promotes surrogate sisterhood and brotherhood as paradigmatic surrogate family relationships because siblings are bound together by shared status in the family and are thus predisposed to engage in the "mingling of hearts" and "soul[s]" he idealizes (3: 165). In contrast, parents and children are confined to roles defined by authority and duty. For example, Sir Charles praises Clementina's mother for being "less of the mother" to Clementina than a "sister" and "friend" (3: 166). As in *Clarissa*, it is the surrogate sibling relationships in the novel that provide the greatest opportunities for characters' moral, intellectual, and emotional growth. Almost every character participates in these fraternal and sororal ties, although to differing degrees. However, for a number of reasons Harriet's surrogate ties are most significant. While Sir Charles also accumulates numerous surrogate brothers and sisters, his infallibility makes it impossible for him to enjoy with anyone the sort of mutually educative relationship characteristic of surrogate siblings. Even with Harriet, his status as surrogate brother often seems more a means of keeping her available in case his on-again, off-again engagement to Clementina falls through than readiness to participate in "the mutual unbosoming of secrets" that "is the cement of faithful Friendship" (3: 165). Harriet, however, is open and frank with her chosen surrogate siblings, particularly Charlotte, whose loyalty to friends, flippancy to everyone else, and irreverence about marriage identify her as the incarnation of her predecessor Anna Howe in *Clarissa*.

The intensity of the bond between Charlotte and Harriet distinguishes it from the somewhat formulaic connections between other surrogate family members in *Sir Charles Grandison*. They meet under dramatic circumstances that encourage complete mutual confidence that ripens into trust and affection. Although it is Sir Charles who rescues Harriet from Sir Hargrave, it is Charlotte who nurses Harriet during her convalescence. During this time Harriet is weak, humiliated, disturbed, and confused about the masquerade and its aftermath. In this impressionable state she "open[s] her whole heart" to Charlotte, an ongoing confession that continues long after she stops worrying about her misadventures with Sir Hargrave and starts focusing all her attention on Sir Charles (4: 22). Charlotte is also ideally situated when she meets Harriet to welcome and confide in a new sister. Her actual sister Lady L is recently married and busy with her own affairs. Charlotte is in particular need of her absent sister because she needs advice about how to deal with her secret engagement to Captain Anderson. These circumstances allow Charlotte and Harriet to forge in a very short time a bond as durable and intense as Anna's long-standing friendship with Clarissa. They consistently describe this connection as sisterly, with Charlotte calling herself Harriet's "elder sister" and insisting Harriet refer to her as "*your Charlotte*" (1: 145). It bothers Charlotte that their connection is only imaginary, and she tries to enforce its validity by claiming Harriet was "found" after being "stolen" from the Grandisons "in her cradle" (148). The fervor of their attachment is also evident in the punctuation of their letters, with Charlotte referring to Harriet as "Sister!" and "Friend!" (3: 202). Charlotte even calls Harriet her "monitoress," echoing one of Anna's favorite terms for Clarissa (7: 267). Additionally, Charlotte writes to Harriet "I love you better, if possible, than I love myself," just as Anna does to Clarissa (6: 30).

Charlotte's and Harriet's love for one another evolves out of their conversations about courtship and marriage. Charlotte asks Harriet to "[r]eveal to me all the secrets of your heart, and how that heart is from time to time affected; that I may know whether you are capable of that greatness of mind in a Love-case, that you shew in all others" (4: 419). In return for Harriet's confidences about her tortured courtship with Sir Charles, Charlotte seeks guidance from Harriet throughout her engagement and early days of her marriage to Lord G. Because of the intensity of this bond, Harriet's marriage to Sir Charles is as important, or possibly even more important, as a means of formalizing her connection to Charlotte, "the friend of [her] heart," than as a model of idealized courtship and marriage (4: 322). After the wedding, Richardson focuses less on Harriet and Sir Charles and more on Harriet and Charlotte. Tellingly, Charlotte congratulates Harriet on her marriage by offering to "embrace my sister, my *real* sister, my sister Grandison" (3: 132).

Harriet's relationship with Charlotte becomes the trunk of the Grandison surrogate family tree; the many branches it supports are grafted onto their sisterhood even though nominally Harriet and Sir Charles are the eldest siblings of this unwieldy brood. It is Charlotte rather than Sir Charles who invites Mrs. Reeves and the rest of Harriet's relations to visit Grandison Hall by "kindly bespeaking a family relation for herself thro' her dear Miss Byron" (1: 148). On Harriet's wedding day, it is Charlotte who stakes a familial claim on Harriet's best friend Lucy as well as Harriet's relations. Harriet's and Charlotte's mutual vows to embrace one another's families and friends as their own—"Ours yours; Yours ours!"—are as solemn as the wedding vows exchanged between Sir Charles and Harriet and project much further into the future. Charlotte promises Harriet to love "your Cousins, and your Cousins Cousins, to the twentieth Generation" since they are now "all of one Family . . . for ever" (6: 230). Similarly, the della Portas are brought into the Grandison family fold by Harriet's proffer of "sisterly love" to her former rival Clementina on behalf of all the Grandison sisters. Echoing Charlotte's earlier praise of Sir Charles for choosing her surrogate sister as his spouse, Harriet thanks him for "giv[ing]" her new "Sisters": a sorority that now includes Clementina (7: 354). Although it is Clementina's brother Jeronymo who invites the Grandisons to Italy so their "one family" may be reunited, it is the bonds of sisterhood originating with Harriet and Charlotte and extending later to Clementina that maintain their connection (7: 383). Harriet promises to exchange letters with Clementina, assuring their families will continue in the future to "mingle souls and sentiments on paper" and thus "not be divided" despite the distance between them (7: 433).

Sir Charles Grandison envisions surrogate families as an endlessly inclusive mechanism uniting every type of family: a complete inversion of *Clarissa*. *Clarissa*'s nuclear and linear families isolate and wound their virtuous members. *Clarissa*'s connection to family members partially compensates her for her exile from her deficient family. However, her connections cannot restore harmony between alienated relations or fully reconcile her to losing her nuclear or lineage family. *Sir Charles Grandison* reverses this situation. In *Clarissa*, Lovelace's offer to become Clarissa's "father, uncle, brother, and . . . *husband* . . . all in one" is menacing (*Clarissa*, 377). When Sir Charles makes the same sort of offer to virtually everyone he encounters, they lionize him for his generosity of spirit. Harriet's absolute freedom to marry anyone she wants in *Sir Charles Grandison* also reverses Clarissa's thralldom to an abusive family.

Given the moderating trajectory Richardson seemed to be taking in regard to family models and marital choice in *Pamela* and *Pamela II*, the all-or-nothing perspective of his last two novels—no choice about a husband or unfettered choice and polarized depictions of family models as entirely opposed or wholly complementary—invites interpretation. Pamela lacks status or wealth, which limits her access to surrogate family members and even her parents. Consequently, her choices are circumscribed, but despite them she is able to choose the husband she loves. Clarissa and Harriet are as virtuous as Pamela, but their improved circumstances do not result in a correlative increase in opportunities. Instead, their experiences are antithetical to one another, and both far removed from Pamela's. One possible explanation for this abrupt shift from moderation to extremities is that Richardson's imagination as an author outran his conventional beliefs about family and gender hierarchies. Placed by his fiction on a path that led away from his ideological convictions, he retreated into fantasy. He comes close to acknowledging this himself in a passage I cite earlier in the chapter. When asked what Clarissa should have done rather than refusing an arranged marriage and running away with Lovelace, his response was evasive and even perplexed. He wrote that no woman ought to "plead" Clarissa's "example for *non-compliance*" with her family's wishes unless she shares "*her* [Clarissa's] *reasons*."[59] In other words, he cannot cite any particular fault in Clarissa, but was alarmed that his readers might demand independence from their families based on a precedent established by his own novel.

Despite the limitations of Richardson's narratives, he developed influential models of courtship, surrogate ties, and women's intellectual adaptability. His work "spawned," as Backscheider argues, "as many revisionary texts as imitative ones by women."[60] The novels that followed would not just revise these concepts, but also re-envision them in significant ways. It was left to women novelists, Haywood and Burney prominent among them, to develop more realistically and deliberately the concept of surrogate families as an opportunity for women to learn to make choices about who to "adopt," and sometimes even to reform bad inclinations based on these decisions, before they make the all-important decision of selecting a spouse.

AN AFFINITY FOR LEARNING

Eliza Haywood's *The History of Miss Betsy Thoughtless* and *The History of Jemmy and Jenny Jessamy*

ELIZA HAYWOOD'S LATER PORTION OF her long career as an author of romances, poetry, periodicals, plays, and novels aligned with Samuel Richardson's emergence as a novelist (*Pamela* was published in 1740, *Pamela II* in 1741, and *Clarissa* in 1748). Given this proximity, it is not surprising that her last two novels, *The History of Miss Betsy Thoughtless* (1751) and *The History of Jemmy and Jenny Jessamy* (1753), focus on issues Richardson also addressed through fiction: the role of women, the appropriate limits of female autonomy, how to balance the authority of parents with ideals of companionate marriage, and appropriate female conduct during courtship and after marriage. Like Richardson and Defoe, one of the ways Haywood addresses these subjects is through the convention of surrogate families.

Haywood's version of surrogate families draws on her predecessors' novels but is also distinctly her own. She incorporates Defoe's tolerance for moral ambiguity, worldly pleasures, and pragmatism with Richardson's focus on domesticity, moral development, and female conduct. Like these earlier authors, Haywood correlates protagonists' choices about surrogate families with their marital prospects. However, in her novels, spousal choice is only one important aspect of an emotionally, socially, and intellectually satisfying life. Surrogate families help Haywood's protagonists live their best lives, not just marry the most eligible suitors. Her vision of surrogate families is outward facing in the sense that it is social and extends beyond the fulfillment of domestic duties. It also has an important psychological component since it promotes introspection and intellectual development for women at every stage of their lives.

I focus on *The History of Miss Betsy Thoughtless* and *The History of Jemmy and Jenny Jessamy* rather than Haywood's romances because I am more interested in her depictions of women's conduct and moral development than of their passionate desires. While remnants of the romance conventions that dominate her early fiction like *Love in Excess* (1719) remain in these later novels, primarily in the form of subplots, Haywood's plots shift gradually over time to align with the bankable themes of female virtue and domesticity. Most scholars now agree that these concerns were central to her final novels but play only a peripheral role in her early romances.[1] For my purposes, I am less concerned with delineating specific changes in her writing over the course of her career than in explicating the ways her later novels revise ideals about women, family, and courtship popularized by Richardson.

In Richardson's novels, surrogate families either supplement or supplant nuclear families, enabling female protagonists to make the best possible decisions about marriage. In Clarissa's case, the best choice is to remain single and await Jesus's perfect love after she dies. Conversely, Harriet in *Sir Charles Grandison* (1754) acts on her own wishes when she marries the Jesus-like Sir Charles. Luckily, her desires coincide perfectly with the advice of her lineage and surrogate families. Surrogate families support both protagonists as they navigate the complex situations engendered by these decisions. However, one thing does not change from one of Richardson's novels to the next: every complex moral conundrum protagonists face is somehow related to the questions of whether to marry, and if so, to whom. While Clarissa, Harriet, and Pamela are rational, moral, and virtuous, these traits are of value only insofar as they help them choose appropriate surrogate family members, meaning surrogate family members who will assist them in finding the right spouses. Richardson credited women with judgment but circumscribed the ways they could use it and still remain respectable. He also idealized parental authority, even though his depiction of the Harlowes demonstrates that he knew not all parents were worthy of veneration. His fiction may be viewed as a sort of bait and switch: young women could be wise and discrete, but if they were, they used their intelligence to select husbands wiser than themselves. Such marriages ultimately rendered their intelligence useless outside the domestic sphere. Specifically, once Pamela becomes Mr. B's wife, she submits to him even in intimate matters such as whether to breastfeed their child. Similarly, Harriet defers to her husband, the godlike Sir Charles, in everything, even inviting the entire family of her former rival for his affections to their home.

Haywood takes Richardson's premise of women's intellectual potential and applies it more broadly.[2] For Haywood, it is still critical for young women to select worthy surrogate family members and spouses. However, it is also vital that they cultivate their minds so they are able to enjoy every aspect of their lives before and after they marry. Haywood's novels include material comfort, a satisfying social life, and a reasonable degree of independence in the inventory of necessities for an enjoyable married life. In her estimation, husbands and children were desirable aspects of women's lives, but not of themselves sufficient to make intelligent women happy. Consequently, surrogate family members in Haywood's fiction help women achieve fulfilling lives rather than just facilitating their marriages.

Haywood resembles Defoe more than Richardson in her emphasis on the pragmatic and worldly value of surrogate sisterhood and motherhood. As I explain in detail in chapter 1, Defoe's female narrators Moll in *Moll Flanders* and Roxana in *Roxana* seek out surrogate mothers and sisters who help them accumulate wealth and status through all sorts of means, including but not limited to marriage. Moll abandons so many husbands and children in her lifelong quest for economic security that most readers lose count of them. She remains loyal only to her surrogate mother the governess, a mentor and coconspirator as delighted by trickery and profit as Moll. Similarly, Roxana discards several inconvenient family members, including her own children, in order to set up house repeatedly with her shrewd surrogate sister Amy.

While Haywood incorporates aspects of Defoe's and Richardson's models of surrogate families into her novels, she uniquely emphasizes the importance of day-to-day pleasures such as entertaining and socializing. Haywood's female characters are not particularly complex, but they display a sort of equilibrium foreign to characters like Moll and Clarissa. They seek balanced, socially and intellectually engaged lives just as women do today. They do not worry themselves overly about theoretical moral issues or propriety in the way Clarissa does. Neither are they contented by wealth or social position alone, as Moll is. Haywood's depiction of marriage is also pragmatic rather than idealistic or ideological. Even the best men have faults, and perfect women do not exist. Consequently, there are no defectless marriages. As Aleksondra Hultquist notes, in Haywood's novels "virtue and submission do not guarantee marital bliss: simply behaving virtuously (though certainly important) is not enough in and of itself to make marriages work."[3] Female protagonists must think and act for themselves, making Haywood's vision of surrogate families a feminist one that takes for granted women's rights to make decisions and to learn from their outcomes, without abandoning moral standards.

As numerous Haywood scholars agree, the version of feminism Haywood espouses in her novels is hardly revolutionary by modern standards. As Juliette Merritt asserts, Haywood's approach to the limitations on women's autonomy was "pragmatic rather than utopian or even idealistic."[4] She was a tactician, not a polemicist. The plots in her novels "frequently emphasized women's impotence in the face of systemic patriarchal power."[5] While she accepted patriarchy as a given, she was a "committed strategist . . . discursively, on behalf of the cause of female agency" insofar as it could be exercised despite the legal, social, economic, and other limitations it imposed on women.[6] For example, Betsy in *Betsy Thoughtless* willfully exploits the power she enjoys over men as an attractive and wealthy young woman, but never expresses any wish to expand her influence into spheres off limits to her because of her gender. She describes her suitors as "meer machine[s]" who must please her regardless of her neglect or rudeness to them but expresses no interest in commanding men in any other capacity.[7] She never, for instance, even imagines what it might be like to study at a university, vote, or become a member of Parliament. Haywood's ambition was not to topple accepted gender norms. Rather, as David Oakleaf observes, she "obliquely" tests their limits to see if women could gain power by manipulating them: more like an accountant seeking tax loopholes than a protester petitioning to abolish the IRS.[8] Because Haywood depicted what was, not what ought to be, her writing provides scholars with what Mary Anne Schofield describes as a "comprehensive picture of woman in early eighteenth-century life."[9] Her late novels offer a window into the complex and gender-coded social world her protagonists navigated.[10]

While Haywood's plots are about courtship, they differ from traditional courtship novels by also focusing on marriage: a subject about which Defoe's and Richardson's best novels provide little insight. Paula Backscheider claims "Haywood led in the movement of fiction away from portraits of courtship to critiques of marriage."[11] Although Richardson attempts to portray marriage in *Pamela* and *Pamela II*, Pamela's account of married life is more conduct book than novel. She models exemplary conduct to female readers rather than accurately portraying the day-to-day trials and tribulations of married life. Defoe's fiction, on the other hand, largely ignores Moll's lived marital experiences. Husbands die, go bankrupt, and turn out to be bigamists and highwaymen. But as long as she stays married to them her narrative comes to a standstill. Only after they leave does she resume her story, providing at most a few breezy details about how costly or profitable each marriage turned out to be, and what loose ends (most often children) she needs to tie up before she can move on to her next adventure.

Although the details of Moll's exploits and Pamela's account of domestic duties obviously differ, Moll and Pamela are similarly static characters, never changing their conception of themselves or the world. Haywood's depiction of surrogate families and marriage diverges from theirs because Betsy's and Jenny's experiences with marriage and surrogate family members change how they understand and react to the world. Their basic personalities do not change any more than Pamela's or Clarissa's, but their judgment matures. As they become more discerning, they make better choices about whom to trust, how to behave, and how to live. Pamela is as judicious as a young servant as she is as a matron. Clarissa and Harriet are wise beyond their years and remain so even as experience tests their resolve. All three adopt the correct surrogate family members and reject improper ones, as well as making the best possible decisions about marriage. However, in Haywood's *Betsy Thoughtless*, Betsy initially selects the wrong surrogate family members and even the wrong husband. Only through suffering domestic humiliations at the hands of an unappreciative husband does she learn to make the sort of choices Pamela seems to make from birth. Betsy's evolving character over the course of many misadventures is conspicuous enough for Lorna Ellis to identify *Betsy Thoughtless* as a female bildungsroman.[12] Jenny is less prone to error than

Betsy, but she learns through experience to marry a detached and worldly man because she does not want her husband to interfere with her social and intellectual pursuits. By depicting maturation as a process rather than a product, Haywood encourages women to become better.

Women's capacity to learn is a necessary premise of their development. Though Haywood's protagonists may not always act rationally, she unequivocally presumes their ability to do so. As Alexander Pettit observes, she did not believe women's inclinations were naturally vicious, instead "regard[ing] . . . female sexuality as susceptible to rational self-control."[13] Education did more for women than reign in their libidos, though. In Haywood's periodicals *The Female Spectator* (1744–1746) and *The Parrot* (1746), she advocates for more rigorous academic education for young women because better-read women were more prepared than their frivolous peers to provide rational companionship to husbands and educational guidance to children. Most significantly, Haywood argues explicitly in her journalism and implicitly in her novels that well-cultivated minds create virtue rather than the other way around.

Christopher Loar asserts that Haywood's periodicals were intended to educate women so that their "chastity . . . bec[ame] rational and principled, not merely habitual."[14] His argument applies equally to her later novels like *Betsy Thoughtless*. All the female victims of seductions and near-rapes in *Betsy Thoughtless* seem insensible to the implications of their actions when they violate social norms.[15] They wander London without chaperones, engage in clandestine correspondence with young men, and socialize in public with female friends who are no better than they should be. Haywood implies that if they understood the world they would act with more discretion. Their virtue would then be safeguarded by their own deliberation rather than just being contingent on others' protection. Betsy learns this lesson the hard way, through an abysmal marriage. But ultimately Haywood rewards her with a better marriage after she learns to behave virtuously: a distinction with a difference from Richardson's formula of virtue rewarded in *Pamela*.

Betsy's experiences in a variety of families are pivotal to her learning. As Naomi Tadmor observes of *Betsy Thoughtless*, its "plot consists of a picaresque ramble through many household-families," with the "flexible structure of the household-family" making it "possible to relocate" Betsy "across the literary scene, whilst . . . assigning her a range of familial roles."[16] Tadmor describes the members of Betsy's various household families as friends, a concept that aligns very closely with my own definition of surrogate families.[17] Friends in *Betsy Thoughtless* are what we would today call family friends: "trans-generational" relationships with people connected to parents but who also extend their "framework of social support and moral virtues" to other family members.[18] According to this definition of friend, a friend extends his or her loyalty to the next generation. In Betsy's case, when her parents die, her father's friend Mr. Goodman and her mother's friend

Lady Trusty become her guardians. The members of Mr. Goodman's and Lady Trusty's household families also end up taking on responsibility for Betsy by proxy. Thus, Mr. Goodman's wife Lady Mellasin, Lady Mellasin's daughter Flora, and Lady Trusty's husband Sir Ralph play significant roles in Betsy's story. Betsy's brothers, Thomas and Francis, are part of her nuclear family but their structural role in the novel is more akin to Tadmor's definition of friends. Specifically, her brothers maintain a household family that intersects with the family Betsy presides over after she marries. (Thomas casts off his live-in mistress, who moves in with Betsy and has an affair with her husband.) This intermixing of families is a plot device that repeats itself frequently in the novel. Betsy's brothers also play the role of friends as Tadmor conceived of the term in that they view themselves as Betsy's natural guardians, and thus attempt to act on their dead father's behalf by directing her decisions about courtship and marriage.

The household families Betsy joins are the source of many of her surrogate family members, especially the undesirable ones. Unlike Pamela or Clarissa, Betsy initially prefers easygoing surrogate family members with lax morals to scrupulous ones like Mrs. Jervis in *Pamela*. Betsy's living situations provide her with opportunities to choose between numerous possible surrogate family members. Much of the novel's courtship plot is made up of the faux pas that occur when she chooses the wrong ones. She learns over the course of the novel to cultivate her relationships with principled surrogate family members and to prune away ties to vicious ones. Betsy's self-directed inward reformation becomes a narrative index for her ability to select an appropriate husband. Her maturity is the novel's prerequisite to its happy ending. Betsy evolves morally over the course of the novel, learning through her experiences in a series of differently constituted households to seek the companionship and heed the advice of virtuous members of her surrogate and nuclear families. Each of these households presents a distinct set of challenges to Betsy and requires her to further develop her judgment in order to avoid its particular pitfalls.

Betsy sets a low bar for prudence in her first household family, leaving her nowhere to go but up when she joins others. This household family is a boarding school, and it differs from Betsy's future families because it is made up of members who have no connection to her nuclear family. Its members are brought together by chance rather than deliberation. Precisely because membership in this household family is unvetted by Betsy's parents or guardians, her decisions about whom to befriend reveal a great deal about her character. Haywood emphasizes Betsy's autonomy while at boarding school by specifying that her widowed father is "indolent" and uninvolved in her moral development when he enrolls her at ten years old (32). He seems to choose the school based on its proximity to his estate (it is less than ten miles away) more than anything else, although Haywood mentions its good reputation. Betsy's father visits her regularly, but she never returns to live with him even during the "breaking-up times" when most the other girls go home (27).[19] The boarding school becomes her real family, and her teachers and classmates thus exert great influence over her.

Betsy's outgoing personality makes her popular enough to choose from a wide variety of potential surrogate family members, from which she selects a girl who shares her most inauspicious traits. Betsy's "particular favorit[e]" is an older girl whose character Haywood discloses through her name, Miss Forward (28). By electing Miss Forward as her closest companion in their shared household family, Betsy elevates her friend to the status of her first surrogate sister. Though Haywood does not specify the reasons Betsy "distinguish[es]" Miss Forward for "intimacy" above any of her other classmates, the novel suggests Betsy discovers in her chosen companion an older and bolder embodiment of her own incipient frivolity and vanity (28). Becoming Miss Forward's best friend cultivates Betsy's levity while discouraging her from developing judgment or prudence. Specifically, by helping Miss Forward exchange letters and arrange meetings with a clandestine suitor, Betsy is at a young age "initiated into the mystery of courtship," including how to behave like a "coquette" and "play at fast-and-loose with [a] lover" (29–30). Haywood reintroduces Miss Forward later as a prostitute, illustrating the worst possible consequences of honing these skills.

Betsy's decision to reject an appropriate surrogate mother provides further evidence of her levity. The "good old gentlewoman" who presides over the school as governess could become a valuable mentor if Betsy were willing to confide in or take direction from her (31). Instead, Betsy treats this potential surrogate mother figure with contempt. The governess attempts to reform Betsy by explaining the many dangers posed by clandestine courtships, but Betsy dismisses her sage advice, attributing it to the "envy" of an "old and ugly" woman long past the age of attracting suitors (31). Betsy's unthinking veto of this possible moral mentor is the antithesis of Pamela's deliberate cultivation of Mrs. Jervis as a surrogate mother in *Pamela*. Betsy's early disdain for authority figures that admonish her in any way, even from the most sincere and altruistic motives, becomes of much greater significance after Betsy's father dies and she moves to London to reside with Mr. Goodman.

The risks Betsy runs by choosing improper surrogate family members escalate in Goodman's household family because the Goodmans are members of London's social elite. They attend numerous public events and entertain so many visitors that Haywood describes their home as a "Babel of mixed company" (59). Spectators from the class into which Betsy will marry surround her at all times, so her choices about how to behave and whom to invite into her surrogate family affect her marital opportunities. The Goodman household is made up of three potential surrogate family members: Mr. Goodman, his wife Lady Mellasin, and Lady Mellasin's daughter by a previous marriage, Flora. Betsy initially welcomes Lady

Mellasin's and Flora's familial overtures, but prolonged affiliation with them reveals their defects and teaches her to be more scrupulous about selecting surrogate mothers and sisters. However, she never warms to Goodman's good-faith attempts to act as a responsible surrogate father. Her disregard for him demonstrates that while she has begun to learn how to judge and act wisely, this process is far from complete.

Lacking her own mother, Betsy sanguinely responds to Lady Mellasin's invitation to adopt her into the family as a fully fledged member who she will treat with the "same affection" as her own daughter (35). Unlike evil stepmothers in fairy tales, Lady Mellasin is neither jealous of Betsy's popularity nor appears to enforce distinctions between her surrogate and biological daughters. This surrogate mother's faults are insidiously attractive to pleasure-loving Betsy. Haywood divulges the nature of these flaws through the observations of Lady Mellasin's foil, Sir Ralph Trusty's wife Lady Trusty. As her surname testifies, Lady Trusty's judgments echo the conventional wisdom of eighteenth-century conduct books. She assesses Lady Mellasin as a "very unfit person to have the care of youth, especially those of her own sex" because of her frivolity and love of admiration (35–36). Not only is Lady Mellasin an unfit role model for any reputable woman, but she is also particularly dangerous to young women at Betsy and Flora's "impressionable age" who, according to the narrator, are "most apt to take the bent of impression, which, according as it is well or ill directed, makes, or mars, the future prospect of [their] lives" (36). Lady Mellasin's behavior eventually results in its own punishment. Her adultery and involvement in a forgery plot lead to her exile from her own household. When Betsy enters the Goodman household, though, Lady Mellasin is still fashionable and respectable, paying and receiving visits from the "most gay and polite of both sexes" and spending her evenings in a "continual round of publick diversions" (36).

Betsy, true to her surname, unthinkingly accepts Lady Mellasin as a surrogate mother, disastrously allowing her to superintend her decisions about courtship. Numerous episodes illustrate Lady Mellasin's culpability for exposing Betsy and Flora to inappropriate suitors. Their family is so permeable to the outside world that it would be difficult for Lady Mellasin to continually monitor Betsy and Flora even if she were inclined to do so, which she is not. Instead, she behaves like one of their confederates. For example, she colludes with Betsy and Flora when they toy with one of Betsy's suitors, Captain Hysom. Additionally, she does not screen the young men who frequent her house, exposing Betsy and Flora to rakes who attempt to seduce both of them. Betsy imitates Lady Mellasin's promiscuous socializing, "suffer[ing] herself to be treated, presented, and squir'd about to all public places, either by the rake, the man of honour, the wit, or the fool, the married, as well as the unmarried, without distinction, and just as [they] fell in her way" (56). Consequently, rumors about Betsy's frivolity circulate throughout London. When a relation of Mr. Trueworth, Betsy's most desirable suitor, asks about Betsy's character, the report she receives is alarming. While Betsy's beauty and charm are widely acknowledged, her informants "[shake] their heads when any of those requisites to make the marriage-state agreeable were mentioned" (223). Consequently, Trueworth's relation advises him against marrying Betsy. News of Betsy's "repeated inadvertencies" even reach the Trustys' country estate, prompting Lady Trusty to write Betsy an admonitory letter (206). Lady Trusty implicitly blames Lady Mellasin for Betsy's indiscretions, lamenting Betsy's lack of a "tender mother, whose precepts and example might keep [her] steady in the paths of prudence" (207). As Betsy's surrogate mother, Lady Mellasin is supposed to do this, but her vanity, love of promiscuous company, and indifference to Betsy's moral development leave Betsy worse than motherless.

While Betsy enjoys the social whirl of the Goodman household, she eventually realizes there are drawbacks to having a permissive surrogate mother. These disadvantages range from the mundane to the consequential. In keeping with Haywood's pragmatic concerns about day-to-day life, Betsy has stepmother problems. Lady Mellasin wants Betsy to look drab so her less-attractive daughter gets more attention from suitors. For example, when Lady Mellasin goes shopping with Flora and Betsy, she convinces Betsy to buy an unflattering fabric while helping Flora select something attractive (60). This is a minor concern, easily remedied, although by featuring it Haywood implicitly asserts that these everyday events are important to women's lives. Lady Mellasin is also a deficient surrogate mother because she is too dissipated and selfish to provide reliable and conscientious guidance to Betsy about courtship. Betsy correctly predicts this and avoids confiding in her at all. She realizes that if she turns to Lady Mellasin for sincere guidance about relationships, Lady Mellasin is more likely to "turn her complaints into ridicule" than to "afford her that cordial and friendly advice she stood in need of" (42). Betsy's household situation does not allow her to break entirely with Lady Mellasin, but she takes steps to distance herself from her surrogate mother. She takes control of her own pin money so she is able to purchase what she likes (61). She also keeps her affairs largely to herself. Overall, Betsy learns from her relationship with Lady Mellasin that it is important to probe authority figures' ulterior motives rather than assume they have her best interests at heart.

Betsy's embrace of Flora as a surrogate sister is even more damaging to her reputation than her connection to Lady Mellasin. While Lady Mellasin's neglect creates propitious conditions for courtship misadventures, it is Betsy's confederacy with Flora that transforms these possibilities into plot. It is natural that Betsy would become intimate friends with Flora since they are both members of Mr. Goodman's household family, their ages are similar, and they "lay together" in the same bed (63). Betsy and Flora also share the same coquettish temperament. Outward similarities make them almost indistinguishable to some of their suitors, a few of whom (such as Mr. Gayland and Mr. Saving) woo them both at different times. What distinguishes them, aside from Betsy's larger fortune, is that Betsy is vain, while Flora is lascivious. In other words, Flora is what Betsy only appears to be. Betsy discovers Flora's licentiousness early in the novel when she spies Flora lying in bed beside Mr. Gayland (63). This is only one of the numerous incidents of Flora's unchasteness witnessed by Betsy. While Betsy inwardly condemns Flora for the "indecency" of her behavior, she does not seriously meditate on what it means about Flora's character, nor does it deter her from socializing with Flora (63). Neither does she confront Flora about her conduct. Instead, Betsy's "good nature" prevails, and she disregards the obvious threat publicly associating with Flora presents to her own reputation (64).

Betsy is untroubled by Flora's faults because she assumes they will not affect her, but experience teaches her otherwise. When Flora and Betsy visit Oxford together, Flora leaves Betsy alone in a room with a rakish young man. As a consequence, Betsy's "ruin" is almost "completed," the rape attempt interrupted only because Betsy's brother Francis happens to providentially intervene (73). The full extent of Flora's profligacy only emerges later in the novel. However, this early episode provides ample evidence that it is as much of a "distemper" as the capriciousness Betsy accuses her of, and far more likely to taint Betsy's reputation by "having it always so near her" (168). Betsy maintains her friendship with Flora even after this near-rape, largely because at this point she is still more averse to the potential criticism a friend of more "serious deportment" might direct at her own "gay and volatile . . . temper" than to the possible consequences—the worst of which she experiences when she is almost raped—of her proximity to Flora (215). Betsy's recognition of Flora's faults proves she is capable of honing her judgment based on experience. Such moments of realization demonstrate she is teachable, even if she is not yet willing to act on her hard-won knowledge.

Betsy's feckless decision to reunite with her boarding school surrogate sister Miss Forward provides further evidence of her unwillingness to take her reputation seriously. It would be difficult for Betsy to distance herself from Flora while they live in the same household. But she could easily reject Miss Forward when she reappears under suspicious circumstances. Miss Forward is so similar to Flora that Helen Thompson describes them as sharing a "transitive likeness."[20] Both are vain, frivolous young women who become involved in sexual affairs. Miss Forward sends a letter to Betsy hoping to revive their friendship. Betsy obliges, visiting her immediately. Miss Forward's living conditions suggest she has fallen in the world. She lodges up several flights of stairs in a boarding house. The foreboding name of its proprietor, Mrs. Nightshade, foretells Miss Forward's later descent into the lowest rungs of prostitution. Miss Forward readily confesses to Betsy that one of her admirers has already seduced, impregnated, and abandoned her and that her father has disowned her. The narrator applauds Betsy's "good-nature" for sympathizing with Miss Forward and giving her money (121). Haywood treats charity as a desirable quality regardless of the morality of the recipient. However, giving Miss Forward money is different than socializing with her.

Beneficence is laudable but associating publicly with a fallen woman like Miss Forward precipitates a disastrous outcome for Betsy. Trueworth discovers Betsy at Miss Forward's lodgings and is horrified to find his "beloved object so intimate with a common prostitute" (229). Although he does not believe, as his companion Sir Bazil does, that Betsy is a prostitute, he questions Betsy's principles because he "could not . . . conceive there was a possibility for true virtue to take delight" in an abandoned woman's company (229). He gives up his courtship entirely after Betsy attends a play with Miss Forward against his explicit warnings. (An anonymous letter he receives from Flora offering specious evidence that Betsy is the mother of a bastard child only confirms this decision.)

Betsy's refusal to repudiate her vestigial connection to Miss Forward jeopardizes not just her reputation, but also her virtue. She is almost raped by one of Miss Forward's patrons. When Betsy returns to Miss Forward's lodgings after the play, a visitor of Miss Forward's who "looked on Miss Betsy as a woman of the town, by seeing her with one that was so" attacks her during their carriage ride home (240). Betsy's terror at this incident is compounded by humiliation when her would-be rapist desists only to censure her conduct, telling her a "young lady more endangered her reputation, by an acquaintance with one woman of ill fame, than by receiving the visits of twenty men, though professed libertines" (241). These incidents directly result from Betsy's stubborn refusal to act on certain knowledge of Miss Forward's fallen status. As Theresa Braunschneider argues, Haywood depicts promiscuity as an "infectious disease" that Betsy will contract regardless of her own innocence if she remains in Miss Forward's company.[21] Just as Betsy's disrelish for criticism prolongs her friendship with Flora, vanity prompts her to defy others' advice and maintain this friendship. As a young, beautiful, and well-connected woman, Betsy thinks she should be able to do exactly as she likes, and that it is the responsibility of her suitors to admire her regardless of her folly.

Only experience is able to overcome Betsy's partiality for faulty surrogate sisters like Flora and Miss Forward. In Flora's case, one of Betsy's former suitors reveals to Betsy the extent of her surrogate sister's treachery. Mr. Saving informs Betsy that his father sent him abroad after an anonymous letter informed him of his son's plans to marry Betsy. The letter describes Betsy as poor in both "fortune" and "reputation," warning Mr. Saving's father against a potential daughter-in-law known to be "gay, vain, and passionately fond of gaming" (198). After returning to England and marrying the woman selected for him by his father, Mr. Saving finds the letter and recognizes the handwriting as Flora's. He shows it to Betsy, who finally understands she has been "harbouring a snake in [her] bosom" (200). It is impossible for Betsy to avoid Flora entirely since it would be impractical to "immediately quit" Goodman's house "and choose another guardian," so she wisely modifies their relationship as much as she is able to, avoiding Flora's company in public and refusing to "communicate anything to her, which she would not wish should be made public" (243). It is much easier for Betsy to ostracize Miss Forward because they do not live in the same household or have the same friends. But it still takes Betsy almost being raped to sever their connection. Betsy's reformation does not blunt her sympathy, however. She later sends Miss Forward enough money to get out of debtor's prison and begin a new life, suggesting compassion, as long as it is from a distance, is the proper attitude for upright women to take toward prostitution or promiscuity.[22] Close female friends, on the other hand, ought to testify to each other's mutually unblemished reputations, as Clarissa's connection to Anna does in Richardson's *Clarissa*.

Betsy converts to a more Richardsonian model of surrogate sisterhood by replacing Flora and Miss Forward with Mabel, a woman whose "principles and behaviour" are the "very reverse of Miss Flora" (215). Initially, Betsy avoids socializing with Mabel because Mabel expects her to behave in a conventionally feminine manner. Betsy does not wish to emulate Mabel's "modest" and "reserved" behavior (215). However, once Betsy fully acknowledges to herself the high cost of intimacy with women who exacerbate her worst faults, she comes to appreciate a friend who will censure her conduct. Mabel never belongs to Betsy's household family, so their status as surrogate sisters is based on other aspects of their relationship. The most important of these is that Betsy seeks Mabel out to replace her other surrogate sisters. Additionally, Mabel and Betsy become related to one another in a complex way by the conclusion of the novel, with Betsy marrying Mabel's husband's sister's widower (Trueworth). This future family connection retroactively adds significance to their budding friendship. Although Betsy and Mabel's relationship is structurally analogous to Anna and Clarissa's, it is not as nuanced. Rather, Betsy's increasing affection for Mabel bluntly signifies Betsy's reform. Like Flora and Miss Forward, Mabel is an instrumental character, fairly undeveloped but important insofar as she indexes a stage in Betsy's gradual maturation. Betsy discovers that being friends with Mabel is not only good for her reputation but is also pleasurable. Mabel is not prudish and sour, but rather "reserved without austerity, cheerful without levity," and "compassionate and benevolent in her nature" (215). In short, she shares in and encourages Betsy's admirable qualities. Just as Anna cultivates her own best self by subjecting herself to Clarissa's judgment in *Clarissa*, Mabel mirrors back Betsy's own best self in *Betsy Thoughtless*. Consequently, Betsy learns to sincerely "prefer the conversation of Mabel, to most of her acquaintance" (215).

Betsy is slower to appreciate the scrutiny of vigilant surrogate parents, preferring to assert authority over her own affairs even though, ironically, her decision to do so ultimately leaves her fewer and worse choices about marriage than if she heeded their advice. Most significantly, Betsy consistently ignores the guidance of her surrogate father, Goodman, and her surrogate mother, Lady Trusty. Goodman attempts to vet Betsy's suitors in order to protect her from fortune hunters and rakes. Betsy refuses his help, blaming his "scrupulousness" for thinning the number of her admirers (127). Just as Betsy refuses to act on her surrogate father Goodman's admonitions, she similarly ignores the ministrations of her "second mother," Lady Trusty (412). Lady Trusty advises Betsy to marry Trueworth, the very thing Betsy wishes she had done, after it is too late to accept him. Betsy understands that Lady Trusty's and Goodman's motives are pure, unlike Lady Mellasin's. They try to help Betsy because they intend to honor their ties to her dead parents. However, she deliberately ignores them because, although she occasionally laments having "no parent to direct" her through the "labyrinth of life," she also enjoys the freedom her orphaned state allows (203).

Betsy still has a lot to learn about appropriate conduct when she leaves the Goodmans to establish her own household. Her decision to go out on her own is based on a combination of inclination and circumstances. She is wealthy enough once she comes of age to rent and staff her own lodgings, and she welcomes the social freedom she enjoys as mistress of the house. No one in her household outranks her, so she is able to come and go whenever she pleases and socialize with anyone she chooses. Although this living situation suits her tastes, there are other reasons beyond her control that she sets up house on her own. Lady Mellasin and Flora leave Goodman's household after he discovers his wife's infidelity and (even worse in his eyes) her attempts to financially defraud him. Betsy remains with Goodman for a while but is forced to leave when he becomes ill. She would be better protected from designing suitors and her poor decision-making if she lived with her guardians or brothers. However, the Trustys live in the country rather than London, and her brothers do not invite Betsy to live with them. Betsy's unusual amount of independence gives Haywood the opportunity to imagine the possible consequences of giving unmarried daughters greater latitude than they generally had in structuring their social lives. It also begs the question of whether Betsy's family members (her brothers), surrogate parents (the Trustys), or Betsy herself ought to be accountable for monitoring her behavior.

Betsy's brothers fail to do their part but blame Betsy for her faulty behavior anyway. As Katrina Clifford observes, novelists frequently use the relationship between brothers and sisters to "examine the place of women in society and the restrictions of the domestic ideal" because "unlike other relationships between men and women in eighteenth-century society, brothers and sisters were not bound together by any particular authority structure," especially "while their parents were alive."[23] Arguably, the death of Betsy's parents grants her brothers more authority over Betsy than they would otherwise have. Still, Betsy is an adult, and the Thoughtless brothers' moral credentials to act as her guardians are suspect. True to the surname they share with Betsy, Thomas and Francis are thoughtless about their obligations to Betsy, though always mindful of her duty to them. The elder brother Thomas inherits a sort of fatherlike authority over Betsy. However, instead of inviting her to live with him, he places his foreign mistress at the head of his London household. Francis is more affectionate toward Betsy than Thomas is, but like Thomas he is a passionate and self-absorbed man about town. As Margaret Croskery observes, both brothers "deman[d] that Betsy display more prudence and good judgement" than they are "able to muster."[24] Francis points out to Betsy with more candor than gallantry that her indiscretions, regardless of whether they actually result in rape or seduction, shame their family more than his do. According to him, Betsy's "reputation is of more consequence to [her] family" than even her virginity because a woman "brings less dishonour upon a family, by twenty private sins, than one public indiscretion" (384).

Taking a typically pragmatic stance, Haywood implies that regardless of Betsy's brothers' flaws, Betsy still ought to at least seek their guidance about her suitors. Her haughty refusal to allow them to "prescribe rules" to her or even be "directed by them" is understandable, but imprudent (386). If she was willing to call upon their guidance, they could help her fend off adventurers and rakes. In the absence of such oversight, Betsy falls prey to the clumsy machinations of a fraudulent suitor. In spite of Francis's explicit warning to beware of the "many imposters in this town, who are continually on the watch for young ladies, who have lost their parents, and live in [an] unguarded manner," Betsy encourages the addresses of a supposed baronet who calls himself Sir Frederick Fineer (386). Sir Frederick behaves suspiciously, but Betsy is so intent on proving her proficiency at minding her own affairs that she ignores numerous signs of his duplicity. She recklessly visits him alone in his lodgings. He tries to force her to marry him, and when that fails he attempts to rape her. Trueworth, in the building by chance, rescues her. The message of this episode is clear. The honorable suitor who courts Betsy publicly after being vetted by her brothers must save her from the suitor who evades these protocols for nefarious reasons. Even lax surrogate parent figures such as Betsy's brothers serve the valuable purpose of shielding an otherwise unprotected young woman from opportunists. Paradoxically, Betsy's attempts to act freely ultimately entrap her since to save her reputation she must marry the only suitor (other than the discredited Sir Frederick) who courts her without seeking her surrogate parents' or her brothers' permission. This suitor, Mr. Munden, proves to be a selfish, callous, and even sadistic husband: traits the novel suggests are manifest in his neglect as a suitor of the traditional responsibility to approach a woman's friends and relations before offering himself to her.

The failure of Betsy's self-brokered marriage provides more evidence for the advantages of seeking guidance about courtship from surrogate and nuclear family members. Mr. Munden, the last suitor standing, becomes Betsy's husband by process of elimination rather than by choice. For several months Betsy accepts his gifts and allows him to escort her around town. Although she welcomes his attentions only out of vanity, he reasonably interprets her receptivity to mean she will eventually marry him. Tired of her trifling, he demands Betsy make a decision about whether to marry him. The near rape by Sir Frederick occurs at this point, uniting all Betsy's family and surrogate family members in their desire to prevent further scandal by marrying her off to her only remaining solvent and respectable suitor. Francis, Thomas, and Lady Trusty (Goodman is dead by this time) press Betsy to marry Munden even though he is a stranger to all of them. Betsy's previous poor choices about courtship convince them marriage is an "absolutely necessary . . . defence" against the consequences of her "ill-conduct" (482). Even if she continues to behave badly after marriage, she will shame her husband rather than her brothers.

Betsy finally learns the value of surrogate parents through the marriage she is backed into by her poor decisions. The unpleasantness of daily life as Mrs. Munden teaches Betsy what she refuses to learn by precept: willfully disregarding legitimate authority isolates rather than empowers her. As a married woman, she is subject to her husband's authority. He behaves autocratically and does not care whether Betsy is happy. All his courtly behavior falls away after the wedding. Once he becomes her husband, he expects to be obeyed. As Haywood writes, Munden views Betsy as an "upper servant, bound to study and obey, in all things, the will of him to whom she had given her hand" (507). Since Betsy has no intention of becoming subservient to him, the marriage quickly sours. Haywood's graphic depiction of this unhappy marriage is, as Deborah Nestor remarks, "one of the most intimate and painful chronicles of the decline of a marriage found in the early English novel."[25] Specifically, Betsy's domestic disputes with Munden over expenses are, as Backscheider similarly notes, some of the "most intense scenes of marital fighting in eighteenth-century fiction."[26] Their disputes range from bickering to psychological abuse to outright violence. When Betsy attempts to reason with Munden about the necessity of budgeting more for household expenses, he demands she use her own pin money to maintain the household. When she argues against this, he reacts violently, at one point even throwing her pet squirrel against the chimney, leaving its "tender frame . . . dashed to pieces" (507). The implied threat of this action is obvious. If Betsy continues to disobey him, he will abuse her just as he did the squirrel. Munden even uses Betsy as bait to entice his patron to advance him at court. Munden, as mundane as he appears to be before he marries, turns out to be just as tyrannical and unreasonable as Clarissa's father is in *Clarissa*. Betsy's captivity in this unhappy marriage shows her again and again that voluntarily heeding the advice of legitimate authority is preferable to the hell she has made for herself by spurning it.

Betsy's response to Munden's abuse demonstrates newfound maturity. In the past, she spurned the advice her surrogate parents gave her. Now she seeks it out.

Without help, Betsy is powerless against Munden's abuse. She is his property. How-ever, with the aid of her surrogate family members she is able to assert some authority. Betsy turns to Lady Trusty several times during her marriage seeking strategies to negotiate with Munden. When these fail, Sir Ralph steps in at Lady Trusty's request and conciliates Munden in order to prevent a public breach between the couple. It is significant that Betsy turns to her surrogate parents to "interpose in [this] affair," and that she takes Lady Trusty's initial advice to try and placate Munden despite her own preference for being "separated for ever, from a person, who, she was now convinced, had neither love nor esteem for her" (511–512).

Some scholars interpret Betsy's dependence on the Trustys as debilitating and even view Lady Trusty as the "voice the patriarchy."[27] While it is true that Lady Trusty initially advises Betsy to placate her boorish husband, this interpre-tation fails to take into account the Trustys' later support for Betsy when she leaves Munden. Lady Trusty does not take the typical stance of a conduct book mouth-piece, which would have been to blame Betsy for her husband's abusive treatment of her. As Chris Roulston notes, wife abuse narratives throughout the eighteenth century were typically "defined by the terms of female virtue," meaning that vir-tuous women were supposed to be able to transform brutal husbands into ideal companions.[28] Instead, the Trustys genuinely sympathize with Betsy's situation. They prescribe ways for Betsy to at least appear as if she is trying to save her mar-riage. When the inevitable rupture comes, Betsy's efforts at least earn her public sympathy. Such a strategy—creating a "paper trail" documenting Betsy's attempts to reconcile with her husband—aligns perfectly with Haywood's pragmatic treat-ment of gender throughout the novel. The Trustys advise Betsy reasonably, and her attempts to act according to their suggestions signify Betsy's increasing "knowl-edge both of self and world" that Ellis associates with the bildungsroman.[29]

Betsy's newfound reliance on family also extends to her brother Thomas, who as her eldest male relation stands in structurally for her parents. Thomas is partially at fault for Betsy's marriage since he would not allow her to live with him. Sir Frederick sought her out because he believed she was unprotected. He prob-ably never would have approached her if she was a member of her brother's household. If Sir Frederick had not attacked Betsy, she would not have been pres-sured into marrying Munden. Thomas is also indirectly responsible for Betsy's domestic problems. He evicts his mistress Mademoiselle de Roquelair and Betsy takes her in. She reciprocates by having an affair with Munden. Although Thomas is partly to blame for Betsy's problems, he also contributes to their solution. Betsy wishes to leave her husband, but rather than act rashly, she does not "do anything precipitately; it was not sufficient, she thought, that she should be justified to her-self; she was willing to be justified in the opinion of her friends" (590). Because she seeks Thomas's guidance rather than spurning it as she used to, he treats her with respect and love, "receiv[ing] her in the most affectionate manner" and "approv[ing] her conduct in regard to her unfaithful husband" (594). He even offers Betsy the "command of his house and family," an unequivocal way of signifying to the world his support for Betsy's separation from her husband (595). This gesture is especially significant because both of them are playing the familial roles they should have adopted in the first place. Literally and figuratively, Betsy takes over her rightful position in Thomas's household from the double-usurper Roquelair (who first displaces Betsy in Thomas's household and then in her own).

In addition to seeking counsel from her brothers and the Trustys about how to deal with her failing marriage, Betsy also consults with her surrogate sister Mabel. This provides additional confirmation of Betsy's reform. While Betsy already has her brother's support for separating from Munden, he is not an authority on the nuances of appropriate female conduct. Mabel, on the other hand, exhibits delicacy in her judgments of her peers. As Haywood writes, Betsy "could not be quite easy till she should hear what judgment" Mabel should "pass on the step she had taken" (595). Mabel's blessing of Betsy's decision rewards Betsy for her voluntary resignation of her own judgment to that of her morally upright surrogate sister. Mabel not only excuses Betsy's decision to leave Munden, but also characterizes it as righteous and just, telling Betsy it "would have been an injustice not only to herself, but to all wives in general" to have stayed with Munden "by setting them an example of submitting to things required of them neither by law nor nature" (595). With the support of all the members of her different types of families, Betsy is able to hide from Munden until he conveniently becomes mortally ill. Betsy rushes to his deathbed in time to reconcile with him and receive the ultimate reward for her submission to her surrogate family and her brothers: Munden's death. As John Richetti points out, the "second chance" Haywood offers Betsy through this narrative contrivance is "unusual" for eighteenth-century courtship novels and extends Betsy's "period of independence."[30] Emily Anderson articulates a general critical consensus that Munden's fortuitous death is a conspicuously "artificial, unrealistic," and "contrived" narrative device.[31] Anderson's observation is unequivocally true, but I would add that this plot twist's peculiarity signals its importance. Betsy regains her independence, but she paradoxically merits this reward because she has learned to rely on and trust her surrogate and nuclear families.

Munden's death allows Betsy to become a member of Haywood's version of a family of the heart. After Trueworth gives up on courting Betsy, he seeks solace from his friendship with Sir Bazil. Sir Bazil is engaged to Mabel. Trueworth falls in love with Sir Bazil's sister, Harriot, and the two couples marry in a double wedding. They all enjoy perfect domestic bliss of the sort Harriet delights in when after she marries Sir Charles in *Sir Charles Grandison*. As Haywood writes, "there were few hours, excepting those allotted by nature and custom for repose, which this

amiable company did not pass together" (401). They discuss literature, the pleasures of the country, and how to act correctly in morally ambiguous situations.
Their conversations are sprightlier than the Grandisons', and Trueworth's amo-
rous humor differs dramatically from Sir Charles's cool demeanor. Despite these
differences, Haywood's admiration for the affectionate coterie closely aligns with
Richardson's ideal of the family of the heart. The differences between the group-
ings reflect the divergent ambitions of these two authors, one a strict moralist and
the other a realistic pragmatist. In both novels, families cordon themselves off
socially from promiscuous society in order to form enclosed circles of warmth and
morality that foster self-improvement. In a narrative that Kelly McGuire wryly
observes "relies extensively upon death as an organizing principle," Harriot's timely
death creates space for Betsy to marry Trueworth.[32]

Betsy's marriage to Trueworth both reflects and facilitates her maturation.
As Hultquist observes, Betsy's second marriage "comes about through her own self-
knowledge rather than as a reward for critical and steadfast virtue."[33] Specifically,
Betsy encounters Trueworth while she is separated from Munden and they both
admit they still love one another. They are in an isolated place, both passionate to
enjoy each other sexually, and Betsy no longer cares for her husband. Despite all
this, Betsy spurns Trueworth's overtures. She exiles Trueworth from her presence
because she has learned to rate propriety higher than self-indulgence. She now scrutinizes even her private actions from Mabel's nice viewpoint and acts accordingly.
Trueworth courts Betsy the first time because he cannot resist her charm and wit
even though he does not approve of her coquettish behavior. The second time, in
a gesture to Richardson's *Pamela*, her "virtue conquer[s]" him because he admires
her chastity (610). In this instance, even the narrator chimes in to "applaud the
conduct of Mrs. Munden" (610).

To the satisfaction of all of Betsy's connections, she resurrects her engagement to Trueworth. Mabel implicitly authorizes their courtship, advising her friend
that there is no reason to ruminate "too deeply" on Munden's death or to "restrain"
from being "easy in [herself], and chearful with [her] friends" (618). Betsy's surrogate mother Lady Trusty also encourages Betsy to marry again once a year of
mourning expires, stating bluntly that by that time she will have "paid all the
regard" to Munden's "memory which could be expected . . . even for a better husband" (629). Betsy spends her mourning period retired in the country with Lady
Trusty. As a widow, it would be socially acceptable for her to set up her own
household in London. Her decision to insulate herself from all the entertainments
and company she previously enjoyed is telling. She enters into a correspondence
with Trueworth but will not allow him to visit her until her mourning ends. By
exchanging letters, they get to know one another intellectually. Their lively correspondence promises a lifetime of more than just sexual compatibility. When
Trueworth finally proposes to Betsy at the Trustys' estate, Francis and Lady Trusty

are both there to approve of and witness their marriage. This conclusion completes the circle of courtship perfectly, permanently bringing together not just the couple, but also Betsy's surrogate family members and her brothers. Trueworth claims Francis as his "brother" and Sir Ralph and Lady Trusty arrange the final legal details necessary to place Betsy in Truewoth's "good hands" (632–633). Betsy is so committed to her companionate marriage with Trueworth that she expects her surrogate relations and her brothers to "take a second place" to him in her affections (628). Still, they will all socialize in a surrogate family that expands, Grandison-like, to include Betsy's surrogate sister Mabel and Mabel's husband Sir Bazil.

The *History of Jemmy and Jenny Jessamy* starts where *Betsy Thoughtless* leaves off: with a wise and thoughtful female protagonist capable of selecting her own spouse, but respectful enough of her families' wishes not to do so recklessly. Jenny closely resembles the mature Betsy. She is wealthy, attractive, and independent, so she has no need to elevate herself through surrogate families as Pamela does in *Pamela* or Defoe's protagonists in *Moll Flanders* (1722) and *Roxana* (1724). Jenny's parents arrange her marriage before they die and Jenny is content with the spouse they select, so her only business is to marry him. The novel's plot is thus not about Jenny's courtship, but rather about how she applies her judgment of others' courtships and marriages to her own situation. She analyzes numerous couples, intending to use what she learns from them to create a domestic life that suits her needs and interests. Jenny is the most intellectual of Haywood's characters. She seeks knowledge not just to apply to her own situation, but also for its own sake. She is observant, curious, and sociable. She is not romantic, but neither is she cynical. The way Pamela and Harriet idolize their husbands would likely strike her as ridiculous and vulgar, but she is no bohemian. She wants a marriage that provides sufficient companionship, appears respectable to others, and leaves her enough freedom to pursue her own interests. Like Millamant in William Congreve's *The Way of the World* (1700), Jenny does not want to be laughed at, pitied, or lose her independence.

The courtship narratives in this novel are largely episodic, featuring a variety of Jenny's close friends who in many cases also qualify as surrogate sisters. She belongs to many of their households, at least temporarily, since she spends much of the novel staying or traveling with friends. In a significant departure from earlier courtship novels, there are no surrogate parent figures in *The History of Jemmy and Jenny Jessamy*. Jenny does not need guidance or social sponsorship. She is already as mature and socially and economically well off as Betsy is at the conclusion of *The History of Miss Betsy Thoughtless*. Although Betsy has several surrogate sisters, these inchoate relationships are notably different from the intense connections Harriet and Clarissa foster with their surrogate sisters or even the developmentally crucial affiliation between Betsy and Mabel. Jenny's surrogate sisters teach her things, but these lessons derive from Jenny's observations about their behavior rather than any explicit counsel her surrogate sisters give. Jenny is so detached that at times she seems to be reading her surrogate sisters' stories rather than participating in them. Through witnessing their tribulations, she experiences by proxy the pitfalls of courtship and marriage. What Karen Cajka describes as "multiple vignettes of marital relationships" subsume the central plot, which becomes less about Jenny and Jemmy's courtship than about "watch[ing]" and "discuss[ing]" others' mistakes in courtship and marriage.[34] Many of these episodes are what I call elsewhere "punitive subplots," meaning that their protagonists are punished in some way for making poor choices about courtship and marriage.[35] In other eighteenth-century novels these subplots are often tragic, resulting in disease and death: but not Haywood's rendition of them. Haywood portrays the outcomes of poor decision-making as comparatively mundane. Bad behavior might result in the loss of money or status, but not in a protracted and painful death.

Many of these punitive subplots are diminished or abbreviated versions of popular plot conventions in other novels, particularly *Pamela* and *Clarissa*. But Haywood revises them to align with Jenny's pragmatic perspective. For example, one subplot is a "retelling," as Nestor describes it, of Clarissa's imprisonment in Sinclair's brothel in *Clarissa*.[36] Haywood's version of an episode that is hundreds of pages long in *Clarissa* is an inset narrative lasting about thirty pages. Its protagonist recounts it to Jenny, who is never directly involved. In this case as with the numerous other anecdotes that make up the bulk of Haywood's novel, she transforms plots Richardson designed to be tragic into instructive situations that provide insight into human nature. Jenny watches, judges, and adds what she learns from each incident to her stock of knowledge about love, marriage, and the world. She is a "philosopheress," applying what she learns from them to her understanding of the world rather than concretely using it to reform herself.[37]

According to Haywood, a philosopheress like Jenny does not aspire to the type of marriage Richardson idealizes. Jenny does not need surveillance and protection. Her cool temperament and strong judgment insulate her from the moral contamination Richardson ascribes to associating closely with morally fallible or dissolute surrogate sisters. She does not need oversight during courtship and will not tolerate it as a wife. She and Jemmy will live in the world after their marriage, just as they do before it. They are likely to have separate social calendars and their own friendships. It is impossible to imagine Jenny radiating her morality outward from a domestic space presided over by a patriarch, as Harriet does after she marries Sir Charles. Haywood's vision of an ideal marriage is practical and social. She focuses on how women can enjoy marriage given its limitations. Most husbands are not replicas of Sir Charles, and most marriages are not going to satisfy all of women's social and intellectual needs. Haywood believes in the modern aphorism "happy wife, happy life." A happy wife from her perspective is one who knows how to take advantage of the social and economic benefits marriage conveys without depending overly on it to provide personal fulfillment.

Jenny's peculiar static nature combined with the marriage her parents arrange for her virtually at birth—a plot device that places her apart from all the couples she encounters who are in the process of making decisions about marriage—makes her an anomalous figure for a courtship novel, but an ideal one for promoting worldliness. Her own courtship is a stage-managed affair initiated by her family when she is an infant. It is a condensed and formulaic rendition of rituals meant to connote affection and devotion. For Jenny, these gestures are empty signifiers. At the direction of their parents, Jenny and Jemmy call one another husband and wife "even while in [their] cradles," give each other gifts selected by their parents, and write letters to one another from their boarding schools (9). Haywood portrays this social engineering as largely successful, cultivating not passion, but instead an affection at "least somewhat more than is ordinarily found between a brother and a sister" (9). In fact, their close familial relationship, signified by their shared family name even before they marry, makes the relationship almost asexual. Because of her unusual situation, Jenny does not navigate the marriage market. Her judgment is never clouded by the excitement of being admired by a wide variety of potential suitors. In the absence of these disruptive social and emotional forces she quietly cultivates her reason. The prosaic unfolding of her future marriage is the antithesis of Clarissa's tumultuous courtship with Lovelace.

Haywood's plot is about observation more than participation. After Jenny's and Jemmy's parents die, the young couple is at liberty to maintain or break their engagement. Jemmy lets Jenny decide what to do. At her request, he agrees to stay engaged but delay their wedding until they "know a little more of the world" by witnessing the courtship and marital "mistakes of others" (27, 31). They even plan meetings to "communicate to each other all the discoveries" they make (32). This "project," as Jenny soberly calls it, transforms what might otherwise have been assignations into seminars intended to analyze raw data. Given wives' vulnerability to husbands whose only legal obligation was to feed and shelter them, it was, as Kathleen Lubey argues, imperative for "women, even more than men" to "seek out new experiences."[38] In this same vein, Jenny describes London as "an ample school" of human nature (31). This characterization revises Richardson's notion of London as a morally perilous place for unprotected young women. Haywood does not depict London as menacing, but rather as a place full of object lessons about how to court and marry properly. Richardson's notion of "properly" is weighted with high-minded moral concerns, but for Jenny it means not appearing sentimental or ridiculous. Jenny is far more concerned about being "laugh'd at" than seduced or raped (31).

Just as Haywood's depiction of London is more subdued than Richardson's, Jemmy is also a cut-rate Lovelace figure. Her portrayal of Jemmy conveys how little she romanticizes men or marriage. While Jenny takes information gathering seriously, more often than not the excursions Jemmy supposedly undertakes for learning's sake turn into sexual affairs. As Charles Hinnant observes, in all Haywood's fiction the "inconstancy of the male libertine is a given," and Jemmy is no exception.[39] He is one in a long line of "libertines who live to prove their privilege."[40] Accordingly, Jemmy sententiously lectures Jenny on the dangers of gambling because a woman he lends money to at a gaming table has sex with him to settle her debts. Similarly, after attempting another liaison he waxes poetic about the "charm" of female "innocence" which he claims is "more attracting to a nice and delicate heart than any other perfection whatsoever" (247). He owes this Richardsonian revelation to his diminished desire for a naïve young virgin he attempted to seduce at university after she is corrupted by the high society she gains access to by marrying his best friend's wealthy, aged uncle (247). Even in her tarnished state he intends to have sex with her, though he ultimately decides against it because the resulting pregnancy might disinherit his friend.

When Jemmy is not indulging his most voracious appetite, he satisfies others. For example, he makes a prolonged complaint to Jenny about the wife of his friend because while she was supposed to be preparing and serving a meal she instead spent the entire night praying. Jemmy's grievances about this overcooked meal sound more like whining than serious reflections on marriage, but even so Jenny takes them seriously. She plays along with this absurd complaint, responding that "[r]eligion . . . does not enjoin us to be rude or unkind to our friends" and that performing "social duties" is more important than prayer when guests are visiting (81). The intellectual alchemy she performs in transforming Jemmy's faultfinding into a valuable lesson reflects as well on her as it does poorly on him.

Jenny's encounters are far more philosophical than Jemmy's, emphasizing her open-mindedness and desire to learn for its own sake. She treats the world as a stage and views herself as its critic. She resides and travels with several young women who function as surrogate sisters. This proximity gives rise to ideal conditions for surrogate family relationships to develop. However, surrogate sisterhood is different for Jenny than it is for Betsy because of their distinct personalities. Jenny's relationship to her surrogate sisters is a quotidian version of surrogate sisterhood in Richardson's novels. While she still chooses her surrogate sisters, she keeps them at an emotional distance, treating them more like specimens to examine than confidantes. She advises them occasionally, but rarely seeks guidance from them. Their status as surrogate sisters is based on other narrative cues. Jenny lives and travels with them and they apparently view her as an intimate friend because they disclose so many secrets to her. Given Jenny's characteristic aloofness with everyone, it makes sense to assess these relationships based on their perspective rather than hers.

Jenny's boarding school friend Sophia most closely approximates Betsy's surrogate sisters in *Betsy Thoughtless*. Sophia's character is an uneasy mixture of

Betsy's dangerous surrogate sister Miss Forward and her morally upright surrogate sister Mabel. Sophia is not inherently depraved, but she is inexperienced and overly passionate, making her susceptible to seduction. When Sophia's brother becomes disenchanted with England after ending a disastrous courtship with a woman who had already clandestinely married another man, Sophia is left alone to manage her own fortune and arrange her own marriage.[41] Jenny leaves her in this situation until she reappears 200 pages later. Sophia encouraged a suitor for the wrong reasons, because he was "handsome—well-made,—genteel" and had an "abundance of wit and vivacity" (321). Following her heart rather than using her head, she lends him 1,000 pounds of her 2,500-pound fortune to advance his career. He not only refuses to repay the money or to marry her, but also tricks her into spending the night at a brothel where he unsuccessfully attempts to rape her. This crude reinterpretation of Clarissa's situation in *Clarissa* does not end in death, but neither does it end in marriage. Instead, it concludes in social limbo with a humiliated Sophia departing England for a "convent at Brussels" (336).

Jenny's response to her surrogate sister's story is typical of her reflections on all the aborted courtships or failed marriages she encounters throughout the novel. Initially, she cannot "help thinking it both strange and blameable" in Sophia "to entertain so violent a passion for a man whose character she knew so little of" (337). Upon further reflection, however, she regains her philosophical composure and considers the possibility that given the "same circumstances" she might "have acted in the same manner" (338). Ultimately, she is thankful to her dead parents for saving her from making any choice at all about marriage by "training [her] up to love" Jemmy (338). Despite Jenny's skeptical self-assessment, she is so emotionally detached it is difficult to imagine she would ever become involved in a dubious courtship. She rejects this opportunity to praise herself at her faulty surrogate sister's expense because of her pragmatic view of the world rather than because she identifies with Sophia's poor decisions. In Haywood's estimation, Sophia is foolish rather than vicious. This is a distinction with a difference because it veers away from Richardson's moral absolutism.

Jenny treats all the women she encounters with the same leniency. For example, when her group of friends encounters a strange woman trying to sell a snuffbox, they listen sympathetically to her story although she admits she is a runaway daughter fleeing an arranged marriage to a perfectly decent man. Jenny offers the unknown woman several guineas to help her overcome her "misfortunes," and even gives her a "cordial embrace" before they part (198–199). Significantly, although this character leaves her father's house to avoid a marriage far more tolerable than the one that drives Clarissa into Lovelace's protection in *Clarissa*, Haywood rewards rather than punishes her. Much later in the novel Jenny meets her a second time, after her marriage to the son of the rejected suitor. The father who once aggressively courted her now affectionately calls her "daughter" (393). This highly contrived episode earns the entire company's "admiration" despite the fact that it originates as an act of defiance against a decent father (393). This anonymous protagonist and her new family are all blithely happy together (393). In contrast, Clarissa is so traumatized when she disobeys her father that she fears damnation. This sort of story repeats itself numerous times in *The History of Jemmy and Jenny Jessamy*, with Haywood again and again deflating the tragic potential of Richardson's plots.

Jenny's observations about marriage are as unsentimental as her conclusions about female virtue and courtship. Reflecting on the numerous unhappy marriages she witnesses, she blames them on the ritualistic idolatry expected of suitors during courtship. Wives assume they will receive the same treatment from husbands as from suitors, but as Jenny points out, marriage transforms "goddesses" into "mortals" overnight (39). Betsy in *Betsy Thoughtless* reaches the same conclusion, but only after hundreds of pages and her own miserable marriage to Munden. Unlike Betsy, Jenny is able to discern this contradiction through research, analysis, and induction. Jenny's "happy turn of mind," as Haywood describes it, allows her to "convert every thing which she either saw or heard of to her own advantage, and to make fresh improvements in herself by the misbehaviours of others" (141). She heeds the complaints of her married friends about husbands who tyrannize them in domestic matters, take mistresses, or simply neglect them socially and sexually. Rather than scrutinize these faulty marriages from the perspective of a conduct book, Jenny treats them as pieces of evidence to be gathered in her ongoing study of what marriage is rather than what it is supposed to be.

After visiting this museum of marital catastrophes, Jenny is prepared to assess marriage realistically and consequently to accept without illusions Jemmy's likely shortcomings as a husband. Haywood's pragmatism about men's flaws is stark enough across genres to merit Pettit's appraisal of it as a "mordant commentary on men generally."[42] Haywood is not a tragedian, though. She depicts what women can expect from an institution that erases their legal personhood and grants ownership of them to men who are unlikely to match up to the standards of Richardson's perfect specimen of manhood, Sir Charles. Jemmy, as Jenny learns when she receives a letter intended for his mistress but misdirected to her, is no Sir Charles. But neither is Jenny a Harriet Byron. Rather than upbraid Jemmy or break with him after reading his outpourings to his mistress, Jenny civilly requests of him "that when we marry you will either have no amours, or be more cautious in concealing them," promising "not be so unreasonable as to expect more constancy from you than human nature and your constitution will allow" (288). While Jenny's tolerance in advance of Jemmy's prospective amours is not a feminist stance, it is businesslike and commonsensical. Jenny negotiates to achieve what matters most to her—the appearance of domestic peace—by capitulating ahead of time to Jemmy's likely infidelities. Since she has already seen how little power wives have to prevent or punish husbands' indiscretions, she knows that she is not really losing anything by acknowledging this ahead of time. Her sober acceptance of conditions she cannot control and of Jemmy's character flaws demonstrate her facility for "thinking, . . . judging," and "comparing" under circumstances otherwise more prone to emotional than rational consideration (359).

Jenny is a reader, just as Clarissa is in *Clarissa*. Both use their reading to hone their minds and to judge themselves and others. However, *Clarissa* applies her wisdom almost exclusively to domestic life. She wishes to understand how to properly perform her duties as a daughter, friend, and eventual wife and mother. Similarly, Pamela in *Pamela II* reads Locke in order to help her educate her children, not simply to learn for the sake of learning itself. Jenny reads in order to understand the world. The ways Jenny takes in information, analyzes it, and makes conclusions based on it allow her to purposefully contemplate any subject. She reads widely, at one point applying her interpretation of Jonathan Swift's *Gulliver's Travels* (1726) to the problems apparent in one of the unhappy marriages she witnesses. She is also familiar enough with the works of this "excellent author" to synthesize his themes and apply them to her own life (143). Significantly, she concludes based on her reading of Swift that "the mind . . . ought to be the chief object of our attention; it is there alone we are either beautiful or deform'd" (143). Her commitment to intellectual development suggests that once she is married, she will continue to devote a great deal of time to reading and thinking. In some ways, marrying Jemmy makes this task easier since he is neither possessive nor doting. Unlike Sir Charles, he is unlikely to monopolize his wife's time or to expect her to account to him for how she spends it when they are apart. Though *The History of Jemmy and Jenny Jessamy* ends in marriage, marriage is not really its object. Marriage to Jemmy is merely the conduit to a rewarding lifetime of thinking, learning, and socializing.

Haywood's morally flexible protagonists in *The History of Betsy Thoughtless* and *The History of Jemmy and Jenny Jessamy* provide a model for later female novelists such as Frances Burney, the subject of the next chapter. In her novels *Evelina* (1778) and *Cecilia* (1782), Burney builds on the notion that surrogate families help women learn about themselves and the world rather than just act as a moral barometer of a protagonist's worthiness for marriage. Her protagonists, Evelina and Cecilia, resemble Defoe's in that they choose surrogate family members who help them advance in society. Like Clarissa in Richardson's *Clarissa*, Evelina and Cecilia replace their nuclear families with surrogate family members. Burney's hybrid version of surrogate families is better than the sum of its parts for her female protagonists. For example, Evelina and Cecilia are more able to discard undesirable families of origin than Betsy. They also exercise the same sort of prerogative as Clarissa to cobble together families for themselves. The difference is that they are not punished for either. They are as self-determined as Defoe's protagonists, although they confine their ambition to the conventional outcome of a lifelong marriage. Burney also innovates the convention of surrogate families in her own distinctive way. Evelina and Cecilia discover their own desires and interests by experimenting with different types of surrogate families. Their emotional and social antennae help them locate the right sort of home; searching for surrogate families helps them better understand themselves.

F RANCES BURNEY'S *EVELINA* (1778) AND *CECILIA* (1782) build on Defoe's, Richardson's, and Haywood's models of surrogate families while also reshaping this plot convention. Surrogate families in *Evelina* and *Cecilia* do not just displace or supplement nuclear and lineage families; they replace them.[1] These earlier novelists gesture toward the amount of freedom Haywood's protagonists enjoy to create their own families. However, they either treat surrogate families as a means to some other ends or impose limitations on protagonists' volition. Moll and Roxana in Defoe's *Moll Flanders* (1722) and *Roxana* (1724) have hardly any nuclear family members to begin with, so deciding whether to replace them with surrogate family members is largely a nonissue. Richardson's novels offer limited freedom for young women to choose appropriate surrogate families, but not at the expense of honoring obligations to their nuclear and lineage families. Haywood's protagonists in *The History of Betsy Thoughtless* (1751) and *The History of Jenny and Jemmy Jessamy* (1753) are orphans so, like Moll and Roxana, their nuclear families are of negligible importance.

Evelina and Cecilia are even more independent than these characters because of their circumstances: in addition to both being orphans, Evelina is an apparent bastard, and Cecilia is an heiress. Their situations place them at opposite ends of the social spectrum. However, these extreme positions create the same experience of profound aloneness for both. Evelina's namelessness is profoundly isolating, making her quite literally the "nobody" Mr. Lovel derisively calls her at a private ball.[2] As Martha Brown observes, being "nobody" and "belong[ing] to nobody" creates opportunity as well as risk; her obscurity allows her to "be anybody and belong to anybody."[3] Cecilia in *Cecilia* appears to be Evelina's opposite. Although she is an orphan, her status as an heiress means she is unquestionably a somebody. However, just as Evelina's lack of a name segregates her from others, Cecilia's power to name another through marriage also distances her from peers and mentors. She is, as Catherine Gallagher puts it, "overburdened" by her "name" and the exceptionality it bestows.[4] For both these characters, detachment from society is a burden, but also offers unique opportunities for self-definition.

Evelina's and Cecilia's isolation also makes them ideal narrative vehicles to critique ideologies of gender. As Julia Epstein argues, Burney's protagonists "embody a set of contradictions so paradigmatic of the later eighteenth century that they might be said to define the ideological tensions inhering in the period's complex demarcations of women's social place."[5] Both characters critique gendered codes of behavior, although in different ways. Wolfram Schmidgen notes that bastard characters such as Evelina are in a "position to make social structure visible" because they are "both inside and outside society."[6] The treatment they receive from others becomes a means for authors to "disclose" the "conventions by which society maintains itself."[7] As an heiress who will bestow her surname on her husband, Cecilia occupies a liminal position between masculinity and femininity. As Margaret Doody asserts, Burney uses these betwixt and between protagonists to scrutinize the "immense effects of social divisions and categories" such as "gender, class," and "wealth."[8]

Evelina has even greater access than Cecilia to diverse companions. As an apparent orphan who moves between numerous household families, she encounters a wide variety of suitors and mentors. She is raised by a country clergyman, travels to London with a wealthy and socially prominent landed family, stays with her social-climbing lower-class grandmother, and then lives with an acquaintance from the country in a household frequented by members of the titled nobility. Each of these household families provides Evelina with potential surrogate family members. As Susan Greenfield and Sarah Spence note, being an orphan and particularly losing a mother is a common fate for female protagonists of eighteenth-century novels.[9] As Barbara Zonitch points out, all "Burney's heroines" are "separated from family and familial community."[10] But Evelina's situation is an exaggerated version of this familiar convention. In order to divine "to whom," as she puts it, she "most belong[s]," she first has to discover who she is (353).

Evelina defines herself not just by choosing surrogate family members most suited to her, but also by rejecting the ones who are not, even when they turn out to be members of her nuclear or lineage families. Over the course of the novel Evelina accumulates a grandmother, several cousins, a half-brother, and a father. This "kin-collecting," as Toby Olshin describes it, is not all bad because it culminates in the desirable outcome of Sir John acknowledging Evelina's legitimacy.[11] Overall, however, the novel's thematic progression is based on selective kin-disposal. As Caroline Gonda writes, Evelina "spends at least as much time shedding new relations as she does acquiring them."[12] While Evelina's relations assert kinship-based claims to her allegiance, she only honors attachments based on what Martha Koehler describes as "affective" ties.[13] Zonitch makes the similar claim that *Evelina* implicitly asserts that "family bonds should be based on feeling rather than solely on blood," a central premise of Richardson's family of the heart.[14] According to Burney, Evelina's real family members, the ones who dictate her opportunities on the marriage market, are not her dead mother, her profligate father, her coarse cousins, or her embarrassing grandmother. Rather, she marries an ideal suitor because of the training and social opportunities provided by her surrogate family members, most importantly her surrogate father Mr. Villars and her surrogate mother Mrs. Mirvan. Burney ultimately depicts marriage itself as a surrogate relationship, with Evelina's spouse, Lord Orville, proposing to his "new-adopted sister" on the basis of her surrogate ties rather than her birth (367).

Evelina's choices about surrogate mothers express her class aspirations and ideals about feminine conduct. Evelina rejects her maternal grandmother, Madame Duval, most forcefully. By birth, her grandmother belongs to Evelina's lineage family. Evelina also lives with her grandmother for about one-fourth of the novel, making them members of the same household family. The only type of family Evelina is able to exclude Duval from is her surrogate family. From Evelina's first unpropitious meeting with her grandmother (Duval is abandoned and alone at night outside a puppet theater and Evelina's party allows her to join them in their carriage), she is instinctively embarrassed by their connection. She is oddly incurious about her grandmother's life or interests. Her antipathy is reflexive rather than considered. She relates the story of her first meeting with Duval in a horrified tone, asking Villars to pity her for "discover[ing] so near a relation in a woman who thus introduced herself" (53). Evelina never scrutinizes her motives for shunning her grandmother, a lack of introspection especially noticeable in an epistolary novel. In contrast, in *Clarissa*, Clarissa repeatedly tries to explain to Anna her reasons for disliking Sinclair and the courtesans who pose as her daughters. Scholars have attempted to fill in this gap with their own interpretations of Duval's role in the novel. They call attention to Duval's shortcomings. Emily Allen points out that she is "public, violent, and loud," to which Jeanine Casler adds that she is "lacking in a crucial area: education."[15] Although two marriages to wealthy men have made Duval rich, her behavior marks her as still belonging to the class (she is a barmaid when she meets Evelina's grandfather) she is supposed to have left behind. Consequently, if Evelina associates herself closely with Duval she accepts as her birthright the lower-class status her behavior and appearance convey. While Evelina does not articulate this rationale explicitly, the intuitive distance she tries to place between herself and her grandmother suggests she senses Duval's vulgarity is contagious.

Evelina's obscure birth makes her particularly vulnerable to damning conclusions about her connection to Duval. Described as "vulgar and illiterate" as well as "uneducated and unprincipled" in the first two letters of the novel exchanged by its moral arbiters Villars and Lady Howard, Burney identifies Duval as a threat to Evelina's prospects long before she meets Evelina (14, 15). Burney dramatizes the threat Duval presents to Evelina's status and marital opportunities in numerous episodes in which Duval is debased figuratively and, in some instances, literally. When her carriage leaks, she retreats "covered with mud" to Ranelagh where she responds to Captain Mirvan's taunts by "stamp[ing]" her feet and "sp[itting] in his face" (66–67). Her filthy appearance and lower-class behavior both threaten to injure Evelina's reputation since potential suitors witness this humiliating spectacle. A similar episode reinforces Duval's lower-class origins in a graphic manner. After being attacked by Captain Mirvan, Duval is so covered with "dirt, weeds, and filth" that she "hardly look[s] human" (150). Ruth Yeazell describes this scene as a revelation, a reverse Cinderella moment when the woman who marries well turns back into the "components and dirt" from which she rose.[16] Evelina is metaphorically dirtied by her connection to a mother figure Burney consistently associates with filth. The best example of the potentially detrimental effect she has on Evelina's marital prospects occurs when Evelina returns to London under Duval's chaperonage. In a scene that echoes an episode in *The History of Miss Betsy Thoughtless*, a group of prostitutes Duval mistakes for "real fine ladies" attach themselves to her party (247). Duval's inability to distinguish ladies from ladies of the evening suggests she is in some fundamental way akin to them.

By rejecting Duval, Evelina attempts to escape the dreadful future she would be subjected to as Duval's acknowledged granddaughter. Duval believes she is entitled to Evelina's fealty, which includes submitting to her choice of a husband. Duval attempts to arrange a match between Evelina and her bumbling middle-class nephew Tom Branghton so she can "leave [her] fortune between" the two branches of the family (242). Duval's connection to the Branghtons also exposes Evelina to the overtures of a silly and conceited suitor named Mr. Smith who baselessly assumes any young woman would be lucky to "catch" him as a husband (226). Even Duval's French beau Du Bois attempts to clandestinely court Evelina while they all share a household. Evelina dismisses all these suitors out of hand, just as she does her grandmother's efforts to conscript her into the Duval family circle. The disagreeable consequences of Duval's connection to Evelina extend beyond laughable proposals such as Tom's. Wealthy and titled suitors like Sir Clement and Lord Orville dismiss her as a legitimate marital prospect after they see her in the company of her grandmother, cousins, and the low company their parties attract.

Evelina would theoretically be able to refuse to marry any suitor selected for her by Duval. However, when her mother Caroline tried to veto the husband Duval proposed for her, Duval harassed her so much that in order to avoid capitulating she was forced into a Clarissa-like elopement with Evelina's father. He then disowned and abandoned her. This possible outcome lurks in the novel's background, with Sir Clement constantly trying to make Evelina his mistress. As an apparent bastard, Evelina is living proof of the detrimental effects of being a member of the wrong family. Bizarrely, by repudiating Duval Evelina ends up getting everything her grandmother has to offer. Duval leaves when Evelina refuses to marry Tom. However, when she is informed of the brilliant marriage Evelina arranges for herself she makes her granddaughter her sole heiress.

Evelina chooses Mrs. Mirvan as her surrogate mother to replace her faulty grandmother. A wealthy and socially connected member of the country gentry, Mrs. Mirvan is the antithesis of Duval. Duval is aggressive, loud, and conspicuous, while Mrs. Mirvan is gentle, maternal, and conventional. Mrs. Mirvan is like a paper doll cut from a conduct book, so proper and feminine as to become a virtual nonentity. Kristina Straub sums her up as "well-intentioned but ineffectual" and Sir Clement more bluntly describes her as an "amiable piece of still-life" (334).[17] Evelina prefers Mrs. Mirvan's blandness to Duval's flamboyance because it offers her the camouflage of normalcy while she learns how to act as if she were born into the class the Mirvans occupy by right. She covers herself socially in the cloak of Mrs. Mirvan's proffered protection, frequently referring to her as "mamma Mirvan" (30). Her desire to legitimate this imaginary daughterhood is so acute she even suggests a familial connection between Villars and Mrs. Mirvan, writing to him that Mrs. Mirvan is so kind "one would think she was your daughter" (74). In contrast, whenever Duval or the Branghtons attempt to assert their relatedness to Evelina she is so "ashamed" she goes to dangerous lengths to conceal their connection (88). Choosing the Mirvan family over Duval offers Evelina access to a propitious group of wealthy and elite suitors inaccessible to her "low-bred and vulgar" relations (95).

Mrs. Selwyn, the last of Evelina's potential surrogate mother figures, paradoxically does not even try to adopt her. She has no maternal tendencies, making her an odd candidate for the role Burney assigns her. Selwyn is a country gentlewoman who lives near Villars. She is unmarried and independent. She only qualifies as a surrogate mother because Evelina becomes her ward and lives with her in a household family for the last third of the novel. She becomes Evelina's guardian and host in Bristol Hotwells, where she travels primarily for pleasure. Evelina accompanies her because Villars hopes the trip will help her regain her health and spirits. In this resort town, Selwyn reintroduces Evelina to the sort of company she took for granted while living with the Mirvans. Then she largely ignores her. In these circumstances, Evelina learns to "judge" and to "*act* for [her]self," advice Villars offers her early on but that she does not take until Mrs. Selwyn's neglect compels her to do so. Evelina explicitly and repeatedly rejects Selwyn as a surrogate mother, a part Selwyn has no intention of auditioning for in any case. Specifically, Evelina reacts with consternation when one of the company asks her if Selwyn, who he describes as "that queer woman," is her mother (275). She criticizes Selwyn's "*masculine*" wit, wishing she could replace her with her beloved Mrs. Mirvan (269). Selwyn treats her "as an equal," but "does not," as Evelina laments, "raise and support [her] with others" as Mrs. Mirvan does (293). Paradoxically, Selwyn's aloofness is necessary for Evelina to establish the intimate friendship with Lord Orville that leads to their marriage. In the absence of active mothering, Evelina learns to converse openly with Lord Orville and overcome his "depreciating opinion" of her (296). Her virtue, intelligence, and companionate domesticity flourish in this vacuum of authority and Lord Orville ultimately decides he loves her enough to propose to her even without taking the prudent step of making "minute inquiries" into her "family and connections" (389). Evelina's preference for her chosen surrogate mother Mrs. Mirvan makes her worthy of Lord Orville, but Selwyn's lack of mothering compels her to reveal her true character to him, and thus prompts his proposal.

Just as Evelina favors her surrogate mother over her grandmother, she also stays loyal to her surrogate father Villars even after Sir John acknowledges her as his daughter. Sir John is a notorious rake who abandons Evelina's pregnant mother Caroline and burns their marriage certificate. He disappears, apparently with no intention of ever acknowledging Evelina. However, he is not quite as bad as he seems. When Selwyn confronts him, she accuses him of being as evil as "Nero or Caligula" (366). Instead, it turns out that Sir John has tried, albeit lazily, to rectify his desertion of Caroline. He acknowledged a baby he falsely believed to be his daughter. His efforts to raise this pretended Evelina are underwhelming. He outsources her education to a convent and then duels with the man she elopes with (who turns out to be his son and thus Evelina's half-brother). After he learns that Evelina is his actual daughter he readily acknowledges her. Evelina does not reject him outright as she does Duval. There is even a hint of Clarissa's blind father worship in her desire to be blessed by him. Their brief reunion is formulaic and theatrical. They weep decorously, virtually trip over each other seeking the other's blessing, and then Sir John rushes out of the room with no plans to remain involved in Evelina's life (386). He sees in Evelina only the ghost of his widow, the "Poor unhappy Caroline," not a distinct person (383). For her part, Evelina venerates the "revered name" of father more than Sir John himself (371). He neither affects Evelina's marital prospects nor brokers the details of her marriage; Lord Orville proposes to Evelina before Sir John acknowledges her and Selwyn arranges their wedding.

Evelina refers to her surrogate father Villars, not Sir John, as the "parent of [her] heart" (336). Their relationship is based on love, trust, and long-standing intimacy rather than blood.[18] He raises and educates Evelina, personally superintending her studies and moral development. David Oakleaf describes him a "counter-father" to the disengaged Sir John, teaching Evelina to reason, empathize, and judge: the very qualities that attract Lord Orville to her.[19] Evelina cares so deeply for Villars that Gonda describes their connection as "more powerfully binding" than "any other relationship in the novel."[20] Burney demonstrates the vast difference between Evelina's connection to Villars and Sir John through their disparate responses to her distress. Sir John is too paralyzed by his own regret and shame to comfort Evelina during their meeting, but when she is need of solace at Berry Hill, Villars provides it regardless of his own agitation. In response to her melancholy and reserve, Villars coaxes her into telling him why she is upset and then "fold[s]" her "to his heart," offering "words of sweetest kindness and consolation" that "soo[the]" and "tranquilli[se]" her (266). His consideration and empathy make Villars Evelina's "*more* than father" and the "[p]arent [her] heart acknowledges" (131, 350). The novel's conclusion provides the strongest evidence of Villars's primacy over Sir John. Rather than travel to one of Sir John's or Lord Orville's estates, or any other probable destination, the new-married couple chooses to spend their honeymoon in Berry Hill with Villars.

Evelina's marriage to Lord Orville is modeled on brotherhood.[21] As Peter DeGabriele asserts, Lord Orville gains Evelina's trust and love by becoming her "surrogate brother."[22] The early stages of their relationship when they meet only in public emphasize Lord Orville's mentorship of her. He is "assiduously attentive to please and to serve all who are in his company," particularly Evelina who has frequent need of his forbearance (74). He also protects her from the consequences of her many social gaffes, pretending he asked her to dance when she uses him as an excuse to turn down another partner, offering her his carriage to save her from a dangerous situation, and even challenging Mr. Lovel to a duel when he repeatedly humiliates her in public. When concealing her mistakes is not sufficient to protect Evelina from herself, he corrects her gently and thoughtfully. After seeing her accompanied by prostitutes at a public garden, he apologizes beforehand for the advice he gives to avoid them in the future. He softens his censure even further by presuming "their characters must be unknown" to her (241).

Lord Orville's fraternal mentoring of Evelina becomes more pointed and ardent when they are brought into closer quarters. While Lord Orville is never a member of Evelina's household family, he spends most of his time in Bristol Hotwells at Clifton House, where Evelina stays with Selwyn. While she lives there, several men sexually harass her. When one of them becomes so drunk that he attacks her publicly, she pleads for a brother to protect her from him. Lord Orville eagerly takes the opportunity to invite her to "think of me as if I were indeed your brother" (314). He shows how earnest he is about enacting this role by escorting Evelina and his actual sister Lady Louisa into the house, one on each arm. Lord Orville continues to refer to Evelina as his sister until he proposes (314). As in *Sir Charles Grandison*, the couple's brothering and sistering becomes a way of expressing familial intimacy before their engagement gives them any formally recognized claim to it. As Doody observes, one of the primary ways female protagonists in early novels are able to express erotic feelings acceptably is by characterizing suitors as brothers.[23] Brotherhood, with its emphasis on mutual duty and affection rather than passion, also offers an idealized model for domestic marriage. The disappearance of Evelina's birth family provides additional evidence for the primacy of surrogate families over nuclear or lineage families in *Evelina*. While Duval, the Branghtons, and Sir John disappear, Evelina and Sir John stay connected to her surrogate father Villars and, presumably, to Villars's neighbor and Evelina's surrogate mother Mrs. Mirvan.

Bizarrely, Evelina's half-brother Macartney is the only member of her nuclear or lineage family that plays an appreciable role in the afterlife of the novel. Macartney marries the imposter Evelina, whom Lord Orville makes "co-heiress" to Sir John's fortune (386). Lord Orville invites the married couple to honeymoon at one of his estates and then make a lengthy visit. Macartney's continuing significance begs the question of what distinguishes him from Evelina's other relations. Just as Sir Charles's cousin Everard in *Sir Charles Grandison* only rates as a real family member after Sir Charles dubs him a surrogate brother, Evelina's intense connection to Macartney is based on choice, not blood. In the first half of the novel, Evelina seizes Macartney's pistols, believing he intends to commit suicide with them. (In reality, he plans to turn highwayman to pay his debts.) This harrowing experience explains the tenacity of their bond to one another (263).[24] Macartney is Evelina's surrogate brother, a member of her family of the heart. His membership in her surrogate family is more meaningful to her than their ties by blood and marriage.

Cecilia begins where *Evelina* leaves off, just as Haywood's *The History of Jemmy and Jenny Jessamy* starts where *The History of Betsy Thoughtless* ends. Cecilia's parents die when she is young, but an uncle whose household family she joins skillfully directs her education. He is a more worldly version of Evelina's surrogate father Villars. He has a prominent position in the Anglican church and socializes frequently, giving Cecilia the opportunity to study etiquette and conversation alongside morality and academic subjects. Consequently, she develops strong judgment and social self-assurance before he dies. His will places her in the custody of what Doody describes as an "unholy mess of guardians."[25] Cecilia must live with one of the three guardians until she reaches her majority and takes control of her fortune. Each household family has its own pitfalls and offers potential surrogate family members. Thus far, the novel is fairly conventional. What really distinguishes it from earlier courtship fiction is that Cecilia loses rather than gains money and status over the course of the novel. Her marriage completes this painful process by forfeiting her entire inheritance. Defoe would probably assess her gains—a surrogate mother she worships and a husband she admires—as unimpressive. A cost-benefit analysis of her decisions would have to conclude that she makes the wrong ones again and again, with her disadvantageous marriage being the final coup de grâce.

The novel's conclusion demands explanation because it is, as Julian Fung describes it, so famously "glum."[26] Numerous scholars have obliged. Meghan Jordan argues that the conclusion "ironizes the complacency of the courtship plot."[27]

Stephanie Russo and A. D. Cousins explicate the unhappy ending as a critique of society rather than literature, asserting that "Burney does not set out to 'punish' women with power, but, instead, to demonstrate how social forces attempt to curtail and circumvent their possessing it."[28] Most of these interpretations implicitly accept the Defoevian premise that any marriage that costs a protagonist too much is necessarily tragic, or at least foolish. They do not accept Cecilia's characterization of her own situation: that it is "imperfect," but still provides "all the happiness human life seems capable of receiving."[29]

Cecilia is happy because she belongs to a family she cares for rather than because she marries an ideal husband. Burney is at pains throughout the novel to emphasize Cecilia's husband's flaws. Neither are these masculine infirmities of character limited to him. As Katharine Rogers observes, every man Cecilia encounters is to some degree "undisciplined, irresponsible, wrong-headed, or stupid."[30] Not only does Burney deflate the assumption of courtship novels that the right husband is the passkey to every other good, she also displaces the centrality of the surrogate father-brother relationship of marriage. None of the men in *Cecilia* are cast in the mold of Villars or Lord Orville. In the absence of worthy surrogate brothers or fathers, Cecilia seeks out a nurturing surrogate sister and a sagacious surrogate mother. The purpose of courtship is no longer husband hunting but finding companionship that is not just feminized (as the ever-thoughtful Lord Orville is), but female. In fact, Cecilia marries Mortimer more to procure his mother Augusta as her mother-in-law than anything else. This formulation inverts the conventional notion of marriage as a means of reinforcing bonds between men. In *Cecilia*, Mortimer is an instrument whose marriage fortifies bonds between women.

Cecilia's familial experiments cycle her through the households of three unsuitable guardians: the fashionable Mr. Harrel, Mortimer's high-born father Compton Delvile, and the miserly Mr. Briggs. They are all potential surrogate father figures since she resides with Harrel and Compton, and at one point intends to live with Briggs. All three view themselves as superior to the others and consequently feel authorized to manage Cecilia's money and choose her husband. Their advice is uniformly bad. Briggs invests her fortune advantageously but refuses to give her access to any of it since he believes "girls [know] nothing of the value of money and ought not to be trusted with it" (180). Against her explicit wishes, he also tries to arrange her marriage, or as he puts it "get [her] a careful"—which is to say rich—husband (96). Harrel takes literally Briggs's figurative notion of Cecilia as a financial instrument to be traded by men. He settles a gambling debt by offering marriage to Cecilia as payment, combining in this one action financial and marital malfeasance. Compton recommends several marriages to Cecilia that would purchase her a title. He considers himself too important to become involved in her sordid financial concerns. Instead of helping her gain access to some of her money in order to pay her debts to a bookseller, he sententiously tells her to confine her reading to didactic periodicals such as "*The Spectator, Tatler* and *Guardian*" until marriage provides her access to her future husband's library (186). Taken together, these three father figures are so atrocious Fung argues they "cause more financial and psychological harm than anyone in *Evelina*," including Sir John.[31]

Even the father figures Cecilia seeks out for herself, Mr. Monckton and Mr. Albany, turn out to be fundamentally selfish and untrustworthy. Monckton cultivates Cecilia's friendship under the guise of a mentor. However, he views Cecilia's "youth, beauty, and intelligence" as "his future property" (9). As he awaits his aged wife's death he grooms Cecilia to replace her. In order to keep her from marrying elsewhere he is willing to endanger and humiliate her. He stalks her at a masquerade, aborts her private marriage to Mortimer, and then duels with Mortimer. Cecilia's friends call Albany, her second father figure, the "man-hater" because he frequents public places in order to reprimand wealthy pleasure-seekers for spending their money frivolously instead of helping the poor (68). They just try to avoid him, but Cecilia is awed by his moral seriousness. He accosts her rudely, demanding in front of a large party of her friends that she "seek the virtuous" (presumably not among her company) and "relieve the poor" (68). In hopes of learning how to act and spend correctly she asks him to become her "monitor" and almoner (708). However, she is just a tool for Albany, who tries to make amends for seducing and abandoning a woman in his youth by hounding and harassing the rich. Seeking approval, Cecilia instead finds in Albany a Harlowe-like insatiability for control over her actions. Whenever she spends time and money on her own interests he castigates her. Ultimately, all these surrogate fathers are deficient.

Cecilia's chosen surrogate brother and future husband Mortimer is as inadequate in his way as Cecilia's available surrogate fathers. He is the son of Compton, one of Cecilia's guardians. Cecilia temporarily becomes a member of Compton's household family during an extended visit. As a ward of Mortimer's father, Cecilia occupies a sisterlike position in relation to Mortimer. As Lord Orville does in *Evelina*, Mortimer cultivates this fraternal role. He comes to Cecilia's aid when she is in danger, saving her from a thunderstorm and protecting her from harassment at a masquerade. However, that is where the similarities between Lord Orville and Mortimer end. Even at his best, Mortimer never lives up to Lord Orville at his worst. First, he is oddly peripheral to *Cecilia*. Whereas Lord Orville participates in most of the central events of *Evelina*, Mortimer says less and appears in fewer scenes than minor comic characters like Mr. Meadows. As for Cecilia, far from swooning over Mortimer in the way Evelina does over Lord Orville, she sensibly intends to marry him because their union would satisfy both "inclination" and "propriety" (253). When Mortimer courts Cecilia despite his parents' prohibition, he is a reluctant lover at best. He reveals his affection for her only under duress, and in episodes that are often more ludicrous than heroic.

For example, he places himself in the path of a spilled pot of tea otherwise destined for Cecilia's lap.

Furthermore, Mortimer is suspicious and narcissistic. While Lord Orville presumes Evelina must be unaware that the women he sees her with at a pleasure garden are prostitutes, Mortimer distrusts Cecilia so much that even after they marry he concludes she is having an affair when he finds her at the house of a rival. The consequences of the duel he rashly initiates in response to his mistaken assumption leave Cecilia unprotected, impoverished, and so ill she loses her intellect and forgets who she is. Even though he is at fault for her breakdown, his response when he finds her is to cry out in despair "Cecilia, I am content to part with thee!" (907). Better she be dead than that he should be saddled with an incapacitated wife. As her illness continues he "spends almost all his time upon the stairs" outside her room rather than sitting with her (909). When his family doctor tries to discuss Cecilia's condition with him, he "fear[s]" to hear "his opinion" so he "snatche[s] up his hat, and rushe[s] . . . out of the house to avoid him" (910). In previous courtship novels including *Evelina*, identifying a suitor as a brother means he will make an ideal husband. In *Cecilia*, it is more ironic than accurate when Cecilia's friend and surrogate sister Henrietta asserts to Cecilia that she is so similar to Mortimer that she "must be his sister" (776).

Cecilia's surrogate sister Henrietta is supportive in all the ways Mortimer is not. Although Henrietta is initially just one of Cecilia's close friends, they become potential surrogate family members after Cecilia invites Henrietta to live with her in the country. In these circumstances, their intimacy becomes sororal. Henrietta is a far better surrogate sibling than Mortimer. Whereas Mortimer is guarded and secretive, Henrietta is "artless, ingenuous, and affectionate" with a mind "informed by intuitive integrity" (345). In contrast to Cecilia's childhood friend Mrs. Harrel, who also lives with Cecilia, Henrietta altruistically interests herself in promoting Cecilia's happiness. In Henrietta, Cecilia finds a "friend to oblige, and a companion to converse with" whose "sweetness . . . revived her spirits, and gave her a new interest to her existence" (794). This passage is reminiscent of Moll's description of the existential revival she experiences when she meets her surrogate mother the governess. Anticipating Burney's language, Moll recounts how just talking to the governess "put new Life and new Spirit into my very Heart."[32]

Burney contrasts Mortimer's and Henrietta's behavior by placing them in similar situations in which they are called upon to help Cecilia. Mortimer becomes enraged when he believes Cecilia prefers Henrietta's brother and his friend Mr. Belfield to him. Henrietta is theoretically Cecilia's rival for Mortimer's affection. However, when Cecilia confides in her about Mortimer's intention to marry her despite his parents' opposition, Henrietta displays "unaffected tenderness" for Cecilia and "thank[s] her most gratefully for reposing such trust in her" (813). The most significant contrast between Henrietta and Mortimer is their reactions to

Cecilia's mental and physical collapse. Rather than fleeing Cecilia's sickroom as Mortimer does, Henrietta refuses to leave Cecilia alone. When the doctor tries to send her away she sternly tells him "I will hold by this dear hand,—I will cling to it till the last minute; and you will not, I know, you will not, give orders to have it taken away from me!" (914). She remains with Cecilia day and night until she recovers, taking on Mortimer's rightful responsibilities. Much like Moll's governess, Henrietta disappears after the protagonist recovers and retreats into her insular married life.

Unlike *Moll Flanders*, *Cecilia* does not depict the exchange of surrogate sister for surrogate brother as an unconditional promotion. Even after accepting Cecilia's marriage to his son, Compton continues to resent her as an interloper. Since the Delviles keep largely to themselves, Cecilia is now permanently trapped in their claustrophobic family. The novel ends on a bittersweet note with Cecilia thankful for the "general felicity" she enjoys as Mortimer's wife while acknowledging the "partial evil" of belonging to such a family (941). As Terry Castle observes, this conclusion is "profoundly at odds with [Cecilia's] bright beginnings and . . . essentially hopeful narrative."[33] No husband, Burney implies, answers every question and solves every problem. Cultivating self-knowledge and philosophical wisdom of the sort Cecilia displays by accepting the shortcomings of her marriage with "chearfullest resignation" (the last words in the novel) is more attainable than finding in marriage a perpetual utopia of the sort that Evelina expects to enjoy with Lord Orville (941).

The courtship plot in *Cecilia* focuses on the protagonist's relationship with her surrogate mother Augusta more than her surrogate brother Mortimer. Cecilia feels more passion for and instant attraction to Augusta than Mortimer. Their first meeting is love at first sight: "thus mutually astonished and mutually pleased, their first salutations were accompanied by looks so flattering to both, that each saw in the other, an immediate prepossession in her favour, and from the moment that they meet, they seemed instinctively impelled to admire" (155). The progress of their affection as it "ripens into esteem" also mimics romantic attachment (160). Cecilia experiences the complications and entanglements typical of courtship plots with Augusta rather than with Mortimer. For example, Augusta punishes Cecilia with "cold civility" for neglecting to visit her, but Cecilia's reassurances to her rekindle "those glowing and delightful sensations which spring from a cordial renewal of friendship and kindness" (353, 359).

The same back-and-forth romantic tug-of-war recurs throughout the second half of the novel as Augusta wavers about allowing Mortimer to marry Cecilia. Augusta frequently declares her love for Cecilia in enraptured exclamations, referring to her as a "noble creature" and an "angel" (425, 674). Cecilia loves and obeys Augusta as if she rather than Mortimer were her husband. Cecilia promises to act as a sort of vassal to Augusta, ceding to her all control over her decisions and actions:

"[a]s my own Agent I regard myself no longer; if, as yours, I can give pleasure, or be of service, I shall gladly receive your commands" (646–647). Cecilia later reiterates the same pledge, assuring Augusta she will be "ruled by you wholly" and "commit to you every thing" (650). Additionally, it is the "praise of Mrs. Delvile," not Mortimer, that is "alone sufficient to make [Cecilia] happy" (426).

Cecilia and Augusta's courtship plot shifts from romantic to familial as they find in one another what their nuclear families lack: a mother for Cecilia and a daughter for Augusta. As the novel progresses, Augusta increasingly describes her affection for Cecilia as "maternal" (501). Even as she forbids Cecilia from marrying her son, she refers to her as "[d]aughter of my mind" and "daughter of my affection" (651, 830). When Augusta finally consents to Mortimer marrying Cecilia she is more enthusiastic about gaining a daughter than she is about her son's prospective happiness. Mortimer seems to be an afterthought when she informs Cecilia of her change of heart and urges her to rush to her side so "that I may bless the daughter I have so often wished to own!" (821). It is likely Cecilia rather than Mortimer who is the first of the "two objects" Augusta describes in the same letter as most dear to her "maternal heart" (821). Similarly, what Cecilia loves best about Mortimer is that he is a conduit through which she can legitimately become Augusta's daughter. She is most attracted to him when he displays "filial enthusiasm" for Augusta, who they agree is the "first among women" (820). The primacy of Cecilia's attachment to Augusta continues after she marries Mortimer. It is telling that she first identifies the "warm affection of Lady Delvile" as the source of her marital happiness and then adds as an addendum that she also continues to feel "unremitting fondness" for her husband (941).

Cecilia's relationship with her surrogate mother Augusta provides her with the intellectual and moral guidance marriage typically offers in courtship novels. Augusta is widely "hated" in society because she spurns frivolous conversation and promiscuous company (155). Unlike the Harrels and their friends, Augusta does not gossip or discuss public places, clothing, and money. Her "discourse," as Cecilia describes it, is serious and morally instructive (160). Even more than Lord Orville (who is willing when necessary to calibrate his conversation to whatever company he finds himself in), Augusta expects her conversational partners to listen attentively, think before responding, and demonstrate accurate judgment. She is an ideal mentor for Cecilia because, as Jane Spencer notes, Cecilia is naturally "introspective" and "reflective."[34] Burney emphasizes Cecilia's receptiveness to Augusta's teaching by contrasting her ductility to the "idle humour" of Augusta's niece Lady Honoria who is "without even a desire of improvement" and has "no view and no thought but to lau[gh] at whatever goes forward" (497). Lady Honoria sports with Augusta, repeating slander about Mortimer just to provoke her. When Augusta reprimands her for "lower[ing] her own dignity" by recounting unverified stories, Lady Honoria flippantly responds that Augusta should be glad for their "quarrel" because otherwise neither would know what to "do for conversation" (356). In contrast, Cecilia is "cruelly depressed" and "[g]rieved" when she offends Augusta (357). She apologizes and attempts to reform. Cecilia's eagerness to please and be mentored by Augusta mimics an eighteenth-century wife's idealized subservience to her husband just as Augusta's pedagogical instincts toward Cecilia mirror eighteenth-century notions of a husband's responsibility to educate his wife.

Burney suggests Cecilia's marriage itself will be an extended conversation with Augusta in which Mortimer will participate only occasionally. Cecilia experiences a preview of married life when she stays with the Delviles during the Easter holidays. She initially hopes staying with the family will help her become more intimately acquainted with Mortimer, but instead he makes a "scrupulous and pointed" effort to avoid her (459). Compton is absent much of the time. Few neighbors visit because they resent the Delviles' "arrogance" (460). Consequently, Cecilia and Augusta are left alone to talk for whole days during which Cecilia finds in "the conversation of Mrs. Delvile a never-failing resource against languor and sadness" (460). Given the Delviles' preference for privacy and domesticity over entertaining and social engagements, Cecilia's married life is likely to bring more of the same. Her daily life will be an ongoing conversational seminar led by Augusta and attended on most days only by Cecilia.

By prioritizing bonds between surrogate mothers, sisters, and daughters over ones to surrogate fathers, brothers, and sons, Burney harkens back to several of the novels I discussed in earlier chapters. In *Moll Flanders* and *Roxana* the protagonists confide more freely and seek more support from their surrogate mothers and sisters than their husbands. Moll confides in the governess; Roxana in Amy. Pamela seeks advice and protection from her surrogate mother Mrs. Jervis. The most significant difference between these novels and *Cecilia* is that in *Cecilia* surrogate relationships between women are not a means to an end. Cecilia sacrifices money and power to procure Augusta as her surrogate mother. In contrast, Defoe's and Richardson's protagonists improve their status, fortunes, and potential to marry wealthy men through their relationships with their surrogate mothers and sisters. The governess helps Moll marry a banker and then later to reunite with Jemy in Newgate. Similarly, Amy schemes on Roxana's behalf so that Roxana can marry her way into a title. In *Pamela*, Mrs. Jervis tries to convince Mr. B Pamela is morally upright, paving the way for her surrogate daughter's virtue to be rewarded through her marriage. In contrast, Cecilia is rewarded with education and self-improvement at the expense of marrying an inferior suitor. She marries in order to procure a surrogate mother who is able to provide these things, rather than because she expects her husband to supply them.

Richardson's later novels *Clarissa* and *Sir Charles Grandison* also value women's education and moral development but depict them as attainable only via marriage or death. Clarissa finds solace in her surrogate sister Anna Howe and her surrogate mother Mrs. Lovick but ultimately must "marry Jesus" through death in order to attain fulfillment. Harriet's marriage to Sir Charles concludes Harriet's story more optimistically, but Sir Charles is still a sort of Jesus figure under whose tuition Harriet places herself for life. His moral and intellectual guidance of her is similar to what Cecilia expects from Augusta as a consequence of marrying Mortimer. In *Clarissa* and *Sir Charles Grandison* surrogate families are the bridge protagonists must cross in order to achieve ideal marriages. Regardless of how significant the surrogate ties a female protagonist forms in these novels, they are still preparatory to marriage. If no worthy husband is available, as in Clarissa's case, the only legitimate conclusion for a woman is death.

Haywood depicts surrogate families as a mechanism for learning rather than as a way to prove her protagonists' inherent superiority. By choosing a variety of surrogate family members, both Betsy in *The History of Miss Betsy Thoughtless* and Jenny in *The History of Jemmy and Jenny Jessamy* learn about themselves and the world. The enlightenment they attain through this process prepares them for a desirable marriage. Haywood's view of marriage is practical and social, in contrast to Richardson's. Betsy is perfectly suited to Mr. Trueworth because they both enjoy society and entertaining. She learns over the course of the novel to be selective about the company she keeps. However, she does not intend to wait at home by the window for Trueworth to return from the hunt or make him jams and jellies, as Pamela claims she will do for Mr. B in *Pamela*. Jenny is even more independent than Betsy. She knows her husband is imperfect. She accepts his faults and looks to herself, her friends, and intellectual pursuits to create the happiness Richardson equates with an ideal marriage. For Betsy, wisdom is a precondition to achieve an ideal marriage rather than a product of it, and for Jenny the most sagacious wife is the one who does not expect too much from her husband.

What is different about Burney's novels and especially *Cecilia* is her emphasis on a woman's education as its own reward and her placement of surrogate motherhood at the center of the novel. Even in the more conventional *Evelina* it is Evelina's "natural love of virtue" and "mind that might adorn *any* station, however exalted" that convinces Lord Orville to propose to her regardless of her birth (346). Education in *Evelina* is important primarily because it is the means to the predictable end of marrying an ideal surrogate brother. Surrogate sisters and mothers provide Evelina with access to her future husband; having served this purpose they disappear. Marriage is of secondary importance to *Cecilia*, displaced by the novel's central relationship between Cecilia and her surrogate mother Augusta. Augusta, not her son, will be Cecilia's mentor. This novel radically departs from the long tradition of the courtship novel as a quest for a surrogate brother who provides whatever the protagonist lacks: status and money in Defoe's novels, moral authority in Richardson's, and an engaging companion in Haywood's. In *Cecilia*, finding a surrogate mother is the purpose of courtship rather than the means by which courtship proceeds.

Cecilia is significant to the history of the courtship novel because it marks the transition from marriage as the sole purpose of the genre to marriage as a means to women's self-awareness and self-improvement. Jane Austen develops this concept even further, and it becomes a centerpiece of Victorian novels such as *Middlemarch* (1871) and *Jane Eyre* (1847). While these future developments are beyond the scope of this project, it is worth briefly glancing sideways at contemporaneous novels that involve surrogate families but do not fit the criteria specified by my project. Henry Fielding's *Tom Jones* (1749) and Sarah Scott's *Millenium Hall* (1762) are two such novels. Much of *Tom Jones*'s plot focuses on Tom's experiences in surrogate families. As a man, he is able to join all sorts of surrogate families without damaging his marital prospects. Although he remains largely unchanged by them, he acts within them as an unmoved mover. Contact with him influences their prospects and values. I attribute this inversion to Tom's masculine privilege. The families that adopt him cast him in the role of a surrogate father or brother, providing him more structural power than surrogate sisters or mothers have. These masculine positions empower him to shape his adopted families rather than be transformed by them. In Scott's novel, women's failed courtships and marriages, as well as their deficient nuclear and lineage families, are preconditions for the creation of the commune for single women for which the novel is named. The residents of Millenium Hall form a surrogate family headed by three matriarchs whose stories become the novel's backbone. By briefly examining these outlying but relevant novels, I provide additional context and support for my larger arguments.

I HAVE EXAMINED TEN NOVELS BY Defoe, Richardson, Haywood, and Burney, all of which fit specific criteria. Each one has a female protagonist and a plot centering on courtship and marriage, and features surrogate families. I developed my typology of surrogate families based on these parameters. It is worth briefly considering novels that are similar enough to the ones included in this study to be instructive, but different enough to test my conclusions. Henry Fielding's *Tom Jones* (1749) and Sarah Scott's *Millenium Hall* (1762) are two such novels.

Tom Jones and *Millenium Hall* overlap in significant ways with the novels I examine. Neither checks every box for inclusion in this study. *Tom Jones* is not exclusively about marriage, but marriage is an important theme in the novel and also its denouement. Additionally, *Tom Jones* includes numerous surrogate families. But Tom is a man. Surrogate families play a different role in his adventures than they do in stories about female protagonists. *Millenium Hall* has even more in common with the novels included in this study than *Tom Jones*. First, Millenium Hall itself functions as a surrogate family. Furthermore, the novel that describes it recounts the life stories of four women who have all outlived numerous courtships and marriages. The novel is the mirror image of *Tom Jones*; the lack of the same thing Fielding's novel has too many of—men—disqualified *Millenium Hall* from my consideration. Only women are allowed to belong to the Millenium Hall family, so its members are not able to adopt surrogate fathers or brothers. Since marriage evolves from paternal and fraternal relationships, conventional courtship plots do not occupy center stage in a novel set in a women's commune. Together, these two novels complement one another by probing the role of gender in the plot convention of surrogate families.

Numerous other novels are also worth considering. I briefly discuss one of them, Henry's sister Sarah Fielding's *David Simple* (1744). Her novel is apposite to my discussion of *Tom Jones* because it focuses on a male character who, like Tom, constructs surrogate families on his way to finding a spouse. One of the most important characteristics of surrogate families is their potential to displace or supplant patriarchal nuclear or lineage families. It would be interesting to broaden this study's scope to compare and contrast surrogate families with other literary conventions that serve similar purposes. For example, Charlotte Lennox's *The Female Quixote* (1752) raises interesting questions about family models in eighteenth-century British fiction. Her protagonist, Arabella, adheres to romance conventions that prolong courtship indefinitely. As Aaron Hanlon notes, scholars often interpret her "quixotic" behavior as a means of achieving "feminine empowerment."[1] Whether or not she intentionally deploys these conventions in a "goal-driven" manner to "manipulate the men in her world to get what she wants" (Zak Watson's formulation of the critical consensus about Arabella), her eccentricity gives her power.[2] It prevents her uncle from exercising authority over her and slows her cousin's courtship to a crawl. Her delusions empower her to make her own choices, just as surrogate families do for protagonists in the novels I examine. In addition to *The Female Quixote*, many other novels involve female choice, courtship, and competing family models. Frances Brooke's *The Excursion* (1777), Elizabeth Inchbald's *A Simple Story* (1791), and Jane Austen's *Mansfield Park* (1814) come immediately to mind. I hope others take up this project where I end because there is much more work to be done.

Surrogate families play a significant role in *Tom Jones*. Tom joins three surrogate families. He belongs to Mr. Allworthy's surrogate family while he lives at Paradise Hall, Partridge's surrogate family as they travel together across England, and Mrs. Miller's surrogate family while he resides in her boarding house during his stay in London. Each surrogate family is central to a portion of the novel: Allworthy to Tom's childhood in the country; Partridge to his rambles across country; and Mrs. Miller to his time in London. Tom instigates changes in all his surrogate families. He forces them to interact with people outside their immediate circle and thus precipitates storylines that would otherwise never occur. He brings his insular Paradise Hall family into frequent contact with Black George's family, Western's family, and other members of the community they would prefer to ignore. He conducts a reluctant Partridge through the countryside, where they encounter gypsies, a highwayman, and a hermit.[3] Tom intervenes in the private affairs of Mrs. Miller's family, too, persuading his friend and fellow boarder Nightingale to marry Mrs. Miller's daughter Nancy whom he has seduced.

Adopting Tom opens Allworthy's insular family to the surrounding community. Hilary Teynor characterizes Allworthy's community as a "large extended family emanating from the epicenter of Paradise Hall."[4] While this is true, I would add that the reason it extends outward is because of Tom. On his own, Allworthy shows little inclination to interact with anyone other than his sister, Bridget. He does not gossip and he mostly stays at home. The world sometimes comes to him, but he does not reach out to interact with it. He passes judgment on Partridge, George Seagrim, and Molly because their transgressions are brought to his attention by others. The only time he reaches out voluntarily to participate in the world is when Tom appears in his bed and he entwines "one of his Fingers into the Infant's Hand."[5] The "gentle Pressure" of Tom's touch spontaneously inspires Mr. Allworthy to adopt Tom, making him Tom's surrogate father (30). This episode should be understood metaphorically as well as literally. The "pressure" Tom exerts is centrifugal, pulling Allworthy outward and into his community.

Tom is not just Allworthy's surrogate son; he is a better version of Allworthy. Allworthy invites this interpretation by giving Tom "his own name of Thomas" (54). Fielding repeatedly emphasizes their closeness. Allworthy "suffers himself to be called" father by Tom (88). He calls Tom "his own Boy," raising him "on an intire Equality" with his legitimate nephew and heir, Blifil (91). The entire neighborhood assumes Tom is actually Allworthy's "own [illegitimate] Child" (203). For his part, Tom feels "filial Obligations" and "more than filial Piety" for Allworthy (144). Tom has Allworthy's best qualities, but unlike Allworthy he is open to the world. He enacts Allworthy's theoretical goodness in practical ways, usually at the expense of his own reputation or safety. He gives money to the Seagrims, takes the blame for George Seagrim's poaching, and saves Sophia from being bucked off a horse. He gallantly helps whoever needs it without worrying about the consequences. Just as Amy in *Roxana* (1724) is so closely aligned with Roxana that they become alternate selves, Tom is a counterpart to Allworthy.

Tom also resembles female protagonists such as Evelina in *Evelina* (1778) in that he benefits substantially from his connections to high-status surrogate family members. The difference is that while Tom welcomes the advantages he gains through his connection to Allworthy, he does not rely on him. Evelina must belong to Mrs. Mirvan's and Mrs. Selwyn's household families in order to prove her worth to Lord Orville. However, Tom is able to make his way without Allworthy or Allworthy's money. His exceptionally good looks and genteel manners are passports to any company, but much of that company would be off-limits to a woman with the same charms. For example, Forward in *Betsy Thoughtless* (1751) ends up in a situation similar to Tom's after her father ejects her from his household. Despite her beauty and genteel behavior, she has fewer options than he does. Her female body imposes its own limitations on her. She is pregnant, unmarried, and unprotected, and therefore shunned by respectable society. When she turns to prostitution as her only means of support, her downfall becomes inevitable. Tom, on the other hand, struts about London in clothing bought with money he earns as Lady Bellaston's gigolo. While being kept by Lady Bellaston should be reason enough to expel him from reputable society, it pales in comparison to the public shame he later experiences when he is imprisoned for murder. But none of this hinders Tom from becoming engaged to Sophia. The antithetical consequences of Tom's and Forward's parallel situations demonstrate how much more women have at stake when they adopt surrogate family members. Just being associated with Forward is enough to convince Trueworth not to marry Betsy.

But no matter what Tom does or who he does it with, he is still able to marry a woman with a spotless reputation.

Tom's connection to his surrogate father Partridge also has more repercussions for Partridge than Tom. When Tom meets Partridge he believes he is his father. Although Partridge quickly disabuses Tom of this assumption, Partridge still becomes Tom's father by investing in his surrogate son emotionally and financially. He assists Tom by acting as his servant and by paying both of their ways on the road. Like Robinson Crusoe's father in Defoe's *Robinson Crusoe* (1719), Partridge tries to convince Tom to stay put and appreciate what he has. He proposes over and over that Tom return to Paradise Hall. On the other hand, Tom is always in search of something. Sometimes it is adventure and sometimes Sophia, but his impulse is always to move forward. Repeatedly, Partridge unsuccessfully pleads with his surrogate son to linger at comfortable inns. But Tom restlessly insists they leave cozy kitchens and fireplace hearths for unexpected and risky encounters with gypsies, Mrs. Waters, a hermit, and even a highwayman.

Gary Gautier argues that there is a significant difference between Tom and Partridge's experiences on the road and Joseph and Parson Adams's in Fielding's earlier novel *Joseph Andrews* (1742). Joseph and Adams seem to travel past others' stories as if they were regarding a series of satirical "Hogarthian . . . sketches."[6] They are observers more than participants, but Tom becomes involved in the stories he hears. He asks to join the gypsies' celebration, argues with the highwayman, has a tryst with Mrs. Waters, and saves the hermit from a beating. Tom is his surrogate father Patridge's conduit to experience, excitement, and ultimately redemption. It is through Tom that Partridge is eventually restored to his neighborhood, his teaching, and financial security. Even his likely marriage to Tom's former mistress, Molly Seagrim, would not have happened if he had never met Tom.

Tom's association with his surrogate mother Mrs. Miller is likewise more consequential to her than Tom. He and Partridge lodge in her London boarding house, Allworthy's favorite. Like the boarding schools Haywood's Betsy and Jenny attend, this boarding house functions as a household family and source of surrogate family members. Miller takes a maternal interest in Tom, advising him about city life and reprimanding him for allowing Bellaston's late-night visits. She has self-interested motives for prohibiting Tom's carousing because she thinks his behavior will call her daughters' reputations into question and expose her to suspicions that her boarding house is actually a "House of ill Fame" (485). However, she is still attached to Tom for his own sake. In the end, she benefits more from this association than he does. Specifically, at the same time she upbraids Tom for his libertine behavior, his fellow lodger and friend Nightingale is seducing her elder daughter, Nancy. Miller's only recourse after she discovers Nancy's pregnancy is to appeal to Tom to convince Nightingale to marry Nancy. Even though Tom has no obligation to his holier-than-thou former landlady (she forces him to move out because he refuses to curtail Bellaston's late-night visits), he gladly intercedes to help "this little Family of Love" (495). By doing so, he implicitly accepts the role Miller envisions for him as her surrogate son.

Miller ultimately owes the health and happiness of her nuclear and lineage families to her surrogate son. He convinces Nightingale to marry Nancy and even intercedes with Nightingale's mercenary father (who has already arranged an advantageous match for his son) to consent to the match. By doing so he prevents the "Ruin" of Miller's "poor, little, worthy, defenceless Family" (497). He also unwittingly saves Miller's cousin and nephew. Miller confides to Tom that her cousin and her newborn baby are ill and too poor to get help. Without even knowing who Miller's relation is, Tom donates twenty guineas (of his admittedly ill-gotten gains from becoming Bellaston's gigolo) to pay for food and medical care. Miller's cousin turns out to be married to Mr. Anderson, the highwayman who attempts to rob Tom and Partridge. Fielding emphasizes Tom's altruism by acknowledging how unusual, even deviant, his voluntary generosity will appear to readers. The narrator imagines readers will "censure" Tom's "Folly for thus troubling himself with the Affairs of others," but explains his hero is incapable of being "an indifferent Spectator of the Misery or Happiness of any one; and he felt either the one or the other in greater Proportion as he himself contributed to either" (529). Learning that Tom is his family's benefactor, Anderson enthusiastically echoes Miller's praises of their honorary family member, calling Tom an "Angel from Heaven" and the "worthiest, bravest, noblest of all human Beings" (470).

Although Tom's benevolence ultimately redounds to himself, he is never motivated by self-interest. Simply by acting according to his extroverted and magnanimous nature he collects enough advocates to reconcile Allworthy to him. Because he saves Miller's family from disaster, he earns his surrogate mother's loyalty. Consequently, she defends him to Allworthy as "one of the worthiest Creatures breathing," and assures Allworthy that Tom still loves him like a father (570). Likewise, Mrs. Waters—Tom's supposed mother—rewards Tom for saving her from an attacker and for preserving her reputation when they are caught in bed together at an inn by testifying to Allworthy that Tom is actually his sister Bridget's son. Tom keeps incriminating information about his former tutor Square to himself. Square recompenses his kindness by confessing to Allworthy that he participated in Blifil's scheme to disinherit Tom. All these stories converge at once, condemning Blifil to exile and restoring Tom to Allworthy's favor. As the acknowledged son of Allworthy's sister, Tom even becomes Allworthy's heir.

Fielding's utopian conclusion brings together all Tom's surrogate family members in one place. Tom marries his beloved Sophia and lives in his father-in-law's estate near Allworthy. Partridge keeps a school in the same neighborhood. Nightingale purchases a nearby estate where he lives with his wife, children, and mother-in-law. Each family individually enacts domestic tranquility and the "most agreeable Intercourse subsists" between all of them (640). Tom becomes a Sir Charles Grandison figure, presiding as paterfamilias over his extended surrogate family. Therein lies a great part of the difference between the significance of surrogate families to male versus female protagonists. Tom does not need them as much as they need him. Neither do any of his scandalous adventures diminish his ability to marry the woman he loves or to be respected as a husband, father, and landowner. Surrogate family members assist him along his way, just as they do female protagonists. However, they do not define or confine him.

Tom's experiences with surrogate families contrasts in instructive ways with David's in Sarah Fielding's *David Simple*. Together, they provide further evidence that gender, not just increasingly egalitarian ideals of nuclear and lineage families, is at stake in depictions of surrogate families. *Tom Jones* and *David Simple* are both stories about young men that end with marriage. But because the gendered characteristics of these two protagonists are so different, surrogate families play disparate roles in their narratives. As Lori Walk observes, David is a "feminized hero."[7] He is not motivated by conventionally masculine traits like competitiveness or ambition. Linda Bree argues that Sarah was highly critical of "drinking and womanizing," behavior Henry sanctions in *Tom Jones* as manifestations of Tom's high spirits and good nature.[8] She further asserts that Sarah viewed these widely accepted masculine prerogatives as "symptoms of serious moral faults" rather than "natural characteristics of an innocent and naïve young man"[9] Expanding on Bree's argument, it is fair to interpret David an anti-Tom: a man who thinks and acts like one of Richardson's female protagonists. The novels provide ample evidence for this approach. David and Tom begin in comparable circumstances. They are members (Allworthy adopts Tom) of well-off nuclear families. They have scheming brothers who betray them for profit. However, they have antithetical, gendered responses to these events. Tom fulfills eighteenth-century readers' expectations about how a man ought to act. He gets angry, but then he gets on with his life. But David suffers a sort of post-traumatic stress after losing his brother. He cannot get beyond his grief (he is too passive to be angry), so he embarks on a quest to replace his brother with what he calls a true friend. Malcolm Kelsall, editor of an early edition of *David Simple*, believes the true friend David seeks is actually a wife.[10] However, Bree disagrees with him, arguing that in *David Simple*, "far from friendship being regarded as a surrogate for romantic love, in this novel the reverse almost seems to be the case."[11] In other words, what David really wants is a sister.

David's courtship and marriage align with this familial goal. Consequently, the courtship aspect of the narrative is so tepid that Bree characterizes *David Simple* as not even "primarily a courtship novel."[12] David marries Camilla, the bride of his choice. However, Richard Terry describes their relationship as so "amicable" and "sexless" that it is difficult to imagine them involved with any sort of coupling other than a meeting of the minds.[13] While Tom earns Sophia's love through physical prowess and chivalry, Camilla marries David because he "love[s] her brother."[14] Not just David's courtship, but also his marriage is a surrogate family affair. Camilla's brother marries David's friend Cynthia and the two couples become a family unit. They pool their finances, parenting responsibilities, and day-to-day lives. They are neither a conventional nuclear family nor a household family. As scholars frequently remark, they are a surrogate family. Walk describes the two couples and their children in Richardsonian terms as a "family of love."[15] Similarly, Joseph Bartolomeo describes them as an "ideal family of [David's] own choosing."[16] Bryan Mangano even calls them a "surrogate family."[17] Some aspects of David's marriage are reminiscent of Burney's *Cecilia* (1782). Like Cecilia, he marries in order to fasten himself to surrogate family members (Augusta Delvile in her case) rather than using them as a launching pad from which to propel himself into marriage. This likeness suggests that it is conventional masculinity of the sort displayed by Tom rather than simply being a man that makes surrogate families incompatible with marriage. The patriarchal family model of a nuclear family—the normative outcome of marriage—precludes other configurations of the sort David seeks out. Tom would never share his status as head of his family with another man, as David does.

Millenium Hall is an interesting test case for my arguments about gender and surrogate families. Its permutation of surrogate families is the antithesis of *Tom Jones*'s, but several steps further down the path from *David Simple*. For the founders of Millenium Hall, courtship and marriage are just steps along the way to their common destination: a women's commune. This commune becomes so large and includes so many different types of women that it is best described as a village-sized household family modeled on the bonds between the surrogate sisters and mothers who establish it. The very scope of Millenium Hall's operations makes it an unwieldy subject for a novel. Scott's approach to solving this narrative challenge is to alternate between the frame narrative describing Millenium Hall and inset stories about its founders. The frame narrative is closer to a utopia than a realistic novel, describing the organization's rules, recruiting strategies, economic operations, and mission statement. In contrast, the embedded personal narratives resemble courtship novels, but with mostly unhappy endings. They invoke plot conventions made familiar to readers by Richardson and other contemporaneous novelists. Despite *Millenium Hall*'s narrative idiosyncrasies, it relies heavily on well-established literary conventions, surrogate families most prominent among them.

Sarah Scott's life likely inspired her depiction of surrogate families in *Millenium Hall*. Although she married, she separated from her husband within a year and lived with her friend, Lady Barbara Montagu. Although the reasons for her separation are unclear, she obviously found married life uncongenial. Over the course of her adult life Scott belonged to numerous household families as she and

Lady Barbara moved house, traveled, and visited together. As Ann Van Sant observes, Scott "routinely (even insistently)" called her "co-resident groups 'families.'"[18] Given these experiences, it is not surprising that *Millenium Hall* focuses on all-female surrogate families. Scott's commitment to female communities and friendship also derives from her connection to her sister and longtime correspondent, the famous bluestocking Elizabeth Montagu. As Eve Bannet observes, both sisters "felt happiest in the company of other women" and valued "reciprocal, supportive friendships between women."[19]

The frame narrative of *Millenium Hall* concentrates on its large-scale economic and social effects on the surrounding community. These sections are primarily expository. They are told from the perspective of a male narrator who finds Millenium Hall by accident when he seeks shelter from a storm. His awed depiction of a perfect society belongs to the tradition of utopian writing.[20] In minute detail, the narrator describes the inhabitants' daily activities and records his guide's explanations of how the Hall is governed and funded. David Oakleaf's economic analysis suggests this commune is so vast that its founders "preside over combined resources" of approximately 100,000 pounds.[21] It uses these extraordinary means to help women of every rank at every stage of life and income level. The founders educate, raise, and give marriage portions to poor young women, provide a haven for disabled and disfigured women, and generate well-paid employment for local women. While these functions are all important, the organization of the Hall is most germane to my inquiry. Specifically, Millenium Hall is a household family made up of smaller surrogate families and headed up by the founders whose stories Scott portrays in *Millenium Hall*'s narrative sections. The whole organization can be understood as a self-contained and self-supporting surrogate family writ large. It resembles the famous image of Hobbes's leviathan, a creature whole of itself but made up of its individual members. The difference is that in Millenium Hall's case, all these members are mothers, daughters, and sisters.

The founders of Millenium Hall form their own discrete surrogate family, which becomes the basis for the organization as a whole. Scott embeds their stories inside the utopian frame narrative. Nicolle Jordan describes these sections as "four framed narratives delineating the circumstances that led the principal members to found this exclusive women's community."[22] These stories are essentially novellas, incorporating numerous conventions of courtship plots, many of them made popular by Richardson's novels.[23] However, they conclude differently than courtship novels. Surrogate families in these narratives are not a means to the end of marriage, as they are in Richardson's novels, nor are they a prize that accompanies the right marriage, as Cecilia's is in *Cecilia*. Instead, they take the place of marriage as the end point in the founders' stories. Scott relegates courtship, marriage, and family problems to the status of obstacles that must be overcome in order to achieve an ideal surrogate family.

Many aspects of the founders' stories, including their uniformly absent or malicious parents, are indistinguishable from typical courtship novels. Jordan describes these accounts of their lives as "dizzyingly complex tales of orphanhood, mother/daughter separation at birth," and "paternal weakness or turpitude."[24] All their stories involve faulty parents, but as Caroline Gonda notes, Louisa's and Mrs. Morgan's feature the most glaring examples of the "miseries of filial dependence."[25] Louisa is raised by an aunt who dies while she is still young, leaving her homeless, penniless, and alone in the world. When a stranger adopts her, seemingly out of compassion, she marvels at her surrogate father's generosity. This unexpected kindness, were it really motivated by altruism, would counter Scott's theme of parental failure. However, as Louisa finds after she enters adolescence, this "tender affection from one bound to her by no paternal ties" is not fatherly at all.[26] He is grooming her to become his mistress. After he fortuitously dies, this "second father" leaves her as "destitute . . . as he found her" (100). She must support herself by becoming a paid companion and servant until she discovers her real mother.

Morgan, Louisa's surrogate sister from boarding school, embarks on life in seemingly much better circumstances. While her mother dies when she is young, she still has a father and stepmother. However, her father is so easily manipulated by his new wife that he exiles Louisa to boarding school and then forces her, in a Clarissa-like plot, to marry the Solmes-like Mr. Morgan. Their marriage is predictably miserable. The other founders' stories also involve defective or missing parents. Overall, their experiences are emblematic of the difficulties all genteel women face when their families fail to protect them. However, for Scott this vulnerability does not end with marriage. Marriage to an unsuitable husband can be just as bad as childhood with the wrong parents or no parents at all. Instead, the founders' travails justify the need for an all-female society such as Millenium Hall.

Repugnant suitors are stock characters in courtship novels, and the founders' stories in *Millenium Hall* are no exception; the difference is that in most novels they are foils for paragons like Lord Orville or Sir Charles, but in *Millenium Hall* they are the only eligible men available. James Cruise describes the men in the founders' narratives as "dissimulating, malicious, unprincipled, and whimsical."[27] Mangano similarly characterizes them as "sexual predators, tyrannical spouses, and inconsistent suitors."[28] Given this undesirable group of potential husbands, the marriages in *Millenium Hall* are, unsurprisingly, joyless. They resemble the punishments women suffer for immorality in punitive subplots like Miss Forward's in *The History of Miss Betsy Thoughtless*. However, the founders of Millenium Hall are as virtuous as heroines like Pamela, Harriet, and Evelina, who are rewarded with blissful domesticity.

Far from being blissful, Morgan's marriage to her Solmes-like husband is hardly tolerable. He forces her to move with him to the country where she is isolated and tyrannized by his sister. He does not allow her to help the poor or see Louisa. Only on his deathbed does he show any appreciation for his long-suffering wife. Louisa seems to have better prospects. She loves a man worthy of her affection. However, he becomes so distraught when his mother forbids their marriage that he commits suicide by allowing himself to be mortally wounded in combat. On his deathbed he receives a letter granting permission for his marriage. As he writes to Louisa, his "impetuous passions" and "short-sighted reason" have made it impossible for him to take advantage of this auspicious turn of events (153). Other founders' narratives focus on the clumsy attempts of generic rakes to seduce them. Even good suitors turn out to have fatal flaws in *Millenium Hall*. For example, Harriot Trentham's fiancé is a brother figure. Surrogate brotherhood is a propitious model for companionate marriage. However, he becomes captivated by a "compleat coquet, capricious and fantastical" (231). He follows his heart and quickly regrets his poor decision, but only after it is too late. There is one blameless male character in all of the founders' narratives: a scholar who tutors Louisa and Morgan at boarding school. He plays a negligible role. His only purpose seems to be for Scott to avoid the charge of unmitigated misanthropy. However, he is such a nonentity that he is best understood as an exception that proves the rule of men's depravity.

Given this paucity of men worthy of marrying, it makes sense that marriage in Scott's novel is an obstacle to be got over rather than an objective to achieve. Her version of a happy ending is becoming a member of Millenium Hall's extended surrogate family. Louisa and Morgan's surrogate sisterhood becomes the basis for the family-like connections between all the women who choose to live there. Mr. Morgan's deathbed is the unlikely site of their reunion. They rekindle their devotion to one another as they tend to him (he is unconscious so he cannot evict Louisa from his bedside) over the course of several months. As Scott writes, their "joy" in being together again is "not to be imagined by any heart" not capable of feeling the "delicate sensations of friendship" (158).

Once her husband dies, Morgan is wealthy (as is Louisa) and at liberty to choose how and with whom she wishes to live. Together, Louisa and Morgan design and enact their conception of a happy ending. Their plan for Millenium Hall allows them to remain together for the rest of their lives and enjoy a "way of life where all their satisfactions might be rational" (159). They revise the patriarchal hierarchy of conventional household families by structuring Millenium Hall as a commune. Realizing that property rights are what allowed their families and husbands to subjugate them in the past, they do away with them. The desire to own things, like the desire to control others, is in their view "broke[n] down by true friendship" (93). In a surrogate family with no fathers, brothers, or sons, there is no need to perpetuate any version of primogeniture. These sisters, mothers, and daughters will share "all property" in "one undistinguished common" (93).

Louisa and Morgan's sisterly spirit extends outward to all the inhabitants of and community surrounding Millenium Hall. However, Scott specifies that sisterly feelings have nothing to do with actual kinship. For most of the women who live there, their Millenium Hall sisterhood compensates for the failure of kinship. Even the cottagers who presumably live with their own nuclear families embrace this view. As one of them tells the narrator, "we [the women tenants] love one another like sisters, or indeed better, for I often see such quarrel" (67). Although Scott was close to her sister Elizabeth, she had little regard for lineage in general. In one of her letters, she observes "I have not that regard to blood some good people have, perhaps it may be that I have so drained my Veins that certainly there does not remain in my whole body one drop of what I brought into the World with me, therefore I feel little from Relationship, my affection is proportioned to the merits and behavior of my kindred."[29] The frame narrative of *Millenium Hall* also suggests that kinship is far less important than being kindred spirits. The narrator discovers early in the novel that his guide at Millenium Hall is "not only an old acquaintance, but a near relation" (61). The passage of time and their changed appearances have "almost effaced" them from the "other's memory" (61). They are both pleased and surprised to discover this relationship, but nothing more. Her connection to her surrogate sisters at Millenium Hall is the basis for her true family.

Tom Jones and *Millenium Hall* overlap in suggestive ways, even though their protagonists occupy different subject positions in their surrogate families based on their gender. As a man, even without giving any particular thought to it, Tom influences the families he joins more than they influence him. While he uses his masculine position of authority to do good, Scott implies in *Millenium Hall* that men like Tom are, at best, rare, and more likely nonexistent. The founders of Millenium Hall are all women, but as heads of their household family they also occupy a masculine position. As Dorice Elliott observes, they "are not wives or mothers," although many of them were before they founded the Hall.[30] Julie McGonegal argues that as a group they "perform" the "part of [a] paternal figure."[31] They establish the Hall's rules, contribute the seed money for it, inspect the houses and finances of their tenants, and provide "poor marriageable women . . . with dowries" and teach them "the codes of female conduct."[32] These are actions traditionally reserved for men. However, because they are women, they "father" differently. They act as patriarchs are ideally supposed to do, but rarely do, at least in novels. They take full responsibility for the social, intellectual, and physical health of their household members and the surrounding community. According to Scott, the perfect surrogate father, ironically, turns out to be a woman.

Completing a lengthy project such as this is at once a melancholy and celebratory experience. Writing these acknowledgments reminds me how much my ability to get to this point is due to the support of all the friends, family members, and colleagues who helped me along the way. Indeed, I owe an immense debt of gratitude to my own surrogate families from Emory University and Boise State University (BSU), and particularly to my surrogate sisters.

The idea for this project emerged in its earliest form during graduate school at Emory. I developed the initial idea of surrogate families with guidance from my dissertation advisor, John Sitter. While the idea of surrogate families was based on the plots of eighteenth-century novels, my own life showed me on a daily basis that surrogate sisters were far from an anachronism. I could not have made it through my dissertation without my surrogate sisters: Nikki Graves, Elizabeth Rackley Williams, and Margaret Koehler (who will always be Margie to me). We revised together, laughed together, wore bridesmaids' dresses in one another's weddings, were hooded together, and cried in our hearty burgundy at Jaggers together. Our misadventures are some of my best memories of that period of my life.

I am also thankful to my colleagues in the Boise State University English Department for helping me navigate the process of writing and revising this book. I sometimes think that if it weren't for my former MA student, BSU colleague, and good friend Jarrod Hurlbert I might be the only person who willingly read *Pamela* (much less *Pamela II*) in Idaho. He helped me revise every chapter of this book and suggested I work with Kate Parker from Bucknell University Press once I was ready to submit a book proposal. I also thank Matt Hansen and Mac Test for their help with revisions and practical suggestions about how to get on with this process when I got bogged down in details. Most importantly, I thank my surrogate sister Samantha Harvey, who has seen me at my best and worst, often in the same evening. In the true spirit of British literature, she has inspired me to keep calm and carry on with my research all through COVID-19 and the other challenges midlife and midcareer have thrown at us.

Other colleagues have inspired and advised me at American Society for Eighteenth-Century Studies (ASECS) conferences throughout the years. I am particularly thankful to Kit Kincade, Sharon Alker, Katherine Ellison, Sheila

Hwang, Andreas Mueller, Ben Pauley, Teri Doerksen, Chris Vilmar, Elaine Bander, and Hilary Havens. I appreciate their friendship and admire their scholarship.

I am thankful to everyone who has helped me at Bucknell University Press. The director and editors have been an absolute dream to work with throughout the publication process. Kate Parker helped me get my project off the ground and read my first draft. Suzanne Guiod was encouraging and helpful at every stage of the process. My readers gave me excellent advice about how to revise the initial manuscript. Miriam Wallace helped me through the book proposal and contract process. Pam Dailey has helped me to the finish line. Their guidance has made this process a great experience.

Finally, I thank my family for their support throughout my education and career. My husband Robert Adelson met me when surrogate families were an inchoate idea. Years later, he proofread each chapter before I sent the manuscript to Bucknell for final review. I appreciate his support throughout my career. He moved out west to Boise so I could accept a position at BSU and has become a cherished member of the Campbell family. He cooks amazing dinners for my mom, sister, brother-in-law, son, and nephews every Sunday. My son Henry inspires me with his energy and determination. Finally, thank you to my mother Anita for modeling a strong work ethic, professional integrity, and devotion to family every day of her life. She has always supported my ambitions and showed me how to keep working at something regardless of the obstacles.

An earlier version of a portion of chapter 1 appeared as "Strictly Business: Marriage, Motherhood, and Surrogate Families as Entrepreneurial Ventures in *Moll Flanders*," in *Studies in Eighteenth-Century Culture* 43 (2014): 51–68, Johns Hopkins University Press, © 2014 and is reprinted with contractual permission.

INTRODUCTION

1. Naomi Tadmor, *Family and Friends in Eighteenth-Century England: Household, Kinship, and Patronage* (New York: Cambridge University Press, 2001); Ruth Perry, *Novel Relations: The Transformation of Kinship in English Literature and Culture 1748–1818* (Cambridge: Cambridge University Press, 2004).
2. Tadmor, *Family and Friends*, 144–145.
3. Although friendship does not constitute a family model, Tadmor observes that occasionally close friends or important business associates were also referred to as members of lineage families. Tadmor characterizes the use of the "language of kinship" by close friends to refer to one another in letters as a strategy for enforcing family-like obligations on correspondents. Tadmor, *Family and Friends*, 140. Similarly, historian Diana O'Hara uses the term "fictive kin" to refer to unrelated but closely connected individuals who often facilitated and witnessed betrothals and marriages in Tudor England. She argues that the bonds of "fictive kinship" were "formally recognized by the community in an act of ritual acceptance." Diana O'Hara, *Courtship and Constraint: Rethinking the Making of Marriage in Tudor England* (Manchester: Manchester University Press, 2000), 39. Sociologists Charles Ibsen and Patricia Klobus note that it was still common in twentieth-century America to honor close family friends by calling them *uncle* or *aunt*. Charles A. Ibsen, and Patricia Klobus, "Fictive Kin Term Use and Social Relationships: Alternative Interpretations," *Journal of Marriage and the Family* 34, no. 4 (1972): 617.
4. Tadmor, *Friends and Family*, 3. See also Michael McKeon, *The Secret History of Domesticity: Public, Private, and the Division of Knowledge* (Baltimore: Johns Hopkins University Press, 2005), 120–121.
5. Tadmor, *Family and Friends*, 22.
6. Tadmor specifies the importance of household families in Samuel Richardson's *Pamela* and Eliza Haywood's *The History of Miss Betsy Thoughtless*. Tadmor, *Family and Friends*, 47–48.
7. Perry, *Novel Relations*, 2.
8. Perry, *Novel Relations*, 2.
9. Tadmor, *Friends and Family*, 22.
10. Cheryl L. Nixon, *The Orphan in Eighteenth-Century Law and Literature: Estate, Blood and Body* (Burlington: Ashgate Press, 2011), 26.
11. Ann Van Sant, "Historicizing Domestic Relations: Sarah Scott's Use of the 'Household Family,'" *Eighteenth-Century Fiction* 17, no. 3 (2005): 379.
12. William Thackeray, *Vanity Fair: A Novel Without a Hero*, ed. Helen Small (New York: Oxford University Press, 2015), 34.
13. Van Sant, "Historicizing," 383.
14. Irene Brown, "Domesticity, Feminism, and Friendship: Female Aristocratic Culture and Marriage in England, 1660–1760," *Journal of Family History* 7 (1982): 219.
15. Samuel Richardson, *Sir Charles Grandison*, ed. Jocelyn Harris, 7 vols. (New York: Oxford University Press, 1972), 5: 514. Hereafter cited parenthetically.
16. Samuel Richardson, *Clarissa; Or the History of a Young Lady*, ed. Angus Ross (New York: Penguin Books, 1985), 986. Hereafter cited parenthetically.

17. Several critics use some version of the term *surrogate families*, especially in relation to Eliza Haywood's, Frances Burney's, and Ann Radcliffe's novels. See Cheryl Nixon, "The Surrogate Family Plot in the Annesley Case and *Memoirs of an Unfortunate Young Nobleman*," *The Eighteenth-Century Novel* 3 (2003): 4, 11; Emily Patterson, "Family and Pilgrimage Themes in Burney's *Evelina*," *New Rambler* 18 (1977): 45; Susan Greenfield, *Mothering Daughters: Novels and the Politics of Family Romance, Frances Burney to Jane Austen* (Detroit: Wayne State University Press, 2002); David Durant, "Ann Radcliffe and the Conservative Gothic," *Studies in English Literature* 22, no. 3 (1982): 519–530; John Richetti, "The Family, Sex, and Marriage in Defoe's *Moll Flanders* and *Roxana*," *Studies in the Literary Imagination* 15, no. 2 (1982): 19; and Amy J. Pawl, "'And What Other Name May I Claim?': Names and Their Owners in Frances Burney's *Evelina*," *Eighteenth-Century Fiction* 3, no. 4 (1991): 283–299.

18. Richetti, "The Family, Sex, and Marriage," 19.

19. Nixon, *The Orphan*, 18. Nixon also asserts that "foster-parents, guardians, and tutors . . . recreate" a "sort of family—whether negative or positive—for the family-less protagonist" (Nixon, *The Orphan*, 1).

20. Janet M. Todd, *Women's Friendship in Literature: The Eighteenth-Century Novel in England and France* (New York: Columbia University Press, 1980), 57n35.

21. Mark Kinkead-Weekes claims that "Richardson's ideal was the extension of the family into a model of community, and the 'love' at the centre looked through 'courtship' to an extended brotherhood, sisterhood, fatherhood and childhood of the heart." Mark Kinkead-Weekes, *Samuel Richardson, Dramatic Novelist* (Ithaca: Cornell University Press, 1973), 282. To my knowledge, Richardson does not use the specific term "family of the heart" in *Sir Charles Grandison*, but he uses close approximations of it such as "family of love" and "family of harmony and love" (Richardson, *Sir Charles Grandison*, 1: 133, 3: 201).

22. Jacqueline Elaine Lawson, *Domestic Misconduct in the Novels of Defoe, Richardson, and Fielding* (Lewiston: Edwin Mellen Press, 1994), 35.

23. Lawson, *Domestic Misconduct*, 107. Several other scholars have noted the presence of substitute family members in *Clarissa* and *Sir Charles Grandison*. See Betty A. Schellenberg, *The Conversational Circle: Re-reading the English Novel, 1740–1775* (Lexington: University Press of Kentucky, 1996), 59; Rebecca Anne Barr, "Richardson's *Sir Charles Grandison* and the Symptoms of Subjectivity," *Eighteenth Century: Theory And Interpretation* 51, no. 4 (2010): 401–402; Kathleen M. Oliver, *Samuel Richardson, Dress, and Discourse* (Basingstoke: Palgrave Macmillan, 2008), 97; Alex Eric Hernandez, "Tragedy and the Economics of Providence in Richardson's *Clarissa*," *Eighteenth-Century Fiction* 22, no. 4 (2010): 620; Ewha Chung, *Samuel Richardson's New Nation: Paragons of the Domestic Sphere and "Native" Virtue* (New York: Peter Lang Publishing, 1998), 70; and Katherine Binhammer, "Knowing Love: The Epistemology of *Clarissa*," *ELH* 74, no. 4 (2007): 871.

24. Van Sant, "Historicizing," 2; Terri Nickel, "'Ingenious Torment': Incest, Family, and the Structure of Community in the Work of Sarah Fielding," *The Eighteenth Century: Theory and Interpretation* 36, no. 3 (1995): 239, 237.

25. Jennifer Golightly, *The Family, Marriage, and Radicalism in British Women's Novels of the 1790s: Public Affection and Private Affliction* (Lewisburg: Bucknell University Press, 2012), 98. I focus exclusively on British fiction, but that does not mean the device of surrogate families was confined to England. According to Ruth Thomas it spread from England to the continent, appearing as in Madame Riccoboni's French novels and becoming the subject of an entire novel with Johann Goethe's *Elective Affinities* (1809). Ruth Thomas, "'Ma Soeur, Mon Amie': Friends as Family in Madame Riccoboni's Fiction," *New Perspectives on the Eighteenth Century* 5, no. 1 (2008): 13–19.

26. Linda Bree, *Sarah Fielding* (New York: Twayne Publishers, 1996), 32.

27. Bree, *Sarah Fielding*, 32.

28. Helena Kelly, *Jane Austen: The Secret Radical* (New York: Knopf, 2017), 31.

29. T.G.A. Nelson, *Children, Parents, and the Rise of the Novel* (Newark: University of Delaware Press, 1995), 169.

30. See Susan Okin, "Patriarchy and Married Women's Property in England: Questions on Some Current Views," *Eighteenth-Century Studies* 17, no. 2 (1983–1984): 121; Christopher Flint, *Family Fictions: Narrative and Domestic Relations in Britain, 1688–1798* (Stanford: Stanford University Press, 1998), 233; Alan Macfarlane, *Marriage and Love in England: Modes of Reproduction 1300–1840* (Oxford: Basil Blackwell Ltd., 1986), 140; and Randolph Trumbach, *The Rise of the Egalitarian Family: Aristocratic Kinship and Domestic Relations in Eighteenth-Century England* (New York: Academic Press, 1978), 94. The gradual shift toward increasing choice in marriage does not mean that women had unlimited autonomy when it came to selecting a spouse. Katharine Rogers argues that novelists often exaggerate women's independence during courtship. She writes that female protagonists "usually enjoyed freedom real women never had," including "freedom of choice" among several desirable men and "no obligation to observe parents' wishes." Katharine Rogers, *Feminism in Eighteenth-Century England* (Urbana: University of Illinois Press, 1982), 150.

31. Tadmor, *Family and Friends*, 4–6.

32. For Lawrence Stone's definition of companionate marriage as a match made for the purposes of "emotional satisfaction" rather than "ambition for increased income or status," see Lawrence Stone, *The Family, Sex, and Marriage in England 1500–1800* (New York: Harper and Row, 1977), 217. More recently, Laura Thomason argues companionate marriage became a means for eighteenth-century women writers to argue against the sort of mercenary and dynastic matches their families proposed for them. Laura E. Thomason, *The Matrimonial Trap: Eighteenth-Century Women Writers Redefine Marriage* (Lewisburg: Bucknell University Press, 2014), 1–17. Wendy Jones further argues in relation to *Sir Charles Grandison* that Richardson ultimately proposed "sentimental love," or attraction inspired by merit, as an alternative to the implied "prudence and interest" permitted by the concept of companionate marriage. Wendy Jones, "The Dialectic of Love in *Sir Charles Grandison*," in *Passion and Virtue: Essays on the Novels of Samuel Richardson*, ed. David Blewett (Toronto: University of Toronto Press, 2001), 309.

33. Amanda Vickery, *The Gentleman's Daughter: Women's Lives in Georgian England* (New Haven: Yale University Press, 1998), 41.

34. Stone, *The Family, Sex, and Marriage*, 214.

35. Vickery, *The Gentleman's Daughter*, 41.

36. Perry, *Novel Relations*, 5.

37. See also Stephen Parker, *Informal Marriage, Cohabitation and the Law, 1750–1989* (New York: Palgrave Macmillan, 1990), 34–36. He claims that cultural anxieties about marital choice manfisted themselves as a "moral panic over clandestine marriages" apparent in literature, the law, and other forms of public discourse. Novels, as he further notes, "abounded with references to secret weddings," providing strong evidence that authors perceived these threats to be material and immediate. Parker, *Informal Marriage*, 34.

38. Helen Thompson, *Ingenuous Subjection: Compliance and Power in the Eighteenth-Century Domestic Novel* (Philadelphia: University of Pennsylvania Press, 2005), 12.

39. Vickery, *Gentleman's Daughter*, 71.

40. Vickery, *Gentleman's Daughter*, 71.

41. Qtd. in Vickery, *Gentleman's Daughter*, 71.

42. Thompson, *Ingenuous Subjection*, 12.

43. It is true that, as Patricia Meyer Spacks points out, for the most part we "can only surmise . . . what it would have felt like to read novels when they were still in the process of defining their shape for the first time." Patricia Meyer Spacks, *Novel Beginnings: Experiments in Eighteenth-Century English Fiction* (New Haven: Yale University Press, 2006), 24. However, the numerous letters Richardson received from his readers describing how deeply they sympathized with Clarissa and Harriet suggest some eighteenth-century novels encouraged

the sort of close identification between reader and fictional protagonists often associated with contemporary fiction.

44. Nixon, *The Orphan*, 26.

45. Flint, *Family Fictions*, 6.

46. Mona Scheuermann, "Redefining the Filial Tie: Eighteenth-Century English Novelists from Brooks to Bage," *Etudes Anglaises, Grande-Bretagne, Etas-Unis* 37, no. 4 (1984): 386.

47. Margaret J. M. Ezell, *Writing Women's Literary History* (Baltimore, Johns Hopkins University Press, 1993); Susan Staves, *A Literary History of Women's Writing in Britain, 1660–1789* (Cambridge: Cambridge University Press, 2006); Toni Bowers, *The Politics of Motherhood: British Writing and Culture 1680–1760* (Cambridge: Cambridge University Press, 1996); Ellen Pollak, *Incest and the English Novel, 1684–1814* (Baltimore: Johns Hopkins University Press, 2003); Michael McKeon, *The Origins of the English Novel, 1600–1740* (Baltimore: Johns Hopkins University Press,1987). Influential studies of marriage, family, and the novel attest not only to the interconnectedness of inquiries about marriage and family, but also to the significant role literature plays in engaging with both. Some of the most influential of these studies are Laura Thomason's *The Matrimonial Trap: Eighteenth-Century Writers Redefine Marriage*; Jennifer Golightly's *The Family, Marriage, and Radicalism in British Women's Novels of the 1790s: Public Affection and Private Affliction*; Cheryl Nixon's *The Orphan in Eighteenth-Century Law and Literature: Estate, Blood and Body*; Chris Roulston's *Narrating Marriage in Eighteenth-Century England and France* (Farnham: Ashgate Press, 2010); Ruth Perry's *Novel Relations: The Transformation of Kinship in English Literature and Culture, 1748–1818*; Naomi Tadmor's *Family and Friends in Eighteenth-Century England: Household, Kinship, and Patronage*; Christopher Flint's *Family Fictions: Narrative and Domestic Relations in Britain, 1688–1789*; and, of course, Lawrence Stone's foundational study of eighteenth-century English marriage and family, *The Family, Sex, and Marriage in England, 1500–1800*. Regardless of their individual conclusions, these authors all agree about the central role novels play in experimenting with the possible outcomes of historical changes favoring increasing marital choice for young people.

48. Leonore Davidoff and Catherine Hall, *Family Fortunes: Men and Women of the English Middle Class 1780–1850* (Chicago: University of Chicago Press, 1987); Margaret R. Hunt, *The Middling Sort: Commerce, Gender, and the Family in England 1680–1780* (Berkeley: University of California Press, 1996); and Amanda Vickery, *Gentleman's Daughter*.

49. Carol Sherman, *The Family Crucible in Eighteenth-Century Literature* (Aldershot: Ashgate Publishing, 2005), 2–3.

50. Paula Backscheider, "The Novel's Gendered Space," in *Revising Women: Eighteenth-Century "Women's Fiction" and Social Engagement*, ed. Paula Backscheider (Baltimore: Johns Hopkins University Press, 2000), 21.

51. George E. Haggerty, "'Romantic Friendship' and Patriarchal Narrative in Sarah Scott's *Millenium Hall*," *Genders* 13 (1992): 108.

52. Nixon, *The Orphan*, 15.

53. David B. Paxman, "Imagining the Child: Bad Parents in the Mid-Eighteenth-Century English Novel," *Journal for Eighteenth-Century Studies* 38, no. 1 (2015): 137.

54. Christine Van Boheemen, *The Novel as Family Romance: Language, Gender, and Authority from Fielding to Joyce* (Ithaca: Cornell University Press, 1987), 46.

55. The numerous orphans who populate eighteenth-century fiction suggest a high level of cultural anxiety about a lack of familial protection and guidance for young people. As Lawson asserts, fictional depictions of family became a "locus and repository of the stresses and the strains of widespread cultural change." Lawson, *Domestic Misconduct*, 108. I would add that portrayals of a lack of family may be similarly interpreted. Orphaned protagonists raise questions, as Cheryl Nixon argues, about "what defines the family" and what "needs, urges, demands, and desires . . . connect unrelated individuals as family." Nixon, *The Orphan*, 119.

56. Paxman, "Imagining the Child," 137.

57. Frances Burney, *Evelina: Or the History of a Young Lady's Entrance into the World*, ed. Edward A. Bloom (New York: Oxford University Press, 2002), 353.
58. Paula R. Backscheider, "The Rise of Gender as a Political Category," in *Revising Women: Eighteenth-Century "Women's Fiction" and Social Engagement*, ed. Paula Backscheider (Baltimore: Johns Hopkins University Press, 2000), 57.
59. Paxman, "Imagining the Child," 139.

CHAPTER 1 — JUST BUSINESS

Sections of this chapter previously appeared in "Strictly Business: Marriage, Motherhood, and Surrogate Families as Entrepreneurial Ventures in *Moll Flanders*," *Studies in Eighteenth-Century Culture* 43 (2014): 51–68.

1. John Richetti, "The Family, Sex, and Marriage in Defoe's *Moll Flanders* and *Roxana*," *Studies in the Literary Imagination* 15, no. 2 (1982): 19.
2. Brean Hammond specifically addresses Defoe's relationship to the picaresque tradition. He argues that Defoe "selected . . . strands" of the picaresque tradition that suited his aims, while also incorporating "genres and modes of writing very different from it and even alien to it, such as spiritual autobiography, conduct manuals and economic pamphlets." Brean Hammond, "Defoe and the Picaresque," in *The Picaresque Novel in Western Literature: from the Sixteenth Century to the Neopicaresque*, ed. J. A. Garrido (Cambridge: Cambridge University Press, 2015), 149. See also Tina Kuhlisch, "The Ambivalent Rogue: Moll Flanders as Modern Picara," in *Rogues in Early Modern Culture*, eds. Craig Dionne and Steve Mentz (Ann Arbor: University of Michigan Press, 2004), 337–360.
3. David Blewett, "Changing Attitudes Toward Marriage in the Time of Defoe: The Case of *Moll Flanders*," *Huntington Library Quarterly* 44, no. 2 (1981): 82–83.
4. Lawrence Stone, *The Family, Sex, and Marriage in England 1500–1800* (New York: Harper and Row, 1977), 217.
5. Stone, *The Family, Sex, and Marriage*, 217.
6. Laura A. Curtis, "A Case Study of Defoe's Domestic Conduct Manuals Suggested by *The Family, Sex and Marriage in England, 1500–1800*," *Studies in Eighteenth-Century Culture* 10 (1981): 414.
7. Paula R. Backscheider, "Defoe's Prodigal Sons," *Studies in the Literary Imagination* 15, no. 2 (1982): 13.
8. Hal Gladfelder, "Defoe and Criminal Fiction," in *The Cambridge Companion to Daniel Defoe*, ed. John Richetti (Cambridge: Cambridge University Press, 2008), 78.
9. Daniel Defoe, *The Fortunes and Misfortunes of the Famous Moll Flanders*, in *The Novels of Daniel Defoe*, vol. 6, ed. Liz Bellamy, 10 vols. (London: Pickering & Chatto, 2008–2009), 116. Hereafter cited parenthetically.
10. Klaus Peter Jochum, "Defoe's Children," in *Fashioning Childhood in the Eighteenth Century: Age and Identity*, ed. Anja Muller (Burlington: Ashgate, 2006), 158.
11. Ellen Pollak, "Gender and Fiction in *Moll Flanders* and *Roxana*," in *The Cambridge Companion to Daniel Defoe*, ed. John Richetti (Cambridge: Cambridge University Press, 2008), 150.
12. Pollak, "Gender and Fiction," 150.
13. Toni Bowers, "'I Wou'd Not Murder My Child': Maternity and the Necessity of Infanticide in Two Novels by Daniel Defoe," in *Writing British Infanticide: Child-Murder, Gender, and Print, 1722–1859*, ed. Jennifer Thorn (Newark: University of Delaware Press, 2003), 173.
14. Ann Louise Kibbie, "Monstrous Generation: The Birth of Capital in Defoe's *Moll Flanders* and *Roxana*," *PMLA* 110, no. 5 (1995): 1024.
15. Spiro Peterson, "The Matrimonial Theme of Defoe's *Roxana*," *PMLA* 70, no. 1 (1955): 167.
16. Michael Shinagel, *Daniel Defoe and Middle-Class Gentility* (Cambridge: Harvard University Press, 1968), 184; Jacqueline Elaine Lawson, *Domestic Misconduct in the Novels of Defoe, Richardson, and Fielding* (Lewiston: Edwin Mellen Press, 1994), 56.

17. Bowers, "'I Wou'd Not Murder My Child,'" 182.
18. Richetti claims Moll and Roxana demonstrate "coldness" and "even . . . contempt for sexuality." Richetti, "The Family, Sex, and Marriage," 24.
19. Srividhya Swaminathan, "Defoe's Alternative Conduct Manual: Survival Strategies and Female Networks in *Moll Flanders*," *Eighteenth-Century Fiction* 15, no. 2 (2003): 185–206.
20. Marilyn Francus, "'A-Killing Their Children with Safety': Maternal Identity and Transgression in Swift and Defoe," in *Lewd and Notorious: Female Transgression and the Eighteenth Century*, ed. Katharine Kittredge (Ann Arbor: University of Michigan Press, 2003), 270.
21. Kuhlisch, "The Ambivalent Rogue," 344.
22. The observation that Moll is motivated by money, not love, is common in Defoe scholarship. For example, Jacques Sohier argues that Moll is a Machiavellian woman, a "materialist" who "gives precedence to security, status, and wealth over affection." Jacques Sohier, "Moll Flanders and the Rise of the Complete Gentlewoman-Tradeswoman," *The Eighteenth-Century Novel* 2 (2002): 16. This is one of the primary reasons, according to Sohier, that she refuses to confide even in her "close kin and loved ones." Sohier, "Moll Flanders and the Rise of the Complete Gentlewoman-Tradeswoman," 18.
23. James Thompson, *Models of Value: Eighteenth-Century Political Economy and the Novel* (Durham: Duke University Press, 1996), 103.
24. Shirlene Mason, *Daniel Defoe and the Status of Women* (Vermont: Eden Press, 1978), 97.
25. Juliet McMaster, "The Equation of Love and Money in *Moll Flanders*," *Studies in the Novel* 2 (1970): 132.
26. W. Austin Flanders, *Structures of Experience: History, Society, and Personal Life in the Eighteenth-Century Novel* (Columbia: University of South Carolina Press, 1984), 120.
27. There are extensive debates about how to appropriately refer to people Moll calls gypsies. I refer to them using Moll's term because she perceives them as members of this group according to its common usage during the eighteenth-century in England.
28. Samuel Johnson, *An Universal Etymological Dictionary of the English Language* (Edinburgh, 1764), 356.
29. See Daniel Defoe, *The Family Instructor. In Three Parts. With a Recommendatory Letter by the Reverend Mr. S. Wright* (London, 1715).
30. Jane Austen, *Emma*, ed. George Justice (New York: Norton, 2012), 48.
31. Melissa Mowry, "Women, Work, Rearguard Politics, and Defoe's *Moll Flanders*," *The Eighteenth Century: Theory and Interpretation* 49, no. 2 (2008): 105.
32. Gladfelder, "Defoe and Criminal Fiction," 77.
33. Blewett, "Changing Attitudes Toward Marriage in the Time of Defoe," 86.
34. Daniel Defoe, *Religious Courtship Abridg'd: Being Historical Discourses on the Necessity of Marrying Religious Husbands and Wives Only* (London, 1734), iv.
35. Daniel Defoe, *Conjugal Lewdness: Or, Matrimonial Whoredom* (London, 1727), 119.
36. Blewett, "Changing Attitudes Toward Marriage in the Time of Defoe," 87.
37. Mona Scheuermann, "An Income of One's Own: Women and Money in *Moll Flanders* and *Roxana*," *Durham University Journal* 80, no. 2 (1988): 225.
38. David Wallace Spielman, "The Value of Money in *Robinson Crusoe, Moll Flanders*, and *Roxana*," *Modern Language Review* 107, no. 1 (2012): 79.
39. Ashley Marshall, "Did Defoe Write *Moll Flanders* and *Roxana*?" *Philological Quarterly* 89, nos. 2–3 (2010): 211. Mark Vareschi speculates that the changes made to abridgements and adaptations of *Moll Flanders* and *Roxana* "may have been intended to . . . make the novels ideologically match the more widely known Defoe works like *Robinson Crusoe* and *The Family Instructor*." Mark Vareschi, "Attribution and Reception: The Case of Defoe and the Circulating Library," *Eighteenth-Century Life* 36, no. 2 (2012): 39–40.
40. Michael Shinagel, "The Maternal Theme in *Moll Flanders*: Craft and Character," *Cornell Library Journal* 7 (1969): 8; Jochum, "Defoe's Children," 161.

41. David B. Paxman, "Imagining the Child: Bad Parents in the Mid-Eighteenth-Century English Novel," *Journal for Eighteenth-Century Studies* 38, no. 1 (2015): 137.
42. Francus, "'A-Killing Their Children with Safety,'" 262.
43. Lois A. Chaber, "Matriarchal Mirror: Women and Capital in *Moll Flanders*," *PMLA* 97, no. 2 (1982): 219.
44. Chaber, "Matriarchal Mirror," 219.
45. Katerina Kitsi-Mitakou, "Whoring, Incest, Duplicity, or the 'Self-Polluting' Erotics of Daniel Defoe's *Moll Flanders*," in *Genealogies of Identity: Interdisciplinary Readings on Sex and Sexuality*, eds. Margaret Breen and Fiona Peters (Amsterdam: Rodopi B. V., 2005), 87.
46. Robert Erickson describes Moll's governess as her "spiritual mother." Robert Erickson, *Mother Midnight: Birth, Sex, and Fate in Eighteenth-Century Fiction* (New York: AMS Press, 1986), 51.
47. I do not think Moll is being ironic here despite the number of children she discards. Rather, to her way of thinking and feeling, Humphry really is her only child because he is the only one who becomes profitable.
48. Daniel Defoe, *The Fortunate Mistress*, in *The Novels of Daniel Defoe*, vol. 9, ed. P. N. Furbank, 10 vols. (London: Pickering & Chatto, 2009), 160. Hereafter cited parenthetically.
49. Lawson, *Domestic Misconduct*, 35.
50. Kibbie, "Monstrous Generation," 1031.
51. Jochum, "Defoe's Children," 167.
52. Terry Castle, "'Amy, Who Knew My Disease': A Psychosexual Pattern in Defoe's *Roxana*," *ELH* 46, no. 1 (1979): 83–84.

CHAPTER 2 — BUILDING A FOUNDATION FOR THE FAMILY OF THE HEART

1. Mark Kinkead-Weekes, *Samuel Richardson, Dramatic Novelist* (Ithaca: Cornell University Press, 1973), 298.
2. Kinkead-Weekes, *Samuel Richardson, Dramatic Novelist*, 282.
3. Kinkead-Weekes's term is a close approximation of Richardson's definition of a surrogate family in *Sir Charles Grandison* as a "family of love" and a "family of harmony and love." Samuel Richardson, *Sir Charles Grandison*, ed. Jocelyn Harris, 7 vols. (New York: Oxford University Press, 1972), 1: 133, 3: 201. Hereafter cited parenthetically. Kinkead-Weekes, *Samuel Richardson, Dramatic Novelist*, 282.
4. Daniel Defoe, *The Fortunes and Misfortunes of the Famous Moll Flanders*, in *The Novels of Daniel Defoe*, vol. 6, ed. Liz Bellamy, 10 vols. (London: Pickering & Chatto, 2008–2009), 116.
5. Samuel Richardson, *Pamela: Or Virtue Rewarded*, in *The Cambridge Edition of the Works of Samuel Richardson*, vol. 2, ed. Albert J. Rivero, 4 vols. (New York: Cambridge University Press, 2011), 9. Hereafter cited parenthetically.
6. Christopher Flint interprets Pamela as a replacement for Mr. B's dead mother. He argues that B attempts to maintain his connection to his mother through Pamela. Christopher Flint, "The Anxiety of Affluence: Family and Class (Dis)order in *Pamela: or Virtue Rewarded*," *Studies in English Literature* 29, no. 3 (1989): 489–551.
7. Naomi Tadmor, "'Family' and 'friend' in *Pamela*: A Case-Study in the History of the Family in Eighteenth-Century England," *Social History* 14, no. 3 (1989): 300.
8. Flint, "The Anxiety of Affluence," 495.
9. Flint, "The Anxiety of Affluence," 502–503.
10. Terry Eagleton, *The Rape of Clarissa: Writing, Sexuality and Class Struggle in Samuel Richardson* (Minneapolis: University of Minnesota Press, 1986), 37.
11. Samuel Richardson, *Pamela in Her Exalted Condition*, in *The Cambridge Edition of the Works of Samuel Richardson*, vol. 3, ed. Albert J. Rivero, 4 vols. (New York: Cambridge University Press, 2011), 29. Hereafter cited parenthetically.

12. Ball argues that this subplot involving Polly Darnford is a "prototype for the three subplots involving Anna Howe and Mr. Hickman in *Clarissa* and Charlotte Grandison and Lord G and Clementina della porretta and the Count of Belvedere in *Grandison*." Donald L. Ball, "*Pamela II*: A Primary Link in Richardson's Development as a Novelist," *Modern Philology* 65, no. 4 (1968): 336.
13. Kinkead-Weeks, *Samuel Richardson, Dramatic Novelist*, 281.
14. Margaret Anne Doody, *A Natural Passion: A Study of the Novels of Samuel Richardson* (Oxford: Clarendon Press, 1974), 67–68. Donald Ball also observes that *Pamela II* "anticipates the large family circle that is the basic social unit in *Grandison*." Ball, "*Pamela II*," 338.
15. Doody, *A Natural Passion*, 81.
16. Sylvia Kasey Marks, *Sir Charles Grandison: The Compleat Conduct Book* (Lewisburg: Bucknell University Press, 1986), 45.

CHAPTER 3 — PERFECTING THE FAMILY OF THE HEART

1. I will hereafter refer to *Pamela in Her Exalted Condition* as *Pamela II*.
2. Samuel Richardson, *Clarissa; Or the History of a Young Lady*, ed. Angus Ross (New York: Penguin Books, 1985), 62. Hereafter cited parenthetically.
3. David Paxman, "Imagining the Child: Bad Parents in the Mid-Eighteenth-Century English Novel," *Journal for Eighteenth-Century Studies* 38, no. 1 (2015): 142.
4. Hina Nazar, "Judging Clarissa's Heart," *ELH* 79, no. 1 (2012): 87.
5. Bonnie Latimer, "'Apprehensions of Controul': The Familial Politics of Marriage, Choice and Consent in *Sir Charles Grandison*," *Journal for Eighteenth-Century Studies* 32, no. 1 (2009): 1.
6. Mark Kinkead-Weekes, *Samuel Richardson, Dramatic Novelist* (Ithaca: Cornell University Press, 1973), 282.
7. Bonnie Latimer, *Making Gender, Culture, and the Self in the Fiction of Samuel Richardson: The Novel Individual* (Burlington: Ashgate Publishing Company, 2013), 79.
8. Latimer, *Making Gender*, 79.
9. Donatella Montini notes that during the "decade from 1742 to 1754 in which Richardson wrote and published his two bulkiest" novels, he also "increased his [overall number of] epistolary exchanges." Donatella Montini, "Language and Letters in Samuel Richardson's Networks," *Journal of Early Modern Studies* 3 (2014): 178.
10. Terry Eagleton, *The Rape of Clarissa: Writing, Sexuality and Class Struggle in Samuel Richardson* (Minneapolis: University of Minnesota Press, 1986), 13.
11. Tom Keymer notes that scholars are increasingly interested in analyzing the effects of the "predominantly female literary circle with which Richardson surrounded himself when *Clarissa* was published and *Grandison* composed and debated" on these novels. Tom Keymer, "Jane Collier, Reader of Richardson, and the Fire Scene in *Clarissa*," in *New Essays on Samuel Richardson*, ed. Albert Rivero (New York: St. Martins Press, 1996), 141.
12. I will refer to Hester Mulso by her married name, Hester Chapone, for the sake of consistency. She became famous as a writer and a bluestocking under her married name. Laura E. Thomason, *The Matrimonial Trap: Eighteenth-Century Writers Redefine Marriage* (Lewisburg: Bucknell University Press, 2014), 68.
13. Eagleton, *The Rape of Clarissa*, 13.
14. Sylvia Kasey Marks, *Sir Charles Grandison: The Compleat Conduct Book* (Lewisburg: Bucknell University Press, 1986), 45.
15. Qtd. in Caroline Gonda, *Reading Daughters' Fictions 1709–1834: Novels and Society from Manley to Edgeworth* (Cambridge: Cambridge University Press, 1996), 86.
16. For example, Richardson asked Anne Dewes, Mary Granville's sister, to adopt him into her seemingly ideal family. Irene Brown, "Domesticity, Feminism, and Friendship: Female Aristocratic Culture and Marriage in England, 1660–1760," *Journal of Family History* 7

(1982): 408. In one of his letters to Sophia Westcomb he describes his relationship to her as "paternal." John Carroll, ed., *Selected Letters of Samuel Richardson* (Oxford: Clarendon Press, 1964), 66.

17. Samuel Richardson, *Pamela in Her Exalted Condition*, in *The Cambridge Edition of the Works and Correspondence of Samuel Richardson*, ed. Albert J. Rivero, 4 vols. (New York: Cambridge University Press, 2011), 3: 31.

18. Sören Hammerschmidt, "Barbauld's Richardson and the Canonization of Personal Character," *Eighteenth-Century Fiction* 25, no. 2 (2012–2013): 441.

19. Qtd. in Keymer, "Jane Collier," 141.

20. Qtd. in Carroll, *Selected Letters of Samuel Richardson*, 65.

21. For a detailed description and analysis of Chapone's *Letters on Filial Obedience* (1750–1751), see Thomason, *The Matrimonial Trap*, 67–84.

22. Qtd. in Carroll, *Selected Letters of Samuel Richardson*, 97.

23. Qtd. in Carroll, *Selected Letters of Samuel Richardson*, 89.

24. Qtd. in Carroll, *Selected Letters of Samuel Richardson*, 144.

25. Qtd. in Carroll, *Selected Letters of Samuel Richardson*, 145. As Carol Flynn observes, the "early Richardson [of the *Familiar Letters*] dispensed his advice in the simplest of terms. Filial piety, for instance, could not be debated. Children were to obey their parents and guardians absolutely." Carol Flynn, *Samuel Richardson: A Man of Letters* (Princeton: Princeton University Press, 1982), 14.

26. Paula Backscheider, "The Rise of Gender as Political Category," in *Revising Women: Eighteenth-Century "Women's Fiction" and Social Engagement*, ed. Paula R. Backscheider (Baltimore: Johns Hopkins University Press, 2000), 32.

27. Tom Keymer, *Richardson's Clarissa and the Eighteenth-Century Reader* (Cambridge: Cambridge University Press, 1992), 122.

28. Keymer, *Richardson's Clarissa*, 122.

29. Qtd in Keymer, *Richardson's Clarissa*, 122.

30. As Richardson writes in his explanation of the structure of *Clarissa*, "the first and second Volumes . . . are chiefly taken up with the Altercations between Clarissa and . . . her Family" that become the "Foundation of the whole" novel. Qtd. in Keymer, *Richardson's Clarissa*, 123.

31. Cynthia Wolff, *Samuel Richardson and the Eighteenth-Century Puritan Character* (Connecticut: Archon Books, 1972), 93.

32. T. C. Eaves and Ben Kimpel, *Samuel Richardson: A Biography* (Oxford: Clarendon Press, 1971), 251.

33. Kathryn Steele, "Clarissa's Silence," *Eighteenth-Century Fiction* 23, no. 1 (2010): 10.

34. Jerry C. Beasley, "Richardson's Girls: The Daughters of Patriarchy in *Pamela*, *Clarissa* and *Sir Charles Grandison*," in *New Essays on Samuel Richardson*, ed. Albert Rivero (New York: St. Martin's Press, 1996), 42. W. Austin Flanders similarly argues Clarissa's virtually invisible and deliberately unapproachable father represents the "intolerable nature of patriarchal authority . . . based in religion." W. Austin Flanders, *Structures of Experience: History, Society, and Personal Life in the Eighteenth-Century Novel* (Columbia: University of South Carolina Press, 1984), 153.

35. Linda Zionkowski's dismissal of Clarissa's mother as "ultimately irrelevant" in a novel focused on patriarchal authority exemplifies this perspective. Linda Zionkowski, "*Clarissa* and the Hazards of the Gift," *Eighteenth-Century Fiction* 23, no. 3 (2011): 477.

36. Paxman, "Imagining the Child," 141.

37. Katherine Binhammer, "Knowing Love: The Epistemology of *Clarissa*," *ELH* 74, no. 4 (2007): 871.

38. Kinkead-Weekes, *Samuel Richardson, Dramatic Novelist*, 281.

39. Robert Erickson also describes Anna's connection to Clarissa in terms reminiscent of surrogate families. He calls their friendship the "purest heart relationship" in the novel, meaning they are the only characters with the "capacity for mutually shared feeling, for entering

deeply into the distresses of the other." Robert A. Erickson, *The Language of the Heart, 1600–1750* (Philadelphia: University of Pennsylvania Press, 1997), 199.

40. Daniel Defoe, *The Fortunate Mistress*, in *The Novels of Daniel Defoe*, vol. 9, ed. P. N. Furbank, 10 vols. (London: Pickering & Chatto, 2009), 38. Hereafter cited parenthetically.

41. Anna uses this same metaphor to describe Clarissa's superiority over her siblings, describing them as "faint twinklers . . . eclipsed" by Clarissa's "sun" (129).

42. James's taunting of Clarissa might even have been inspired by Richardson's own experiences as a child when his classmates nicknamed him "*Serious* and *Gravity*." Qtd. in Carroll, *Selected Letters of Samuel Richardson*, 231.

43. Alex Eric Hernandez, "Tragedy and the Economics of Providence in Richardson's *Clarissa*," *Eighteenth-Century Fiction* 22, no. 4 (2010): 620.

44. John A. Dussinger, "Love and Consanguinity in Richardson's Novels," *Studies in English Literature* 24, no. 3 (1984): 521.

45. Margaret Anne Doody, "The Man-Made World of Clarissa Harlowe and Robert Lovelace," in *Samuel Richardson: Passion and Prudence*, ed. Valerie Grosvenor Myer (London: Vision Press, 1986), 69.

46. Kathleen Oliver, *Samuel Richardson, Dress, and Discourse* (Basingstoke: Palgrave Macmillan, 2008), 97.

47. Wendy Lee, "A Case for Hard-Heartedness: *Clarissa*, Indifferency, Impersonality," *Eighteenth-Century Fiction* 26, no. 1 (2013): 49.

48. Ewha Chung, *Samuel Richardson's New Nation: Paragons of the Domestic Sphere and "Native" Virtue* (New York: Peter Lang Publishers, 1998), 62. Chung's argument aligns with my own in its emphasis on Clarissa's expanding family-like network of close friends and supporters. However, Chung differs from me in her explanation of this "substitute familial network" as first and foremost a "newly found religious community." Chung, *Samuel Richardson's New Nation*, 67.

49. Derek Taylor, "Samuel Richardson's *Clarissa* and the Problem of Heaven," in *Theology and Literature in the Age of Johnson: Resisting Secularism*, eds. Melvyn New and Gerard Reedy (Newark: University of Delaware Press, 2012), 79.

50. Significantly, Morden interrupts Belford's claim that Mrs. Lovick is as careful of Clarissa as a mother could be with "And *more* careful, too . . . or she is not careful at all" (1350). Morden's comments reinforce my argument that surrogate relations are more important than blood ties in *Clarissa*.

51. Mrs. Smith also to a lesser degree acts as a mother figure to Clarissa. Jacqueline Lawson describes the two of them as twin "maternal figures" who function as a "non-sanguinous family unit" for Clarissa as she dies. Jacqueline Elaine Lawson, *Domestic Misconduct in the Novels of Defoe, Richardson, and Fielding* (Lewiston: Edwin Mellen Press, 1994), 107.

52. Mr. Hickman also acts as a surrogate brother figure to Clarissa. Clarissa calls him her "brother" and "friend," and seals their connection by asking him to carry a kiss she gives him to her surrogate sister Anna (1131).

53. The notable exception to Anna's compassion for Clarissa occurs when Anna believes Clarissa returned willingly to Lovelace. She directs her anger at Clarissa in this instance because she wrongly believes Clarissa has willfully erred.

54. Clarissa looks forward with rapture to her own death, and even to Anna's because after they die they may "meet, never to part again" where they "shall enjoy each other to all eternity!" (1348). They will no longer be divided by suitors and husbands who draw attention away from one another but will instead share equally in the love of one "adorable object," Jesus (1348).

55. James Bryant Reeves, "Posthumous Presence in Richardson's *Clarissa*," *Studies in English Literature* 53, no. 3 (2013): 609.

56. Betty A. Schellenberg, *The Conversational Circle: Rereading the English Novel, 1740–1775* (Lexington: University Press of Kentucky, 1996), 59.

57. Rebecca Anne Barr, "Richardson's *Sir Charles Grandison* and the Symptoms of Subjectivity," *Eighteenth Century: Theory and Interpretation* 51, no. 4 (2010): 401–402.

58. Samuel Richardson, *Sir Charles Grandison*, vol. 1, ed. Jocelyn Harris, 7 vols. (New York: Oxford University Press, 1972), 147. Hereafter cited parenthetically.

59. Qtd in Keymer, *Richardson's Clarissa*, 122.

60. Paula Backscheider, "The Rise of Gender as Political Category," in *Revising Women: Eighteenth-Century "Women's Fiction" and Social Engagement*, ed. Paula R. Backscheider (Baltimore: Johns Hopkins University Press, 2000), 57.

CHAPTER 4 — AN AFFINITY FOR LEARNING

1. Haywood scholarship has largely moved away from the view that her writing shifted dramatically after Pope criticized her in *The Dunciad* (1727). There is now a general consensus that her work was influenced by shifts in readers' tastes, but that it always maintains a characteristic focus on women's desires and men's caddishness. Most Haywood scholars now agree with Aleksondra Hultquist's assertion that a "drastic reformation in style and theme did not really occur" in Haywood's later work and that even her didactic novels include many of the romance conventions that characterize her earliest writing. Aleksondra Hultquist, "Marriage in Haywood; or, Amatory Reading Rewarded," in *Masters of the Marketplace: British Women Novelists of the 1750s*, ed. Susan Carlile (Bethlehem: Lehigh University Press, 2011), 31. Similarly, Patrick Spedding describes the theory that Haywood's early and late work are discontinuous as "dated . . . dichotomous" and "untenable." Patrick Spedding, "Shameless Scribbler or Votary of Virtue? Eliza Haywood, Writing (and) Pornography in 1742," in *Women Writing, 1550–1750*, eds. Jo Wallwork and Paul Bundoora Salzman (Australia: Meridian, 2001), 237.

2. The most straightforward example of Haywood borrowing plot devices from Richardson is her novel *Anti-Pamela* (1741). It revises the plot and characterization of Richardson's *Pamela*. Aleksondra Hultquist describes Haywood's selective borrowing from Richardson as "working within the Richardsonian ideal of delight and instruction" but mingling it with her own "amatory training." Hultquist, "Marriage in Haywood," 33.

3. Hultquist, "Marriage in Haywood," 33.

4. Juliette Merritt, "Reforming the Coquet? Eliza Haywood's Vision of a Female Epistemology," in *Fair Philosopher: Eliza Haywood and The Female Spectator*, eds. Lynn Marie Wright and Donald J. Newman (Lewisburg: Bucknell University Press, 2006), 187. She reiterates and expands on this point in another article as well. Juliette Merritt, "Spying, Writing, Authority: Eliza Haywood's *Bath Intrigues*," *Studies in Eighteenth-Century Culture* 30 (2001): 183–199.

5. Juliette Merritt, *Beyond Spectacle: Eliza Haywood's Female Spectator* (Toronto: University of Toronto Press, 2004), 20.

6. Merritt, *Beyond Spectacle*, 20.

7. Eliza Haywood, *The History of Miss Betsy Thoughtless*, ed. Christine Blouch (Petersborough: Broadview Press, 1998), 101. Hereafter cited parenthetically.

8. David Oakleaf, "Circulating the Name of a Whore: Eliza Haywood's Betsy Thoughtless, Betty Careless and the Duplicities of the Double Standard," *Women's Writing* 15, no.1 (2008): 125.

9. Mary Anne Schofield, "Exposé of the Popular Heroine: The Female Protagonists of Eliza Haywood," *Studies in Eighteenth-Century Culture* 12 (1983): 96. Several Haywood scholars note that Haywood's body of work is of particular significance to the development of the novel because she registers shifts in gender norms and assesses ideals of feminine propriety. For example, Shea Stuart argues *Betsy Thoughtless* is a "microcosm of eighteenth-century social conflicts—emergent versus residual ideologies of patriarchy and of marriage, conduct-book didacticism versus common reality." Shea Stuart, "Subversive Didacticism in Eliza

Haywood's *Betsy Thoughtless,*" *Studies in English Literature* 42, no. 3 (2002): 572. Katrina Clifford similarly claims *Betsy Thoughtless* "contributes significantly to our understanding of . . . notions of authority, equality and female independence." Katrina Clifford, "From Reformed Coquette to Coquettish Reformer: *The History of Miss Betsy Thoughtless* and the History of the Domestic Novel," in *Remaking Literary History*, eds. Helen Groth and Paul Sheehan (Newcastle upon Tyne: Cambridge Scholars Publishing, 2010), 85.

10. As Christine Blouch argues, Haywood "played a key role in the novel's evolution and defined central issues in the portrayal of eighteenth-century female subjectivity." Christine Blouch, "Eliza Haywood and the Romance of Obscurity," *Studies in English Literature* 31, no. 3 (1991): 536.

11. Paula R. Backscheider, "The Story of Eliza Haywood's Novels: Caveats and Questions," in *The Passionate Fictions of Eliza Haywood: Essays on Her Life and Work*, eds. Kirsten T. Saxton and Rebecca P. Bocchicchio (Lexington: University Press of Kentucky, 2000), 33.

12. Lorna Ellis, *Appearing to Diminish: Female Development and the British Bildungsroman, 1750–1850* (Lewisburg: Bucknell University Press, 1999), 65.

13. Alexander Pettit, "Eliza Haywood's Present for a Servant-Maid: The Sexual Polemics of Rotten Food," in *Sustaining Literature: Essays on Literature, History, and Culture, 1500–1800: Commemorating the Life and Work of Simon Varey*, ed. Greg Clingham (Lewisburg: Bucknell University Press, 2007), 213.

14. Christopher F. Loar, "The Exceptional Eliza Haywood: Women and Extralegality in *Eovaai*," *Eighteenth-Century Studies* 45, no. 4 (2012): 574. Hajeong Park makes the similar argument that in Haywood "female virtue can be acquired only through education." Hajeong Park, "Envisioning a History of Women: Female Friendship and a Community of Women in Haywood's Early Fiction," *British and American Fiction to 1900* 16, no. 2 (2009): 53.

15. In her article focused on the numerous rapes and near rapes in *Betsy Thoughtless*, Andrea Austin claims "repeated scenes of Betsy's danger are incrementally juxtaposed with the various interpolated seduction narratives . . . in order to underscore that inequity between the sexes drives the action of the sequence." Andrea Austin, "Shooting Blanks: Potency, Parody, and Eliza Haywood's *The History of Miss Betsy Thoughtless*" in *The Passionate Fictions of Eliza Haywood: Essays on her Life and Work*, eds. Kirsten T. Saxton and Rebecca P. Bocchicchio (Lexington: University Press of Kentucky, 2000), 269.

16. Naomi Tadmor, *Family and Friends in Eighteenth-Century England: Household, Kinship, and Patronage* (New York: Cambridge University Press, 2001), 51.

17. Tadmor, *Family and Friends*, 246.

18. Tadmor, *Family and Friends*, 246.

19. Betsy's father regularly visits her school but otherwise expends no trouble raising her. While Haywood does not explicitly criticize him for his indifference, he is at best "lethargic"—Jennifer Thorn's characterization of him—and at worst neglectful. Jennifer Thorn, "'Althea Must Be Open'd': Eliza Heywood, Individualism, and Reproductivity," *Eighteenth-Century Women: Studies in Their Lives, Work, and Culture* 1 (2001): 117.

20. Helen Thompson, "Betsy Thoughtless and the Persistence of Coquettish Volition," *Journal for Early Modern Cultural Studies* 4, no. 1 (2004): 117.

21. Theresa Braunschneider, *Our Coquettes: Capacious Desire in the Eighteenth Century* (Charlottesville: University of Virginia Press, 2009), 123.

22. Deborah Nestor argues that the Miss Forward subplot encourages the reader to reconsider didactic novels' conventional "black-and-white" assumption that fallen women are "purely wicked" in favor of a more sympathetic understanding of their situations. Deborah J. Nestor, "Virtue Rarely Rewarded: Ideological Subversion and Narrative Form in Haywood's Later Fiction," *Studies in English Literature* 34, no. 3 (1994): 583.

23. Clifford, "From Reformed Coquette to Coquettish Reformer," 77–78.

24. Margaret Case Croskery, "Novel Romanticism in 1751: Eliza Haywood's *Besty Thoughtless*," in *Enlightening Romanticism, Romancing the Enlightenment: British Novels from 1750 to 1832*, ed. Miriam L. Wallace (Surrey: Ashgate Publishing, 2009), 32.

25. Nestor, "Virtue Rarely Rewarded," 584.
26. Backscheider, "The Story of Eliza Haywood's Novels," 34.
27. Stuart, "Subversive Didacticism in Eliza Haywood's *Betsy Thoughtless*," 560.
28. Chris Roulston, *Narrating Marriage in Eighteenth-Century England and France* (Farnham: Ashgate Publishing Company, 2010), 166.
29. Ellis, *Appearing to Diminish*, 185.
30. John Richetti, "Histories by Eliza Haywood and Henry Fielding: Imitation and Adaptation," in *The Passionate Fictions of Eliza Haywood: Essays on Her Life and Work*, eds. Kirsten T. Saxton and Rebecca P. Bocchicchio (Lexington: University Press of Kentucky, 2000), 253.
31. Emily Anderson, *Eighteenth-Century Authorship and the Play of Fiction: Novels and the Theater, Haywood to Austen* (New York: Routledge, 2009), 40.
32. Kelly McGuire, "Mourning and Material Culture in Eliza Haywood's *The History of Miss Betsy Thoughtless*," *Eighteenth-Century Fiction* 18, no. 3 (2006): 282.
33. Hultquist, "Marriage in Haywood," 33.
34. Karen Cajka, "The Unprotected Woman in Eliza Haywood's *The History of Jemmy and Jenny Jessamy*," in *Masters of the Marketplace: British Women Novelists of the 1750s*, ed. Susan Carlile (Bethlehem: Lehigh University Press, 2011), 47.
35. Ann Campbell, "Punitive Subplots and Clandestine Marriage in Eliza Haywood's *The History of Jemmy and Jenny Jessamy*," *Eighteenth-Century Women: Studies in Their Lives, Work, and Culture* 5 (2008): 78–101.
36. Nestor, "Virtue Rarely Rewarded," 590.
37. Eliza Haywood, *The History of Jemmy and Jenny Jessamy*, ed. John Richetti (Lexington: University Press of Kentucky, 2005), 31. Hereafter cited parenthetically.
38. Kathleen Lubey, *Excitable Imaginations: Eroticism and Reading in Britain, 1660–1760* (Lewisburg: Bucknell University Press, 2012), 97.
39. Charles Hinnant, "Ironic Inversion in Eliza Haywood's Fiction: *Fantomina* and 'The History of the Invisible Mistress,'" *Women's Writing* 17, no. 3 (2010): 411.
40. Tiffany Potter, "'A God-like Sublimity of Passion': Eliza Haywood's Libertine Consistency," *Eighteenth-Century Novel* 1 (2001): 96.
41. I describe Sophia's brother's clandestine marriage and its historical context in detail in a previous article. Campbell, "Punitive Subplots and Clandestine Marriage," 84–87.
42. Pettit, "Eliza Haywood's Present for a Servant-Maid," 215.

CHAPTER 5 — ADOPTING TO CHANGE

1. I focus on *Evelina* and *Cecilia* rather than Burney's later novels *Camilla* (1796) and *The Wanderer* (1814) for several reasons. Camilla, the protagonist of *Camilla*, is the opposite of an orphan. As Sarah Austin observes, *Camilla* is the "only Burney novel which provides its heroine with a complete, stable, and indeed idealized family." Sarah Austin, "'All Wove into One': *Camilla*, the Prose Epic, and Family Values," *Studies in Eighteenth-Century Culture* 29 (2000): 292. Camilla's problems arise from having too much family, not too little. As Elaine Bander puts it, families are "always problematic" in Burney's fiction: "damned if you've got 'em, damned if you don't." Elaine Bander, "Family Matters in Burney's *Camilla*," *The Age of Johnson* 22 (2012): 281. But Camilla's particular variety of damnation does not involve surrogate families. It may seem uncharitable to characterize Camilla, as Elisabeth Gruner does, as a "boring daddy's girl." Elisabeth Gruner, "The Bullfinch and the Brother: Marriage and Family in Frances Burney's *Camilla*," *Journal of English and Germanic Philology*, 93, no. 1 (1994): 19. However, it is fair to say that her nuclear and lineage families influence her decisions to such a degree that even if she wanted to construct her own surrogate family, they would not allow her to do so. Juliet, the protagonist of *The Wanderer*, has all the freedom Camilla lacks. She is an orphan who makes her own way in the world. But while *The Wanderer* is technically a courtship novel, it is less about love and marriage than the systemic oppression of women in English society. Juliet's story focuses on the

economic, legal, and political obstacles she must overcome to support herself. Her disadvantageous circumstances make it impossible for her to select surrogate family members.

2. Frances Burney, *Evelina: Or the History of a Young Lady's Entrance into the World*, ed. Edward A. Bloom (New York: Oxford University Press, 2002), 37. Hereafter cited parenthetically.

3. Martha Brown, "Fanny Burney's 'Feminism': Gender or Genre?" in *Fetter'd or Free: British Women Novelists, 1670–1815*, ed. Mary Schofield and Cecilia Macheski (Athens: Ohio University Press, 1986), 32.

4. Catherine Gallagher, *Nobody's Story: The Vanishing Acts of Women Writers in the Marketplace 1670–1820* (Berkeley: University of California Press, 1994), 231. As Terry Castle similarly asserts, Cecilia "represents an unprecedented and potentially disruptive kind of female autonomy" because she can choose never to marry, and if she does marry she will name her husband rather than the other way around. Terry Castle, *Masquerade and Civilization: The Carnivalesque in Eighteenth-Century English Culture and Fiction* (Stanford: Stanford University Press, 1986), 267.

5. Julia Epstein, "Marginality in Frances Burney's Novels," in *The Cambridge Companion to the Eighteenth Century Novel*, ed. John Richetti (Cambridge: Cambridge University Press, 1996), 198.

6. Wolfram Schmidgen, "Illegitimacy and Social Observation: The Bastard in the Eighteenth Century Novel," *ELH* 69, no. 1 (2002): 140.

7. Schmidgen, "Illegitimacy and Social Observation," 140.

8. Margaret Anne Doody, "Burney and Politics," in *The Cambridge Companion to Frances Burney*, ed. Peter Sabor (Cambridge: Cambridge University Press, 2007), 98.

9. Susan Greenfield, *Mothering Daughters: Novels and the Politics of Family Romance: Frances Burney to Jane Austen* (Detroit: Wayne State University Press, 2002), 18; Sarah Spence, "Nurturing: Attachment Theory and Fanny Burney's *Evelina* and *Cecilia*," *The Psychohistory Review* 24, no. 2 (1996): 176.

10. Barbara Zonitch, *Familiar Violence: Gender and Social Upheaval in the Novels of Frances Burney* (Newark: University of Delaware Press, 1997), 31. Christina Davidson, Marcie Frank, Judith Newton, and Irene Fizer make similar arguments. Christina Davidson, "Conversations as Signifiers: Characters on the Margins of Morality in the First Three Novels of Frances Burney," *Partial Answers: Journal of Literature and the History of Ideas* 8, no. 2 (2010): 282; Marcie Frank, "Frances Burney's Theatricality," *ELH* 82, no. 2 (2015): 618; Judith Newton, "Evelina: Or the History of a Young Woman's Entrance into the Marriage Market," *Modern Language Studies* 6, no. 1 (1976): 54; Irene Fizer, "The Name of the Daughter: Identity and Incest in *Evelina*," in *Refiguring the Father: New Feminist Readings of Patriarchy*, eds. Patricia Yaeger and Beth Kowaleski-Wallace (Carbondale: Southern Illinois University Press, 1989), 89.

11. Toby Olshin, "'To Whom I Most Belong': The Role of Family in *Evelina*," *Eighteenth-Century Life* 6, no. 1 (1980): 35.

12. Caroline Gonda, *Reading Daughters' Fictions 1709–1834: Novels and Society from Manley to Edgeworth* (Cambridge: Cambridge University Press, 1996), 127.

13. Martha Koehler, *Models of Reading: Paragons and Parasites in Richardson, Burney, and Laclos* (Lewisburg: Bucknell University Press, 2005), 152.

14. Zonitch, *Familiar Violence*, 43.

15. Emily Allen, "Staging Identity: Frances Burney's Allegory of Genre," *Eighteenth-Century Studies* 31, no. 4 (1998): 440; Jeanine Casler, "Rakes and Races: Art's Imitation of Life in Frances Burney's *Evelina*," *The Eighteenth-Century Novel* 3 (2003): 159.

16. Ruth Bernard Yeazell, *Fictions of Modesty: Women and Courtship in the English Novel* (Chicago: University of Chicago Press, 1991), 133. John Zomchick similarly argues Madame Duval's body is "deconstructed to its elemental components of dirt and mud." John Zomchick, "Satire and the Bourgeois Subject in Frances Burney's *Evelina*," in *Cutting Edges:*

Postmodern Critical Essays on Eighteenth-Century Satire, ed. James Gill (Knoxville: University of Tennessee Press, 1995), 357.

17. Kristina Straub, *Divided Fictions: Fanny Burney and Feminine Strategy* (Lexington: University of Kentucky Press, 1987), 24.

18. Emily Allen describes Villars as one of several "father surrogates" in *Evelina*. Allen, "Staging Identity," 446. Virginia Cope also describes Villars as Evelina's "foster father." Virginia Cope, "Evelina's Peculiar Circumstances and Tender Relations," *Eighteenth-Century Fiction* 16, no. 1 (2003): 59.

19. David Oakleaf, "The Name of the Father: Social Identity and the Ambition of *Evelina*," *Eighteenth-Century Fiction* 3, no. 4 (1991): 352.

20. Gonda, *Reading Daughters' Fictions*, 125. Waldo Glock also suggests Villars is "more loving and concerned for [Evelina's] welfare than her real father." Waldo Glock, "Appearance and Reality: The Education of Evelina," *Essays in Literature* 2 (1975): 33.

21. Mary Severance argues the entire narrative of *Evelina* traces its heroine's "journey from the arms of her loving guardian and 'more-than-father,' Villars, to the enveloping arms of Lord Orville, her fatherly lover and husband." Mary Severance, "An Unerring Rule: The Reformation of the Father in Frances Burney's *Evelina*," *The Eighteenth Century: Theory and Interpretation* 36, no. 2 (1995): 120.

22. Peter DeGabriele, "The Legal Fiction and Epistolary Form: Frances Burney's *Evelina*," *Journal for Early Modern Cultural Studies* 14, no. 2 (2014): 36.

23. Margaret Anne Doody, "Beyond *Evelina*: The Individual Novel and the Community of Literature," *Eighteenth-Century Fiction* 3, no. 4 (1991): 371.

24. Betty Rizzo attributes Evelina's instinctive attachment to the "cri du sang or 'call of blood' topos that is common in French drama of the seventeenth and eighteenth centuries and in the English novel of the second half of the eighteenth." Betty Rizzo, "Burney and Society," in *The Cambridge Companion to Frances Burney*, ed. Peter Sabor (Cambridge: Cambridge University Press, 2007), 131.

25. Doody, "Beyond *Evelina*," 371.

26. Julian Fung, "Frances Burney as Satirist," *Modern Language Review* 106, no. 4 (2011): 945.

27. Meghan Jordan, "Madness and Matrimony in Frances Burney's *Cecilia*," *Studies in English Literature* 55, no. 3 (2015): 561.

28. Stephanie Russo and A. D. Cousins, "'In a State of Terrour and Misery Indescribable': Violence, Madness and Revolution in the Novels of Frances Burney," in *The French Revolution and the British Novel in the Romantic Period*, eds. Stephanie Russo, A. D. Cousins, and Dani Napton (New York: Peter Lang, 2011), 92.

29. Frances Burney, *Cecilia, or Memoirs of an Heiress*, eds. Peter Sabor and Margaret Anne Doody (New York: Oxford University Press, 2009), 941. Hereafter cited parenthetically.

30. Katharine Rogers, *Frances Burney: The World of Female Difficulties* (New York: Harvester Wheatsheaf, 1990), 95.

31. Fung, "Frances Burney as Satirist," 944.

32. Daniel Defoe, *The Fortunes and Misfortunes of the Famous Moll Flanders*, in *The Novels of Daniel Defoe*, vol. 6, ed. Liz Bellamy, 10 vols. (London: Pickering & Chatto, 2008–2009), 141.

33. Terry Castle, *Masquerade and Civilization*, 269.

34. Jane Spencer, "*Evelina* and *Cecilia*," in *The Cambridge Companion to Frances Burney*, ed. Peter Sabor (Cambridge: Cambridge University Press, 2007), 35.

CONCLUSION

1. Aaron Hanlon, "Maids, Mistresses, and 'Monstrous Doubles': Gender-Class Kyriarchy in *The Female Quixote* and 'Female Quixotism,'" *The Eighteenth Century* 55, no. 1 (2014): 77.

2. Zak Watson, "Desire and Genre in 'The Female Quixote,'" *Novel: A Forum on Fiction* 44, no. 1 (2011): 31.

3. There are extensive debates about how to appropriately refer to the group Fielding describes as "gypsies." I refer to them using Fielding's and Tom's term because they perceive them as members of this group according to its common usage during the eighteenth-century in England.

4. Hilary Teynor, "A Partridge in the Family Tree: Fixity, Mobility, and Community in *Tom Jones*," *Eighteenth-Century Fiction* 17, no. 3 (2005): 353.

5. Henry Fielding, *Tom Jones*, ed. Sheridan Baker (New York: Norton, 1995), 30. Hereafter cited parenthetically.

6. Gary Gautier, "Marriage and Family in Fielding's Fiction," *Studies in the Novel* 27, no. 2 (1995): 116.

7. Lori Walk, "Questing for Family in *Joseph Andrews* and *David Simple*," *Eighteenth-Century Novel* 1 (2001): 248.

8. Linda Bree, *Sarah Fielding* (New York: Twayne Publishers, 1996), 33.

9. Bree, *Sarah Fielding*, 33.

10. Qtd. in Bree, *Sarah Fielding*, 42.

11. Bree, *Sarah Fielding*, 42.

12. Bree, *Sarah Fielding*, 42.

13. Richard Terry, "*David Simple* and the Fallacy of Friendship," *Studies in English Literature* 44, no. 3 (2004): 529.

14. Terry, "David Simple," 529.

15. Walk, "Questing for Family in *Joseph Andrews* and *David Simple*," 238.

16. Joseph Bartolomeo, "A Fragile Utopia of Sensibility: *David Simple*," in *Gender and Utopia in the Eighteenth Century: Essays in English and French Utopian Writing*, eds. Nicole Pohl and Brenda Tooley (Aldershot: Ashgate Publishing, 2007), 48.

17. Bryan Mangano, *Fictions of Friendship in the Eighteenth-Century Novel* (Iowa: Palgrave Macmillan, 2017), 94.

18. Ann Van Sant, "Historicizing Domestic Relations: Sarah Scott's Use of 'The Household Family,'" *Eighteenth-Century Fiction* 17, no. 3 (2005): 379.

19. Eve Tavor Bannet, "The Bluestocking Sisters: Women's Patronage, Millenium Hall, and 'The Visible Providence of a Country,'" *Eighteenth-Century Life* 30, no. 1 (2006): 36.

20. See Barbara Schnorrenberg, "A Paradise Like Eve's: Three Eighteenth-Century English Female Utopias," *Women's Studies* 9, no. 3 (1982): 263–273; Crystal Lake, "Redecorating the Ruin: Women and Antiquarianism in Sarah Scott's *Millenium Hall*," *ELH* 76, no. 3 (2009): 661–686; and Nicole Pohl, "'Sweet Place, Where Virtue Then Did Rest': The Appropriation of the Country-House Ethos in Sarah Scott's *Millenium Hall*," *Utopian Studies* 7, no. 1 (1996): 49–59.

21. David Oakleaf, "At the Margins of Utopia: Jamaica in Sarah Scott's *Millenium Hall*," *Eighteenth-Century Fiction* 28, no. 1 (2015): 126.

22. Nicolle Jordan, "A Creole Contagion: Narratives of Slavery and Tainted Wealth in *Millenium Hall*," *Tulsa Studies in Women's Literature* 30, no. 1 (2011): 58.

23. See Vincent Carretta, "Utopia Limited: Sarah Scott's *Millenium Hall* and *The History of Sir George Ellison*," *The Age of Johnson* 5 (1992): 303–325.

24. Nicolle Jordan, "Gentlemen and Gentle Women: The Landscape Ethos in *Millenium Hall*," *Eighteenth-Century Fiction* 24, no. 1 (2011): 33.

25. Caroline Gonda, "Sarah Scott and 'The Sweet Excess of Paternal Love,'" *Studies in English Literature* 32, no. 3 (1992): 523.

26. Sarah Scott, *Millenium Hall*, ed. Gary Kelly (Orchard Park: Broadview Press, 1995), 90. Hereafter cited parenthetically.

27. James Cruise, "A House Divided: Sarah Scott's *Millenium Hall*," *Studies in English Literature* 35, no. 3 (1995): 561.

28. Bryan Mangano, "Institutions of Friendship in Sarah Scott's *Millenium Hall*," *Texas Studies in Literature and Language* 57, no. 4 (2015): 464.

29. Qtd. in Bannet, "The Bluestocking Sisters," 34.

30. Dorice Elliott, "Sarah Scott's *Millenium Hall* and Female Philanthropy," *Studies in English Literature* 35, no. 3 (1995): 542.

31. Julie McGonegal, "The Tyranny of Gift Giving: The Politics of Generosity in Sarah Scott's *Millenium Hall* and *Sir George Ellison*," *Eighteenth-Century Fiction* 19, no. 3 (2007): 301.

32. McGonegal, "The Tyranny of Gift Giving," 301.

Allen, Emily. "Staging Identity: Frances Burney's Allegory of Genre." *Eighteenth-Century Studies* 31, no. 4 (1998): 433–451.

Anderson, Emily Hodgson. *Eighteenth-Century Authorship and the Play of Fiction: Novels and the Theater, Haywood to Austen*. New York: Routledge, 2009.

Austen, Jane. *Emma*. Edited by George Justice. New York: Norton, 2012.

Austin, Andrea. "Shooting Blanks: Potency, Parody, and Eliza Haywood's *The History of Miss Betsy Thoughtless*." In *The Passionate Fictions of Eliza Haywood: Essays on her Life and Work*, edited by Kirsten T. Saxton and Rebecca P. Bocchicchio, 259–282. Lexington: University Press of Kentucky, 2000.

Austin, Sarah. "'All Wove into One': *Camilla*, the Prose Epic, and Family Values." *Studies in Eighteenth-Century Culture* 29 (2000): 273–298.

Backscheider, Paula. "Defoe's Prodigal Sons." *Studies in the Literary Imagination* 15, no. 2 (1982): 3–18.

———. "The Novel's Gendered Space." In *Revising Women: Eighteenth-Century "Women's Fiction" and Social Engagement*, edited by Paula Backscheider, 1–30. Baltimore: Johns Hopkins University Press, 2000.

———, ed. *Revising Women: Eighteenth-Century "Women's Fiction" and Social Engagement*. Baltimore: Johns Hopkins University Press, 2000.

———. "The Rise of Gender as Political Category." In *Revising Women: Eighteenth-Century "Women's Fiction" and Social Engagement*, edited by Paula Backsheider, 32–57. Baltimore: Johns Hopkins University Press, 2000.

———. "The Story of Eliza Haywood's Novels: Caveats and Questions." In *The Passionate Fictions of Eliza Haywood: Essays on Her Life and Work*, edited by Kirsten T. Saxton and Rebecca P. Bocchicchio, 19–47. Lexington: University Press of Kentucky, 2000.

Ball, Donald L. "*Pamela II*: A Primary Link in Richardson's Development as a Novelist." *Modern Philology* 65, no. 4 (1968): 334–342.

Bander, Elaine. "Family Matters in Burney's *Camilla*." *The Age of Johnson* 22 (2012): 281–297.

Bannet, Eve Tavor. "The Bluestocking Sisters: Women's Patronage, Millenium Hall, and 'The Visible Providence of a Country.'" *Eighteenth-Century Life* 30, no. 1 (2006): 25–55.

Barr, Rebecca Anne. "Richardson's *Sir Charles Grandison* and the Symptoms of Subjectivity." *Eighteenth Century: Theory and Interpretation* 51, no. 4 (2010): 391–411.

Bartolomeo, Joseph. "A Fragile Utopia of Sensibility: *David Simple*." In *Gender and Utopia in the Eighteenth Century: Essays in English and French Utopian Writing*, edited by Nicole Pohl and Brenda Tooley, 39–52. Aldershot: Ashgate Publishing, 2007.

Beasley, Jerry C. "Richardson's Girls: The Daughters of Patriarchy in *Pamela*, *Clarissa* and *Sir Charles Grandison*." In *New Essays on Samuel Richardson*, edited by Albert Rivero, 35–52. New York: St. Martin's, 1996.

Binhammer, Katherine. "Knowing Love: The Epistemology of *Clarissa*." *ELH* 74, no. 4 (2007): 859–879.

Blewett, David. "Changing Attitudes Toward Marriage in the Time of Defoe: The Case of Moll Flanders." *Huntington Library Quarterly* 44, no. 2 (1981): 77–88.

————, ed. *Passion and Virtue: Essays on the Novels of Samuel Richardson*. Toronto: University of Toronto Press, 2001.

Blouch, Christine. "Eliza Haywood and the Romance of Obscurity." *Studies in English Literature* 31, no. 3 (1991): 535–551.

Bowers, Toni. "'I Wou'd Not Murder My Child': Maternity and the Necessity of Infanticide in Two Novels by Daniel Defoe." In *Writing British Infanticide: Child-Murder, Gender, and Print, 1722–1859*, edited by Jennifer Thorn, 172–195. Newark: University of Delaware Press, 2003.

————. *The Politics of Motherhood: British Writing and Culture 1680–1760*. Cambridge: Cambridge University Press, 1996.

Braunschneider, Theresa. *Our Coquettes: Capacious Desire in the Eighteenth Century*. Charlottesville: University of Virginia Press, 2009.

Bree, Linda. *Sarah Fielding*. New York: Twayne Publishers, 1996.

Breen, Margaret, and Fiona Peters, eds. *Genealogies of Identity: Interdisciplinary Readings on Sex and Sexuality*. Amsterdam: Rodopi B. V., 2005.

Brown, Irene. "Domesticity, Feminism, and Friendship: Female Aristocratic Culture and Marriage in England, 1660–1760." *Journal of Family History* 7 (1982): 219–236.

Brown, Martha G. "Fanny Burney's 'Feminism': Gender or Genre?" In *Fetter'd or Free: British Women Novelists, 1670–1815*, edited by Mary Schofield and Cecilia Macheski, 29–39. Athens: Ohio University Press, 1986.

Burney, Frances. *Cecilia, or Memoirs of an Heiress*. Edited by Peter Sabor and Margaret Anne Doody. New York: Oxford University Press, 2009.

————. *Evelina: Or the History of a Young Lady's Entrance into the World*. Edited by Edward A. Bloom. New York: Oxford University Press, 2002.

Cajka, Karen. "The Unprotected Woman in Eliza Haywood's *The History of Jemmy and Jenny Jessamy*." In *Masters of the Marketplace: British Women Novelists of the 1750s*, edited by Susan Carlile, 47–58. Bethlehem: Lehigh University Press, 2011.

Campbell, Ann. "Punitive Subplots and Clandestine Marriage in Eliza Haywood's *The History of Jemmy and Jenny Jessamy*." *Eighteenth-Century Women: Studies of their Lives, Work, and Culture* 5 (2008): 78–101.

Carlile, Susan, ed. *Masters of the Marketplace: British Women Novelists of the 1750s*. Bethlehem: Lehigh University Press, 2011.

Carretta, Vincent. "Utopia Limited: Sarah Scott's *Millenium Hall* and *The History of Sir George Ellison*." *The Age of Johnson* 5 (1992): 303–325.

Carroll, John, ed. *Selected Letters of Samuel Richardson*. Oxford: Clarendon Press, 1964.

Casler, Jeanine. "Rakes and Races: Art's Imitation of Life in Frances Burney's *Evelina*." *The Eighteenth-Century Novel* 3 (2003): 157–169.

Castle, Terry. "'Amy, Who Knew My Disease': A Psychosexual Pattern in Defoe's *Roxana*." *ELH* 46, no. 1 (1979): 81–96.

————. *Masquerade and Civilization: The Carnivalesque in Eighteenth-Century English Culture and Fiction*. Stanford: Stanford University Press, 1986.

Chaber, Lois. "Matriarchal Mirror: Women and Capital in *Moll Flanders*." *PMLA* 97, no. 2 (1982): 212–226.

Chung, Ewha. *Samuel Richardson's New Nation: Paragons of the Domestic Sphere and "Native" Virtue*. New York: Peter Lang Publishing, 1998.

Clifford, Katrina. "From Reformed Coquette to Coquettish Reformer: *The History of Miss Betsy Thoughtless* and the History of the Domestic Novel." In *Remaking Literary History*, edited by Helen Groth and Paul Sheehan, 76–86. Newcastle upon Tyne: Cambridge Scholars Publishing, 2010.

Clingham, Greg, ed. *Sustaining Literature: Essays on Literature, History, and Culture, 1500–1800: Commemorating the Life and Work of Simon Varey*. Lewisburg: Bucknell University Press, 2007.

Cope, Virginia. "Evelina's Peculiar Circumstances and Tender Relations." *Eighteenth-Century Fiction* 16, no. 1 (2003): 59–78.

Croskery, Margaret Case. "Novel Romanticism in 1751: Eliza Haywood's *Betsy Thoughtless.*" In *Enlightening Romanticism, Romancing the Enlightenment: British Novels from 1750 to 1832*, edited by Miriam L. Wallace, 21–37. Surrey: Ashgate Publishing, 2009.

Cruise, James. "A House Divided: Sarah Scott's *Millenium Hall.*" *Studies in English Literature* 35, no. 3 (1995): 555–573.

Curtis, Laura A. "A Case Study of Defoe's Domestic Conduct Manuals Suggested by *The Family, Sex and Marriage in England, 1500–1800.*" *Studies in Eighteenth-Century Culture* 10 (1981): 409–428.

Davidoff, Leonore, and Catherine Hall. *Family Fortunes: Men and Women of the English Middle Class 1780–1850.* Chicago: University of Chicago Press, 1987.

Davidson, Christina. "Conversations as Signifiers: Characters on the Margins of Morality in the First Three Novels of Frances Burney." *Partial Answers: Journal of Literature and the History of Ideas* 8, no. 2 (2010): 277–304.

Defoe, Daniel. *Conjugal Lewdness: Or, Matrimonial Whoredom.* London, 1727.

———. *The Family Instructor. In Three Parts. With a Recommendatory Letter by the Reverend Mr. S. Wright.* London, 1715.

———. *The Fortunate Mistress.* In *The Novels of Daniel Defoe*, vol. 9, edited by P. N. Furbank. London: Pickering & Chatto, 2009.

———. *The Fortunes and Misfortunes of the Famous Moll Flanders.* In *The Novels of Daniel Defoe*, vol. 6, edited by Liz Bellamy. London: Pickering & Chatto: 2008–2009.

———. *Religious Courtship Abridg'd: Being Historical Discourses on the Necessity of Marrying Religious Husbands and Wives Only.* London, 1734.

DeGabriele, Peter. "The Legal Fiction and Epistolary Form: Frances Burney's *Evelina.*" *Journal for Early Modern Cultural Studies* 14, no. 2 (2014): 22–40.

Dionne, Craig, and Steve Mentz, eds. *Rogues in Early Modern Culture.* Ann Arbor: University of Michigan Press, 2004.

Doody, Margaret Anne. "Beyond *Evelina*: The Individual Novel and the Community of Literature." *Eighteenth-Century Fiction* 3, no. 4 (1991): 358–371.

———. "Burney and Politics." In *The Cambridge Companion to Frances Burney*, edited by Peter Sabor, 93–110. Cambridge: Cambridge University Press, 2007.

———. "The Man-Made World of Clarissa Harlowe and Robert Lovelace." In *Samuel Richardson: Passion and Prudence*, edited by Valerie Grosvenor Myer, 52–77. New Jersey: Vision Press, 1986.

———. *A Natural Passion: A Study of the Novels of Samuel Richardson.* Oxford: Clarendon Press, 1974.

Durant, David. "Ann Radcliffe and the Conservative Gothic." *Studies in English Literature* 22, no. 3 (1982): 519–530.

Dussinger, John A. "Love and Consanguinity in Richardson's Novels." *Studies in English Literature* 24, no. 3 (1984): 513–526.

Eagleton, Terry. *The Rape of Clarissa: Writing, Sexuality and Class Struggle in Samuel Richardson.* Minneapolis: University of Minnesota Press, 1986.

Eaves, T. C., and Ben Kimpel. *Samuel Richardson: A Biography.* Oxford: Clarendon Press, 1971.

Elliott, Dorice Williams. "Sarah Scott's *Millenium Hall* and Female Philanthropy," *Studies in English Literature* 35, no. 3 (1995): 535–553.

Ellis, Lorna. *Appearing to Diminish: Female Development and the British Bildungsroman, 1750–1850.* Lewisburg: Bucknell University Press, 1999.

Epstein, Julia. "Marginality in Frances Burney's Novels." In *The Cambridge Companion to the Eighteenth-Century Novel*, edited by John Richetti, 198–211. Cambridge: Cambridge University Press, 1996.

Erickson, Robert A. *The Language of the Heart, 1600–1750.* Philadelphia: University of Pennsylvania Press, 1997.

———. *Mother Midnight: Birth, Sex, and Fate in Eighteenth-Century Fiction.* New York: AMS Press, 1986.

Ezell, Margaret J. M. *Writing Women's Literary History*. Baltimore: Johns Hopkins University Press, 1993.

Fielding, Henry. *Tom Jones*. Edited by Sheridan Baker. New York: Norton, 1995.

Fizer, Irene. "The Name of the Daughter: Identity and Incest in *Evelina*." In *Refiguring the Father: New Feminist Readings of Patriarchy*, edited by Patricia Yaeger and Beth Kowaleski-Wallace, 78–107. Carbondale: Southern Illinois University Press, 1989.

Flanders, W. Austin. *Structures of Experience: History, Society, and Personal Life in the Eighteenth-Century Novel*. Columbia: University of South Carolina Press, 1984.

Flint, Christopher. "The Anxiety of Affluence: Family and Class (Dis)order in *Pamela: or Virtue Rewarded*." *Studies in English Literature* 29, no. 3 (1989): 489–514.

———. *Family Fictions: Narrative and Domestic Relations in Britain, 1688–1789*. Stanford: Stanford University Press, 1998.

Flynn, Carol. *Samuel Richardson: A Man of Letters*. Princeton: Princeton University Press, 1982.

Francus, Marilyn. "'A-Killing Their Children with Safety': Maternal Identity and Transgression in Swift and Defoe." In *Lewd and Notorious: Female Transgression and the Eighteenth Century*, edited by Katharine Kittredge, 258–282. Ann Arbor: University of Michigan Press, 2003.

Frank, Marcie. "Frances Burney's Theatricality." *ELH* 82, no. 2 (2015): 615–635.

Fung, Julian. "Frances Burney as Satirist." *Modern Language Review* 106, no. 4 (2011): 937–953.

Gallagher, Catherine. *Nobody's Story: The Vanishing Acts of Women Writers in the Marketplace 1670–1820*. Berkeley: University of California Press, 1994.

Garrido, J. A., ed. *The Picaresque Novel in Western Literature: from the Sixteenth Century to the Neopicaresque*. Cambridge: Cambridge University Press, 2015.

Gautier, Gary. "Marriage and Family in Fielding's Fiction." *Studies in the Novel* 27, no. 2 (1995): 111–128.

Gill, James, ed. *Cutting Edges: Postmodern Critical Essays on Eighteenth-Century Satire*. Knoxville: University of Tennessee Press, 1995.

Gladfelder, Hal. "Defoe and Criminal Fiction." In *The Cambridge Companion to Daniel Defoe*, edited by John Richetti, 64–83. Cambridge: Cambridge University Press, 2008.

Glock, Waldo. "Appearance and Reality: The Education of Evelina." *Essays in Literature* 2 (1975): 32–41.

Golightly, Jennifer. *The Family, Marriage, and Radicalism in British Women's Novels of the 1790s: Public Affection and Private Affliction*. Lewisburg: Bucknell University Press, 2012.

Gonda, Caroline. *Reading Daughters' Fictions 1709–1834: Novels and Society from Manley to Edgeworth*. Cambridge: Cambridge University Press, 1996.

———. "Sarah Scott and 'The Sweet Excess of Paternal Love.'" *Studies in English Literature* 32, no. 3 (1992): 511–535.

Greenfield, Susan. *Mothering Daughters: Novels and the Politics of Family Romance, Frances Burney to Jane Austen*. Detroit: Wayne State University Press, 2002.

Groth, Helen, and Paul Sheehan, eds. *Remaking Literary History*. Newcastle upon Tyne: Cambridge Scholars Publishing, 2010.

Gruner, Elisabeth. "The Bullfinch and the Brother: Marriage and Family in Frances Burney's *Camilla*." *Journal of English and Germanic Philology* 93, no. 1 (1994): 18–34.

Haggerty, George E. "'Romantic Friendship' and Patriarchal Narrative in Sarah Scott's *Millenium Hall*." *Genders* 13 (1992): 108–122.

Hammerschmidt, Sören. "Barbauld's Richardson and the Canonization of Personal Character." *Eighteenth-Century Fiction* 25, no. 2 (2012–2013): 431–454.

Hammond, Brean. "Defoe and the Picaresque." In *The Picaresque Novel in Western Literature: From the Sixteenth Century to the Neopicaresque*, edited by J. A. Garrido, 113–139. Cambridge: Cambridge University Press, 2015.

Hanlon, Aaron. "Maids, Mistresses, and 'Monstrous Doubles': Gender-Class Kyriarchy in *The Female Quixote* and 'Female Quixotism.'" *The Eighteenth Century* 55, no. 1 (2014): 77–96.

Haywood, Eliza. *The History of Jemmy and Jenny Jessamy*. Edited by John Richetti. Lexington: University Press of Kentucky, 2005.

———. *The History of Miss Betsy Thoughtless*. Edited by Christine Blouch. Peterborough: Broadview Press, 1998.

Hernandez, Alex Eric. "Tragedy and the Economics of Providence in Richardson's *Clarissa*." *Eighteenth-Century Fiction* 22, no. 4 (2010): 599–630.

Hinnant, Charles H. "Ironic Inversion in Eliza Haywood's Fiction: *Fantomina* and 'The History of the Invisible Mistress.'" *Women's Writing* 17, no. 3 (2010): 403–412.

Hultquist, Aleksondra. "Marriage in Haywood; or, Amatory Reading Rewarded." In *Masters of the Marketplace: British Women Novelists of the 1750s*, edited by Susan Carlile, 31–46. Bethlehem: Lehigh University Press, 2011.

Hunt, Margaret R. *The Middling Sort: Commerce, Gender, and the Family in England 1680–1780*. Berkeley: University of California Press, 1996.

Ibsen, Charles A., and Patricia Klobus. "Fictive Kin Term Use and Social Relationships: Alternative Interpretations." *Journal of Marriage and the Family* 34, no. 4 (1972): 615–619.

Jochum, Klaus Peter. "Defoe's Children." In *Fashioning Childhood in the Eighteenth Century: Age and Identity*, edited by Anja Muller, 157–167. Burlington: Ashgate Publishing, 2006.

Johnson, Samuel. *An Universal Etymological Dictionary of the English Language*. Edinburgh, 1764.

Jones, Wendy. "The Dialectics of Love in *Sir Charles Grandison*." In *Passion and Virtue: Essays on the Novels of Samuel Richardson*, edited by David Blewett, 295–316. Toronto: University of Toronto Press, 2001.

Jordan, Meghan. "Madness and Matrimony in Frances Burney's *Cecilia*." *Studies in English Literature* 55, no. 3 (2015): 559–578.

Jordan, Nicolle. "A Creole Contagion: Narratives of Slavery and Tainted Wealth in *Millenium Hall*." *Tulsa Studies in Women's Literature* 30, no. 1 (2011): 57–70.

———. "Gentlemen and Gentle Women: The Landscape Ethos in *Millenium Hall*." *Eighteenth-Century Fiction* 24, no. 1 (2011): 31–54.

Kelly, Helena. *Jane Austen: The Secret Radical*. New York: Knopf, 2017.

Keymer, Tom. "Jane Collier, Reader of Richardson, and the Fire Scene in *Clarissa*." In *New Essays on Samuel Richardson*, edited by Albert J. Rivero, 141–161. New York: St. Martin's, 1996.

———. *Richardson's Clarissa and the Eighteenth-Century Reader*. Cambridge: Cambridge University Press, 1992.

Kibbie, Ann Louise. "Monstrous Generation: The Birth of Capital in Defoe's *Moll Flanders* and *Roxana*." *PMLA* 110, no. 5 (1995): 1023–1034.

Kinkead-Weekes, Mark. *Samuel Richardson, Dramatic Novelist*. Ithaca: Cornell University Press, 1973.

Kitsi-Mitakou, Katerina. "Whoring, Incest, Duplicity, or the 'Self-Polluting' Erotics of Daniel Defoe's *Moll Flanders*." In *Genealogies of Identity: Interdisciplinary Readings on Sex and Sexuality*, edited by Margaret Breen and Fiona Peters, 79–94. Amsterdam: Rodopi B. V., 2005.

Kittredge, Katharine, ed. *Lewd and Notorious: Female Transgression and the Eighteenth Century*. Ann Arbor: University of Michigan Press, 2003.

Koehler, Martha J. *Models of Reading: Paragons and Parasites in Richardson, Burney, and Laclos*. Lewisburg: Bucknell University Press, 2005.

Kuhlisch, Tina. "The Ambivalent Rogue: Moll Flanders as Modern Picara." In *Rogues in Early Modern Culture*, edited by Craig Dionne and Steve Mentz, 337–360. Ann Arbor: University of Michigan Press, 2004.

Lake, Crystal B. "Redecorating the Ruin: Women and Antiquarianism in Sarah Scott's *Millenium Hall*." *ELH* 76, no. 3 (2009): 661–686.

Latimer, Bonnie. "'Apprehensions of Controul': The Familial Politics of Marriage, Choice and Consent in *Sir Charles Grandison*." *Journal for Eighteenth-Century Studies* 32, no. 1 (2009): 1–19.

———. *Making Gender, Culture, and the Self in the Fiction of Samuel Richardson: The Novel Individual*. Burlington: Ashgate Publishing, 2013.

Lawson, Jacqueline Elaine. *Domestic Misconduct in the Novels of Defoe, Richardson, and Fielding*. Lewiston: Edwin Mellen Press, 1994.

Lee, Wendy Anne. "A Case for Hard-Heartedness: *Clarissa*, Indifferency, Impersonality." *Eighteenth-Century Fiction* 26, no. 1 (2013): 33–65.

Loar, Christopher F. "The Exceptional Eliza Haywood: Women and Extralegality in *Eovaai*." *Eighteenth-Century Studies* 45, no. 4 (2012): 565–584.

Lubey, Kathleen. *Excitable Imaginations: Eroticism and Reading in Britain, 1660–1760*. Lewisburg: Bucknell University Press, 2012.

Macfarlane, Alan. *Marriage and Love in England: Modes of Reproduction 1300–1840*. Oxford: Basil Blackwell Ltd., 1986.

Mangano, Bryan. *Fictions of Friendship in the Eighteenth-Century Novel*. Iowa: Palgrave Macmillan, 2017.

———. "Institutions of Friendship in Sarah Scott's *Millenium Hall*." *Texas Studies in Literature and Language* 57, no. 4 (2015): 464–490.

Marks, Sylvia Kasey. *Sir Charles Grandison: The Compleat Conduct Book*. Lewisburg: Bucknell University Press, 1986.

Marshall, Ashley. "Did Defoe Write *Moll Flanders* and *Roxana*?" *Philological Quarterly* 89, nos. 2–3 (2010): 209–241.

Mason, Shirlene. *Daniel Defoe and the Status of Women*. Vermont: Eden Press, 1978.

McGonegal, Julie. "The Tyranny of Gift Giving: The Politics of Generosity in Sarah Scott's *Millenium Hall* and *Sir George Ellison*." *Eighteenth-Century Fiction* 19, no. 3 (2007): 291–306.

McGuire, Kelly. "Mourning and Material Culture in Eliza Haywood's *The History of Miss Betsy Thoughtless*." *Eighteenth-Century Fiction* 18, no. 3 (2006): 281–304.

McKeon, Michael. *The Origins of the English Novel, 1600–1740*. Baltimore: Johns Hopkins University Press, 1987.

———. *The Secret History of Domesticity: Public, Private, and the Division of Knowledge*. Baltimore: Johns Hopkins University Press, 2005.

McMaster, Juliet. "The Equation of Love and Money in *Moll Flanders*." *Studies in the Novel* 2 (1970): 131–144.

Merritt, Juliette. *Beyond Spectacle: Eliza Haywood's Female Spectator*. Toronto: University of Toronto Press, 2004.

———. "Reforming the Coquet?: Eliza Haywood's Vision of a Female Epistemology." In *Fair Philosopher: Eliza Haywood and The Female Spectator*, edited by Lynn Marie Wright and Donald J. Newman, 176–192. Lewisburg: Bucknell University Press, 2006.

———. "Spying, Writing, Authority: Eliza Haywood's *Bath Intrigues*." *Studies In Eighteenth-Century Culture* 30 (2001): 183–199.

Montini, Donatella. "Language and Letters in Samuel Richardson's Networks." *Journal of Early Modern Studies* 3 (2014): 173–198.

Mowry, Melissa. "Women, Work, Rearguard Politics, and Defoe's *Moll Flanders*." *The Eighteenth Century: Theory and Interpretation* 49, no. 2 (2008): 97–109.

Muller, Anja, ed. *Fashioning Childhood in the Eighteenth Century: Age and Identity*. Burlington: Ashgate Publishing, 2006.

Myer, Valerie Grosvenor, ed. *Samuel Richardson: Passion and Prudence*. New Jersey: Vision Press, 1986.

Nazar, Hina. "Judging Clarissa's Heart." *ELH* 79, no. 1 (2012): 85–109.

Nelson, T.G.A. *Children, Parents, and the Rise of the Novel*. Newark: University of Delaware Press, 1995.

Nestor, Deborah J. "Virtue Rarely Rewarded: Ideological Subversion and Narrative Form in Haywood's Later Fiction." *Studies in English Literature* 34, no. 3 (1994): 579–598.

New, Melvyn, and Gerard Reedy, eds. *Theology and Literature in the Age of Johnson: Resisting Secularism*. Newark: University of Delaware Press, 2012.

Newton, Judith. "*Evelina*: Or the History of a Young Woman's Entrance into the Marriage Market." *Modern Language Studies* 6, no. 1 (1976): 48–56.

Nickel, Terri. "'Ingenious Torment': Incest, Family, and the Structure of Community in the Work of Sarah Fielding." *The Eighteenth Century: Theory and Interpretation* 36, no. 3 (1995): 234–247.

Nixon, Cheryl L. *The Orphan in Eighteenth-Century Law and Literature: Estate, Blood and Body.* Burlington: Ashgate Press, 2011.

———. "The Surrogate Family Plot in the Annesley Case and *Memoirs of an Unfortunate Young Nobleman*." *The Eighteenth-Century Novel* 3 (2003): 1–37.

Oakleaf, David. "At the Margins of Utopia: Jamaica in Sarah Scott's *Millenium Hall*." *Eighteenth-Century Fiction* 28, no. 1 (2015): 109–137.

———. "Circulating the Name of a Whore: Eliza Haywood's Betsy Thoughtless, Betty Careless and the Duplicities of the Double Standard." *Women's Writing* 15, no. 1 (2008): 107–134.

———. "The Name of the Father: Social Identity and the Ambition of *Evelina*." *Eighteenth-Century Fiction* 3, no. 4 (1991): 341–358.

O'Hara, Diana. *Courtship and Constraint: Rethinking the Making of Marriage in Tutor England.* Manchester: Manchester University Press, 2000.

Okin, Susan. "Patriarchy and Married Women's Property in England: Questions on Some Current Views." *Eighteenth-Century Studies* 17, no. 2 (1983–1984): 121–138.

Oliver, Kathleen M. *Samuel Richardson, Dress, and Discourse.* Basingstoke: Palgrave Macmillan, 2008.

Olshin, Toby. "'To Whom I Most Belong': The Role of Family in *Evelina*." *Eighteenth-Century Life* 6, no. 1 (1980): 29–42.

Park, Hajeong. "Envisioning a History of Women: Female Friendship and a Community of Women in Haywood's Early Fiction." *British And American Fiction to 1900* 16, no. 2 (2009): 49–73.

Parker, Stephen. *Informal Marriage, Cohabitation and the Law, 1750–1989.* New York: Palgrave Macmillan, 1990.

Patterson, Emily. "Family and Pilgrimage Themes in Burney's *Evelina*." *New Rambler* 18 (1977): 41–48.

Pawl, Amy J. "'And What Other Name May I Claim?': Names and Their Owners in Frances Burney's *Evelina*." *Eighteenth-Century Fiction* 3, no. 4 (1991): 283–299.

Paxman, David B. "Imagining the Child: Bad Parents in the Mid-Eighteenth-Century English Novel." *Journal for Eighteenth-Century Studies* 38, no. 1 (2015): 135–151.

Perry, Ruth. *Novel Relations: The Transformation of Kinship in English Literature and Culture 1748–1818.* Cambridge: Cambridge University Press, 2004.

Peterson, Spiro. "The Matrimonial Theme of Defoe's *Roxana*." *PMLA* 70, no. 1 (1955): 166–191.

Pettit, Alexander. "Eliza Haywood's Present for a Servant-Maid: The Sexual Polemics of Rotten Food." In *Sustaining Literature: Essays on Literature, History, and Culture, 1500–1800: Commemorating the Life and Work of Simon Varey*, edited by Greg Clingham, 211–225. Lewisburg: Bucknell University Press, 2007.

Pohl, Nicole, ed. *Gender and Utopia in the Eighteenth Century: Essays in English and French Utopian Writing.* Aldershot: Ashgate Publishing, 2007.

———. "'Sweet Place, Where Virtue Then Did Rest': The Appropriation of the Country-House Ethos in Sarah Scott's *Millenium Hall*." *Utopian Studies* 7, no. 1 (1996): 49–59.

Pollak, Ellen. "Gender and Fiction in *Moll Flanders* and *Roxana*." In *The Cambridge Companion to Daniel Defoe*, edited by John Richetti, 139–157. Cambridge: Cambridge University Press, 2008.

———. *Incest and the English Novel, 1684–1814.* Baltimore: Johns Hopkins University Press, 2003.

Potter, Tiffany. "'A God-like Sublimity of Passion': Eliza Haywood's Libertine Consistency." *Eighteenth-Century Novel* 1 (2001): 95–126.

Reeves, James Bryant. "Posthumous Presence in Richardson's *Clarissa*." *Studies in English Literature* 53, no. 3 (2013): 601–621.

Richardson, Samuel. *Clarissa; Or the History of a Young Lady*. Edited by Angus Ross. New York: Penguin Books, 1985.

———. *Pamela in Her Exalted Condition*. In *The Cambridge Edition of the Works and Correspondence of Samuel Richardson*, vol. 3, edited by Albert J. Rivero. New York: Cambridge University Press, 2011.

———. *Pamela: Or Virtue Rewarded*. In *The Cambridge Edition of the Works and Correspondence of Samuel Richardson*, vol. 2, edited by Albert J. Rivero. New York: Cambridge University Press, 2011.

———. *Sir Charles Grandison*. Edited by Jocelyn Harris. New York: Oxford University Press, 1972.

Richetti, John, ed. *The Cambridge Companion to the Eighteenth-Century Novel*. Cambridge: Cambridge University Press, 1996.

———. "The Family, Sex, and Marriage in Defoe's *Moll Flanders* and *Roxana*." *Studies in the Literary Imagination* 15, no. 2 (1982): 19–35.

———. "Histories by Eliza Haywood and Henry Fielding: Imitation and Adaptation." In *The Passionate Fictions of Eliza Haywood: Essays on Her Life and Work*, edited by Kirsten T. Saxton and Rebecca P. Bocchicchio, 240–258. Lexington: University Press of Kentucky, 2000.

Rivero, Albert, ed. *New Essays on Samuel Richardson*. New York: St. Martin's, 1996.

Rizzo, Betty. "Burney and Society." In *The Cambridge Companion to Frances Burney*, edited by Peter Sabor, 131–146. Cambridge: Cambridge University Press, 2007.

Rogers, Katharine. *Feminism in Eighteenth-Century England*. Urbana: University of Illinois Press, 1982.

———. *Frances Burney: The World of Female Difficulties*. New York: Harvester Wheatsheaf, 1990.

Roulston, Christine. *Narrating Marriage in Eighteenth-Century England and France*. Farnham: Ashgate Publishing, 2010.

Russo, Stephanie, and A. D. Cousins. "'In a State of Terrour and Misery Indescribable': Violence, Madness and Revolution in the Novels of Frances Burney." In *The French Revolution and the British Novel in the Romantic Period*, edited by Stephanie Russo, A. D. Cousins, and Dani Napton, 83–99. New York: Peter Lang, 2011.

———, A. D. Cousins, and Dani Napton, eds. *The French Revolution and the British Novel in the Romantic Period*. New York: Peter Lang, 2011.

Sabor, Peter, ed. *The Cambridge Companion to Frances Burney*. Cambridge: Cambridge University Press, 2007.

Saxton, Kirsten T., and Rebecca P. Bocchicchio, eds. *The Passionate Fictions of Eliza Haywood: Essays on her Life and Work*. Lexington: University Press of Kentucky, 2000.

Schellenberg, Betty A. *The Conversational Circle: Re-reading the English Novel, 1740–1775*. Lexington: University Press of Kentucky, 1996.

Scheuermann, Mona. "An Income of One's Own: Women and Money in *Moll Flanders* and *Roxana*." *Durham University Journal* 80, no. 2 (1988): 225–239.

———. "Redefining the Filial Tie: Eighteenth-Century English Novelists from Brooks to Bage." *Etudes Anglaises, Grande-Bretagne, Etas-Unis* 37, no. 4 (1984): 385–398.

Schmidgen, Wolfram. "Illegitimacy and Social Observation: The Bastard in the Eighteenth Century Novel." *ELH* 69, no. 1 (2002): 133–166.

Schnorrenberg, Barbara. "A Paradise Like Eve's: Three Eighteenth-Century English Female Utopias." *Women's Studies* 9, no. 3 (1982): 263–273.

Schofield, Mary Anne. "Exposé of the Popular Heroine: The Female Protagonists of Eliza Haywood." *Studies in Eighteenth-Century Culture* 12 (1983): 93–103.

———, and Cecilia Macheski, eds. *Fetter'd or Free: British Women Novelists, 1670–1815*. Athens: Ohio University Press, 1986.

Scott, Sarah. *Millenium Hall*. Edited by Gary Kelly. Orchard Park: Broadview Press, 1995.

Severance, Mary. "An Unerring Rule: The Reformation of the Father in Frances Burney's *Evelina*." *The Eighteenth Century: Theory and Interpretation* 36, no. 2 (1995): 119–138.

Sherman, Carol. *The Family Crucible in Eighteenth-Century Literature.* Aldershot: Ashgate Publishing, 2005.

Shinagel, Michael. *Daniel Defoe and Middle-Class Gentility.* Cambridge: Harvard University Press, 1968.

———. "The Maternal Theme in *Moll Flanders*: Craft and Character." *Cornell Library Journal* 7 (1969): 3–23.

Sohier, Jacques. "Moll Flanders and the Rise of the Complete Gentlewoman-Tradeswoman." *The Eighteenth-Century Novel* 2 (2002): 1–21.

Spacks, Patricia Meyer. *Novel Beginnings: Experiments in Eighteenth-Century English Fiction.* New Haven: Yale University Press, 2006.

Spedding, Patrick. "Shameless Scribbler or Votary of Virtue? Eliza Haywood, Writing (and) Pornography in 1742." In *Women Writing, 1550–1750*, edited by Jo Wallwork and Paul Bundoora Salzman, 237–251. Australia: Meridian, 2001.

Spence, Sarah. "Nurturing: Attachment Theory and Fanny Burney's *Evelina* and *Cecilia*." *The Psychohistory Review* 24, no. 2 (1996): 155–180.

Spencer, Jane. "*Evelina* and *Cecilia*." In *The Cambridge Companion to Frances Burney*, edited by Peter Sabor, 23–37. Cambridge: Cambridge University Press, 2007.

Spielman, David Wallace. "The Value of Money in *Robinson Crusoe, Moll Flanders*, and *Roxana*." *Modern Language Review* 107, no. 1 (2012): 65–84.

Staves, Susan. *A Literary History of Women's Writing in Britain, 1660–1789.* Cambridge: Cambridge University Press, 2006.

Steele, Kathryn. "Clarissa's Silence." *Eighteenth-Century Fiction* 23, no. 1 (2010): 1–34.

Stone, Lawrence. *The Family, Sex, and Marriage in England 1500–1800.* New York: Harper and Row, 1977.

Straub, Kristina. *Divided Fictions: Fanny Burney and Feminine Strategy.* Lexington: University Press of Kentucky, 1987.

Stuart, Shea. "Subversive Didacticism in Eliza Haywood's *Betsy Thoughtless*." *Studies in English Literature* 42, no. 3 (2002): 559–575.

Swaminathan, Srivdhya. "Defoe's Alternative Conduct Manual: Survival Strategies and Female Networks in *Moll Flanders*." *Eighteenth-Century Fiction* 15, no. 2 (2003): 185–206.

Tadmor, Naomi. "'Family' and 'Friend' in *Pamela*: A Case-Study in the History of the Family in Eighteenth-Century England." *Social History* 14, no. 3 (1989): 289–306.

———. *Family and Friends in Eighteenth-Century England: Household, Kinship, and Patronage.* New York: Cambridge University Press, 2001.

Taylor, E. Derek. "Samuel Richardson's *Clarissa* and the Problem of Heaven." In *Theology and Literature in the Age of Johnson: Resisting Secularism*, edited by Melvyn New and Gerard Reedy, 71–89. Newark: University of Delaware Press, 2012.

Terry, Richard. "*David Simple* and the Fallacy of Friendship." *Studies in English Literature* 44, no. 3 (2004): 525–544.

Teynor, Hilary. "A Partridge in the Family Tree: Fixity, Mobility, and Community in *Tom Jones*." *Eighteenth-Century Fiction* 17, no. 3 (2005): 349–372.

Thackeray, William. *Vanity Fair: A Novel Without a Hero.* Edited by Helen Small. New York: Oxford University Press, 2015.

Thomas, Ruth. "'Ma Soeur, Mon Amie': Friends as Family in Madame Riccoboni's Fiction." *New Perspectives on the Eighteenth Century* 5, no. 1 (2008): 13–19.

Thomason, Laura E. *The Matrimonial Trap: Eighteenth-Century Women Writers Redefine Marriage.* Lewisburg: Bucknell University Press, 2014.

Thompson, Helen. "Betsy Thoughtless and the Persistence of Coquettish Volition." *Journal For Early Modern Cultural Studies* 4, no. 1 (2004): 102–126.

———. *Ingenuous Subjection: Compliance and Power in the Eighteenth-Century Domestic Novel.* Philadelphia: University of Pennsylvania Press, 2005.

Thompson, James. *Models of Value: Eighteenth-Century Political Economy and the Novel.* Durham: Duke University Press, 1996.

Thorn, Jennifer. "'Althea Must Be Open'd': Eliza Haywood, Individualism, and Reproductivity." *Eighteenth-Century Women: Studies in Their Lives, Work, and Culture* 1 (2001): 95–127.
———, ed. *Writing British Infanticide: Child-Murder, Gender, and Print, 1722–1859*. Newark: University of Delaware Press, 2003.
Todd, Janet M. *Women's Friendship in Literature*. New York: Columbia University Press, 1980.
Trumbach, Randolph. *The Rise of the Egalitarian Family: Aristocratic Kinship and Domestic Relations in Eighteenth-Century England*. New York: Academic Press, 1978.
Van Boheemen, Christine. *The Novel as Family Romance: Language, Gender, and Authority from Fielding to Joyce*. Ithaca: Cornell University Press, 1987.
Van Sant, Ann. "Historicizing Domestic Relations: Sarah Scott's Use of the 'Household Family.'" *Eighteenth-Century Fiction* 17, no. 3 (2005): 373–390.
Vareschi, Mark. "Attribution and Reception: The Case of Defoe and the Circulating Library." *Eighteenth-Century Life* 36, no. 2 (2012): 36–59.
Vickery, Amanda. *The Gentleman's Daughter: Women's Lives in Georgian England*. New Haven: Yale University Press, 1998.
Walk, Lori. "Questing for Family in *Joseph Andrews* and *David Simple*." *Eighteenth-Century Novel* 1 (2001): 237–252.
Wallace, Miriam L., ed. *Enlightening Romanticism, Romancing the Enlightenment: British Novels from 1750 to 1832*. Surrey: Ashgate Publishing, 2009.
Wallwork, Jo, and Paul Bundoora Salzman, eds. *Women Writing, 1550–1750*. Australia: Meridian, 2001.
Watson, Zak. "Desire and Genre in 'The Female Quixote.'" *Novel: A Forum on Fiction* 44, no. 1 (2011): 31–46.
Wolff, Cynthia Griffin. *Samuel Richardson and the Eighteenth-Century Puritan Character*. Connecticut: Archon Books, 1972.
Wright, Lynn Marie, and Donald J. Newman, eds. *Fair Philosopher: Eliza Haywood and The Female Spectator*. Lewisburg: Bucknell University Press, 2006.
Yaeger, Patricia, and Beth Kowaleski-Wallace, eds. *Refiguring the Father: New Feminist Readings of Patriarchy*. Carbondale: Southern Illinois University Press, 1989.
Yeazell, Ruth Bernard. *Fictions of Modesty: Women and Courtship in the English Novel*. Chicago: University of Chicago Press, 1991.
Zionkowski, Linda. "*Clarissa* and the Hazards of the Gift." *Eighteenth-Century Fiction* 23, no. 3 (2011): 471–494.
Zomchick, John. "Satire and the Bourgeois Subject in Frances Burney's *Evelina*." In *Cutting Edges: Postmodern Critical Essays on Eighteenth-Century Satire*, edited by James Gill, 347–356. Knoxville: University of Tennessee Press, 1995.
Zonitch, Barbara. *Familiar Violence: Gender and Social Upheaval in the Novels of Frances Burney*. Newark: University of Delaware Press, 1997.

126–127; plot, 124; surrogate families in, 15, 117, 118, 124–125, 126, 127–128; view of men, 126–127

Moll (character): brothers of, 23–24; coldness of, 27, 136n18; commercial spirit of, 19, 20, 23, 24, 25, 27, 32; criminal activities of, 29, 30; escape to America, 30; experience in household families, 22–23; friends of, 18, 19–20; gypsies and, 20–21, 136n27; half-brother/husband of, 25, 27–28; imprisonment of, 30; marriages of, 22, 28, 30–31, 32, 38, 79; materialism of, 136n22; as matrimonial whore, 25; nuclear family of, 25, 30–31, 38; personality of, 10, 21, 22, 24; practical worldview of, 31; psychological complexity of, 11; relationships with mother, 27; relations with governess, 28–30, 31, 115; resiliency of, 18; self-promotional skills, 21; sense of apartness, 24; social ambitions of, 17, 19, 21–22, 25; surrogate relations of, 5, 13, 19, 20, 28–29, 32, 114; Tom Jones and, 7; travels of, 27–28; treatment of children, 18, 19, 25, 26–27, 28, 31–32, 34, 38, 137n47; view of matrimonial relations, 23, 30–31, 32–33

Moll Flanders (Defoe): adaptations of, 136n39; comparison to *Roxana*, 19, 32; depiction of motherhood, 19, 20, 28–29, 32; erotic scenes, 19, 25; genre of, 9; incest episode, 20, 25, 27–28; role of money in, 26; surrogate family in, 4–5, 12–13, 18

Montagu, Barbara, 124–125
Montagu, Elizabeth, 125
Montini, Donatella, 52, 138n9
Mowry, Melissa, 24

Nelson, T.G.A., 7
Nestor, Deborah, 90, 95, 142n22
Nickel, Terri, 5
Nixon, Cheryl, 4, 5, 9, 10, 132n19, 134n55
novels: depiction of intimacy in, 8–9; depiction of parenting in, 10; development of genre of, 141n9, 142n10; familial attitudes in, 9; gendered distinctions, 6–7; punitive subplots, 95, 126

nuclear families, 1, 2–3, 4, 124

Oakleaf, David, 79, 107, 125
O'Hara, Diana, 131n3

Oliver, Kathleen, 62
Olshin, Toby, 103
orphans, 5, 10, 103, 134n55

Pamela (character): attempted rape of, 44; correspondence of, 47–48; daughterly role of, 42; doppelgänger of, 42; education of, 40; influence of, 48, 49; intimacy between Polly and, 47–48; isolation of, 41, 51; Lady Davers and, 13, 45–46, 48; liberation of, 48–49; lower status of, 13, 74; loyalty of, 48; marriage life of, 44–45, 48–49, 77, 79; moral authority of, 13, 42–43, 44; paternal connection to, 41; reading habits of, 100; rejection of Mrs. Jewkes, 43–44; relationships with servants, 41; search for husband, 40; surrogate mother of, 42, 43, 44, 82, 115; surrogate sister of, 13, 47, 48; vulnerability of, 40–41

Pamela (Richardson), 13, 37, 38, 41, 51, 138n12
Pamela in Her Exalted Condition (Richardson), 13, 39, 45, 46–47, 51
Park, Hajeong, 142n14
patriarchal family, 54, 55–56, 57, 139n25, 139n34
Paxman, David, 10, 11, 27, 50
Perry, Ruth, 1, 8
Peterson, Spiro, 19
Pettit, Alexander, 80, 99
Pollak, Ellen, 9, 18
punitive subplots, 95, 126

Riccoboni, Marie-Jeanne, 132n25
Richardson, Samuel: childhood experience, 140n42; close relationships of, 53; comparison to Defoe, 39–40; correspondents of, 8, 52–54, 133n43, 138n9; depiction of surrogate families, 11, 39, 49, 72, 77; female protagonists of, 52, 54; ideal of family, 132n21, 137n3; ideal of friendship, 67; influence of, 75; literary career of, 1, 76, 138n11; on parental values, 54, 57, 77, 139n25, 139n34; protagonists of, 11–12, 40; self-authored families in fiction of, 52; on sentimental love, 133n32; value of women's education, 115–116; view of marriage, 39–40, 79. See also *Clarissa* (Richardson); *Pamela* (Richardson); *Pamela in Her Exalted Condition* (Richardson); *Sir Charles Grandison* (Richardson)

Richetti, John, 4, 16, 92, 136n18
Rizzo, Betty, 145n24
Rogers, Katharine, 110, 133n30
Roulston, Chris, 91
Roxana (character): authority of, 33; coldness
    of, 136n18; commercial attitudes of, 19,
    32, 34; domestic network of, 32; feeling
    of remorse, 34; financial affairs of, 38;
    imaginary pregnancy of, 36; marriages
    of, 32, 33; psychological complexity
    of, 11; relationship with husband, 36;
    surrogate relations of, 5, 19, 32, 35–38,
    115; treatment of children, 18, 19, 32,
    33–34, 35, 36, 37, 38; wealth of, 32,
    33, 34
Roxana (Defoe): adaptations of, 136n39;
    comparison to Moll Flanders, 19, 32;
    depiction of maternity and domesticity
    in, 19; family models in, 32; mother-
    children relations in, 33–34; surrogate
    relations in, 5, 12, 13, 18, 36–37, 38;
    theme of sexuality, 19
Russo, Stephanie, 110
Ruth Perry, 1

Schellenberg, Betty, 69
Scheuermann, Mona, 9, 25
Schmidgen, Wolfram, 103
Scott, Sarah, 5, 117, 124–125, 128. See also
    Millenium Hall (Scott)
seduction narratives, 80, 85, 86,
    142n15
self-authored families, 52
Severance, Mary, 145n21
Sherman, Carol, 9
Shinagel, Michael, 19
siblinghood, 1, 2, 5
Sir Charles Grandison (Richardson): major
    conflict of, 70; nuclear and lineage
    families in, 4, 50, 69, 70; protagonist,
    40, 51; Sir Charles and Harriet's
    union, 51, 69–70, 71, 72–73, 116;
    surrogate connections in, 4, 14, 39,
    49–52, 69, 70, 71–72, 74; utopia in,
    14; value of kinship, 70; women's
    education and moral development
    in, 115–116
Sohier, Jacques, 136n22
Spacks, Patricia Meyer, 133n43
Spedding, Patrick, 141n1
Spence, Sarah, 103
Spencer, Jane, 114

Spielman, David, 26
Staves, Susan, 9
Steele, Kathryn, 56
Stone, Lawrence, 133n32; The Family, Sex,
    and Marriage in England, 7, 16
Straub, Kristina, 106
Stuart, Shea, 141n9
surrogate brotherhood, 72; as model for
    marriage, 108–109, 127
surrogate families: affection in, 2, 50;
    all-female, 15, 125; as bridge to ideal
    marriages, 116; definition of, 1, 4–5,
    80, 132n17; effects of belonging to,
    49; erosion of, 48; as family of the
    heart, 39; gender and, 123, 124, 128;
    hierarchical relationship in, 46; ideal of
    self-contained, 125; identity and, 14;
    intimacy in, 4; literary depiction of, 1,
    5–6, 11, 12, 118, 125, 132n25; marriage
    and, 16, 125; vs. nuclear and lineage
    families, 3–4, 13, 14–15, 50, 70, 109;
    studies of, 12; typology of, 118; women
    and, 3, 75, 100
surrogate parents, 2, 5, 44–45, 51, 65, 70–71,
    90–91
Swaminathan, Srividhya, 19
Swift, Jonathan: Gulliver's Travels, 100

Tadmor, Naomi, 1, 40, 80, 81, 131n3
Terry, Richard, 123
Teynor, Hilary, 119
Thackeray, William: Vanity Fair, 3
Thomas, Ruth, 132n25
Thompson, Helen, 8, 85
Thompson, James, 19
Thorn, Jennifer, 142n19
Todd, Janet, 5
Tom Jones (character): Allworthy's
    community and, 119–120; altruism of,
    122; attractiveness of, 7; male privilege,
    120–121; marriage of, 15, 121, 122;
    personality of, 6, 120; resemblance of
    female protagonists, 120; search for
    adventures, 121; sexual encounters of,
    6–7, 121; surrogate families of, 6, 15,
    117, 119–122, 123; surrogate mother of,
    121–122; travels of, 121

Van Boheemen, Christine, 10
Van Sant, Ann, 2, 5, 125
Vareschi, Mark, 136n39
Vickery, Amanda, 7, 8, 9

ANN CAMPBELL has published articles about family, courtship and marriage, and pedagogy in *Studies in Eighteenth-Century Culture*, *Eighteenth-Century Life*, *Eighteenth-Century Women*, *Aphra Behn Online*, and *Digital Defoe*. She is a professor of English at Boise State University in Idaho.